Children, Education, and the First Amendment

Children and the Law

General Editor: Gary B. Melton,
University of Nebraska–Lincoln

Editorial Board: Thomas Grisso,
University of Massachusetts–Amherst
Gerald P. Koocher, Harvard University
Robert J. Mnookin, Stanford University
W. J. Wadlington, University of Virginia
Lois A. Weithorn, University of Virginia

Children, Education, and the First Amendment

A psycholegal analysis   David Moshman

University of Nebraska Press: Lincoln and London

The paper in this book meets the minimum requirements of American
National Standard for Information Sciences—Permanence of Paper
for Printed Library Materials, ANSI Z39.48–1984.
Library of Congress Cataloging-in-Publication Data
Moshman, David
  Children, education, and the First Amendment : a psycholegal
  analysis / David Moshman.
  p. cm. — (Children and the law)
  Bibliography: p.
  Includes indexes.
  ISBN 0-8032-3110-5 (alk. paper)
  1. Educational law and legislation—United States.   2. Children
  —Legal status, laws, etc.—United States.   3. Freedom of
  information—United States.   4. Reasoning in children.   I. Title.
  II. Series.
  KF4155.M67 1989
  344.73'07—dc 19
  [347.3047]   88-29094 CIP

to Ruth and Howard

Contents

Preface

I turned 30 in May 1981. One Sunday that month, I read an article in the morning paper about efforts by fundamentalist Christians to eliminate "humanism" from the public schools (Kleiman, 1981). As a psychologist who specializes in the development of reasoning, I was appalled. It seemed clear to me that what fundamentalists called humanism was simply the promotion of rationality, and that the result of eliminating so-called secular humanism would be a curriculum that discouraged independent thinking and critical analysis.

As I began to explore the legal aspects of the fundamentalist attack on secular humanism in public schools, it became increasingly clear that children's intellectual freedom was directly at stake in these matters, that this raised the legal question of children's First Amendment rights, and that application of the First Amendment to children raised empirical questions about children's reasoning and the development of rationality. It also became clear, however, that the issue was not simply fundamentalists vs. public schools. On the contrary, I became increasingly convinced that the fundamentalist critique of secular humanism is not itself the major problem but simply highlights a deeper dilemma inherent in public education in a democratic society: Can government genuinely educate children without infringing on their intellectual freedom? What happens to the ideal of government by the will of the governed when each generation of the governed is systematically educated by that very government?

With these questions in mind, I became concerned that supporters of public schools have been too quick to invoke the First Amendment as a legal weapon against fundamentalists and have often failed to see the deeper First Amendment problems inherent in public education. To put the issue even more broadly, I think we need to pay more attention to the issues of intellectual freedom involved in the socialization of children.

The intent of this book is to propose a general analysis of children's First Amendment rights that can be applied to current issues involving children, especially in public school settings. My central concern is neither to support nor attack public schools, fundamentalists, or any other parties to the current political controversies. My intent is, rather, to highlight the intellectual rights of children and the role of the First Amendment in protecting these rights.

Who will want to read this book? Obviously, the book deals directly with constitutional law and should be of interest to lawyers and law students concerned with child and family law, education law, and/or the First Amendment. In addition, a major thesis of the book is that psychological research on children's reasoning must be considered in applying the First Amendment to issues involving children. The book should therefore also be of interest to psychologists and students of psychology who deal with the use of data from the social and behavioral sciences in addressing issues of law and social policy. Third, the book directly addresses many of the major current controversies concerning public and (to a lesser extent) private schools and thus may be of interest to teachers, librarians, administrators, and school board members. Although the book is intended more as a scholarly analysis than as a popular exposition, I have tried to make it accessible to professionals in a variety of disciplines by avoiding or explaining jargon and concepts specific to law, psychology, or education. I hope that, as a result, the book will be accessible to parents who are concerned about their children's intellectual rights at home and at school and perhaps to some adolescents as well.

Readers interested in learning about the current First Amendment rights of children as recognized by U.S. courts will find a brief overview in Chapter 1 and detailed coverage of many cases, including the major Supreme Court decisions, in Chapter 4. I should note in advance, however, that the primary purpose of this book is to present and defend my own analysis of children's First Amendment rights. Most of the book (and especially Chapter 2) should thus be read not as a summary of current case law but as a theory of why and how the First Amendment should be applied to children.

The essence of my approach to children's First Amendment rights appears in Tables 1 and 2 as a set of proposed principles. These principles are adapted from a set I originally presented in my own chapter of a book I edited several years ago (Moshman, 1986). I thank Jossey-Bass for permission to adapt sections of my earlier discussion of these principles and related issues for inclusion in the present volume.

I am grateful to Gary Melton and Lois Weithorn for detailed critiques of the entire manuscript; to Chuck Tremper, Harvey Siegel, and Gerald Koocher for additional comments; and to the students in my fall 1987 seminar on children's intellectual rights—Jim Ogloff, Kathy Benes, Steve Hultman, Andy Nichols, Susan Limber, Stacy Etheredge, and Susan Resz—for lively discussion of an earlier draft. As for those with whom I have had other useful discussions about children's First Amendment rights and related issues, I couldn't even begin to name them all—and I won't try.

Congress shall make no law
respecting an establishment of religion,
or prohibiting the free exercise thereof;
or abridging the freedom of speech,
or of the press;
or the right of the people peaceably to assemble,
and to petition the government for a redress
of grievances.

The First Amendment to the United States Constitution
Passed by Congress, September 25, 1789
Ratified by the States, December 15, 1791

Table 1 : Children's First Amendment Rights: Proposed Principles

1. *Free Expression*. (a) Government may not hinder children from forming or expressing any idea unless the abridgment of belief or expression serves a compelling purpose (e.g., to prevent disruption of education) that cannot be served in a less restrictive way. (b) *Freedom of Nonexpression*. Government may not require children to adopt or express a belief in any idea.

2. *Free Exercise of Religion*. Government may not restrict children from acting in accord with their religious beliefs unless the restriction serves a compelling purpose (e.g., to prevent a perceived establishment of religion in a public school) that cannot be served in a less restrictive way.

3. *Freedom of Access*. Government may not restrict a child's access to ideas and sources of information unless the restriction serves a compelling purpose (e.g., to prevent demonstrable harm to the child) that cannot be served in a less restrictive way.

4. *Freedom of Association*. Government may not hinder children from associating with others of their own choice, nor require undesired associations, unless the abridgment of free association or nonassociation serves a compelling purpose (e.g., to enable education) that cannot be served in a less restrictive way.

5. *Limited Inculcation*. (a) *Legitimate Purpose*. Government may inculcate ideas and values, but only when it has a legitimate purpose for doing so (e.g., to produce educated citizens). (b) *Religious Neutrality*. Gov-

ernment inculcation may not have, as its purpose or principal effect, the advancement or hindrance of any religion or of religion in general. (c) *Nonindoctrination*. Government may not indoctrinate–that is, it may not inculcate ideas or values in a way that unnecessarily limits the possibility of critical or rational analysis.

6. *Nonarbitrary Distinction of Child from Adult.* Protection of children from harm due to their limited rationality may be a compelling reason for limiting First Amendment rights provided it can be shown that (a) the children in question are less rational than a minimally normal adult; (b) the difference in rationality is of a nature and extent such that substantial harm is likely unless First Amendment freedoms are abridged; and (c) the potential harm outweighs countervailing parental and First Amendment interests.

Table 2 : Children's Intellectual Rights: Proposed Principles

7. *Free Expression II*. (a) Children have a right to form, express, and communicate any ideas. (b) *Freedom of Nonexpression II*. Children have a right not to adopt or express belief in ideas they do not wish to hold or express.

8. *Free Exercise of Religion II*. Children have a right to act in accord with their religious beliefs except where restriction serves a compelling purpose (e.g., to prevent harmful or illegal behavior) that cannot be served in a less restrictive way.

9. *Freedom of Access II*. Children have a right of access to all ideas and sources of information. Those responsible for their development have an affirmative obligation to provide access to diverse sources of information and a reasonable diversity of opinions and perspectives.

10. *Freedom of Association II*. Children have a right to associate with others of their own choice, and to avoid undesired associations.

11. *Limited Inculcation II*. Children have a right not to be subjected to inculcation except for legitimate reasons, and not to be indoctrinated.

12. *Nonarbitrary Distinction of Child from Adult II*. Restrictions on children's intellectual rights should be limited to those necessitated by the individual child's circumstances and intellectual limitations.

13. *Right to Education*. To the extent that their rights are restricted on the basis of limited rationality, children have a right to the sort of environment that will facilitate their intellectual development and thus render such restriction unnecessary.

1 : Children and the First Amendment

An overseas country has just set up a network of "education centers." All citizens are required to report to them for six hours each day, five days per week, for ten years, in order to receive a government-sponsored "education." The education is "compulsory."

Most Americans would immediately be skeptical. This sounds like the sort of indoctrination program one would expect from an ideological group that has just won political control, perhaps through violent revolution, and is seeking to ensure unquestioning popular support.

Compulsory government-sponsored education is, however, the norm in most countries, and is widely viewed as a benefit rather than a threat. Article 26 of the Universal Declaration of Human Rights, approved by the General Assembly of the United Nations on December 10, 1948, explicitly mandates that "elementary education shall be compulsory." Education is compulsory in every state of the United States, typically from age 6 or 7 to age 16 (van Geel, 1987).

Why is compulsory education generally seen as a human right rather than a threat to liberty? One relevant factor is that it usually applies only to children. Of course, given that everyone begins life as a child, a long-standing program of compulsory education applies to everyone. Nevertheless, it applies to each of us only during the period of our childhood.

This in itself, however, should not be sufficient to relieve our concern. If a government wished to systematically indoctrinate its citizens in certain religious or political ideologies and had the option of beginning a ten-year program of education at any age, it would almost surely choose to begin in early childhood. Young children are far less able than adults to recognize and resist indoctrination and thus may be far better targets. The fact that education is compulsory for children rather than adults should, if anything, increase our concern about it. Compulsory education during the period of our lives when we are most intellectually vulnerable gives government substantial power to indoctrinate. Even if it has no intent to indoctrinate, government may guide children's thinking in ways that affect them for the rest of their lives. Compulsory, government-controlled education is a genuine threat to intellectual freedom.

It does not follow from this that education should not be compulsory. On the contrary, education is so critical in the modern world that an individual lacking a basic education probably would be unable to earn a living or fulfill the basic responsibilities of citizenship in a democratic society. Given that young children may not fully understand the long-term implications of inadequate education and that parents may not always act in their children's best interests, it is reasonable to require some sort of education even in cases where the parents or child do not desire this.

Acceptance of compulsory education, however, does not mean one may be complacent about its threat to intellectual freedom. On the contrary, there appears to be good reason for serious scrutiny of how government uses its educational powers. A major thesis of this book is that, in the United States, the First Amendment provides the central legal basis for such scrutiny.

The question of government influence on children in public schools is, of course, a subset of the much broader question of adult influence over children in general. If ten years of daily education can have a substantial impact, parental control from birth through adulthood probably has far greater potential to direct the course of development. Although parental control of children may fall outside the scope of the First Amendment (a point to be further discussed), it is nevertheless useful to consider First Amendment issues within the context of a broader consideration of intellectual rights. It may be helpful at this point to consider the sorts of questions that arise in this area.

Who should decide what children see, hear, and read? Do they have a right to read books, listen to music, or see movies adults disapprove of? Is it proper to remove a book from a school library or curriculum because of its political views? Is it proper to remove a book because it shows women in nontraditional roles? Because it shows women in traditional roles? Because it has a religious theme? Because it has an anti-religious theme? Because it is vulgar? Because it is racist? Because it presents a point of view (such as evolution) some religions disapprove of? Because it shows a point of view (such as "scientific" creationism) scientists disagree with?

What about children's own expression? Should there be limits on what they are allowed to say? On what they are allowed to write? On what they publish in student newspapers? Should they be permitted to criticize the government, their schools, their teachers, their parents, or their peers?

Do children have a right to hold, express, and act on their own religious beliefs? Should they be permitted to pray in school? Should they be allowed to meet in school facilities for religious activities? Should public schools be required, permitted, or forbidden to set aside time and/or facilities for religious activities?

May adults inculcate ideas and values in their dealings with children? Should they do so? May adults *require* children to believe or express certain things? Should schools be value-neutral? Can they be?

Are we justified in distinguishing children from adults for the purpose of according or restricting rights? Should children have special privileges (such as free education) simply because they are children? Should they be subject to special limitations (such as restrictions on expression) simply because they are children? Is the child's age a relevant consideration?

What all of these questions have in common is that they involve the right to use and develop one's intellect, including access to information and ideas, freedom to believe what one chooses, freedom to express one's beliefs, and freedom to act in accord with those beliefs. In short, they raise the issue of children's *intellectual rights* (Moshman, 1986). Although the concept of intellectual rights illuminates important links among the above questions, we will see throughout this book that it is itself a multifaceted construct, drawing on at least four major disciplines: law, philosophy, psychology, and education.

The First Amendment: A Summary of Current Law

In the United States, the constitutional basis for intellectual rights is the First Amendment. In fact, intellectual freedom is usefully regarded as the underlying thread that ties together the First Amendment's three major sections.

Freedom of religion

The first section of the First Amendment includes two distinct clauses concerning religious liberty. The establishment clause forbids government to promote religion; the free exercise clause forbids government to restrict religion. Thus, the First Amendment protects intellectual freedom by forbidding government to interfere with one's religious beliefs, either directly, by restricting the exercise of those beliefs, or indirectly, by promoting alternative beliefs. The Supreme Court has generally construed the two clauses, taken together, as requiring a government policy of strict neutrality with respect to religion (Beschle, 1987; Laycock, 1986)[1] and a wall of separation between church and state (Pfeffer, 1984).[2]

Application of these broad principles to actual cases is, of course, complex and controversial. Notwithstanding the general concepts of government neutrality and separation of church and state, the Court has generally addressed religion cases by classifying them as either establishment or free exercise issues and has elaborated a distinct body of case law with respect to each.

With respect to establishment, the general standard is a three-part test established in *Lemon v. Kurtzman* (1971).[3] To qualify as constitutional under the establishment clause a law (a) must have a secular purpose; (b) must not, as its principal effect, either advance or inhibit

1. Everson v. Board of Education, 330 U.S. 1 (1947)
2. Reynolds v. United States, 98 U.S. 145 (1878)
3. Lemon v. Kurtzman, 403 U.S. 602 (1971)

religion; and (c) must not foster "an excessive government entanglement with religion."[4] Although the Court has wavered in its use of
this test—setting it aside, for example, in order to permit legislative
chaplains for historical reasons[5]—the *Lemon* test remains the major
approach to establishment issues (Simson, 1987).[6]

As for free exercise, the most clearcut violation of the free exercise
clause would be for the government to ban religion, to restrict a particular religion simply because it disapproves of its theology, or to
interfere with particular religious practices simply because they are
associated with a disfavored religion. Actual free exercise cases are
almost always more subtle than this. The typical case involves a law
that appears strictly secular in its purpose and principal effect but
that is nevertheless alleged to infringe on the practice of a minority
religion.

The general approach to such cases involves two steps. First the
Court examines whether there is indeed a significant burden on the
free exercise of religion. In assessing this the Court avoids delving
into theological issues such as the truth or falsity of various religious
views or the proper interpretation of a religious ideology. Rather it
considers factors such as the sincerity of belief[7] and the centrality of
the belief or practice to the religion in question.[8]

If the religious burden is deemed significant, the burden of proof
shifts to the government to show that the law in question furthers a
compelling state interest that will be seriously compromised if religious exemptions are granted. If the governmental interest is not
sufficiently compelling, or if it can be achieved in a manner less re-

4. Lemon, *supra*, quoting Walz v. Tax Commission of New York, 397 U.S. 664, 667
(1970)
5. Marsh v. Chambers, 463 U.S. 783 (1983). See also Lynch v. Donnelly, 465 U.S. 668
(1984)
6. Witters v. Washington Department of Services for the Blind, 474 U.S. 481 (1986);
Wallace v. Jaffree, 472 U.S. 38 (1985); Aguilar v. Felton, 473 U.S. 402 (1985); Grand
Rapids School District v. Ball, 473 U.S. 373 (1985); Estate of Thornton v. Caldor, Inc. 472
U.S. 703 (1985)
7. Thomas v. Review Board of the Indiana Employment Security Division, 450 U.S. 707
(1981)
8. Wisconsin v. Yoder, 406 U.S. 205 (1972)

strictive of religious liberty, then the abridgment of free exercise is unconstitutional.[9]

Not only do the standard tests for the establishment and free exercise clauses differ but the normal remedies differ as well. In general, when a law violates the establishment clause it is simply struck down as an unconstitutional establishment of religion. In free exercise cases, on the other hand, the problem is usually not inherent in the law itself but in its application to particular individuals or religious groups. The usual remedy, then, is not to strike down the law but to require the government to allow certain exceptions.

Freedom of expression

The next section of the First Amendment, guaranteeing freedom of speech and of the press, extends the scope of intellectual freedom to all ideas, not only those of a religious nature. These clauses refer most directly to the expression of ideas. It is clear, however, that one cannot *express* ideas unless one *has* ideas, and that one cannot *have* ideas unless one *forms* them. Thus the right to form and hold beliefs is implicit in the right to express them (Arons, 1983; Haiman, 1981; van Geel, 1983).[10]

It may be added that one obviously is hindered in forming ideas if one has no access to the ideas of others. Moreover, one's expression is meaningless unless others have access to what one expresses. Thus access to ideas is also directly entailed in the free expression clauses.[11] It is important to note, however, that nothing in the First Amendment requires government to *promote* access to ideas, *encourage* the formation of new ideas, or *facilitate* expression. Government is only *forbidden to restrict* one's freedom to receive, form, hold, and express ideas (Haiman, 1981).

Freedom of expression is not absolute, however. On the contrary, a variety of governmental restrictions on speech and press are judicially permitted (Zacharias, 1987). One of the most important categories of

9. Sherbert v. Verner, 374 U.S. 398 (1963)
10. Rogers v. Okin, U.S.L.W., CA. 75-1601-T, District Court of Massachusetts, slip opinion, p. 68
11. Virginia State Board of Pharmacy v. Virginia Citizens Consumer Council, Inc., 425 U.S. 748 (1976)

exception is obscenity, which has been ruled by the Court as falling outside the boundary of the First Amendment and thus subject to extensive government regulation and restriction.[12] Recognizing the danger of removing an entire category of speech from constitutional protection, the Court has attempted to define obscenity clearly and to limit it to speech of no conceivable social or political significance,[13] though its efforts have been much criticized and the task of defining obscenity is regarded by some as hopeless.[14]

Another important category of exception is libel, involving a lawsuit by one individual against another for publishing a false and defamatory statement. But what about when the allegedly defamed individual is a government official? The Supreme Court recognizes that open criticism of governmental and social policy, a core First Amendment value, may be stifled if potential speakers must protect themselves against potentially expensive libel suits. It therefore has held that government or public figures who allege libel must prove "actual malice"—that is, that a speaker not only has harmed them by publishing a false statement but that the speaker either knew the statement was false or published it with a reckless disregard for its truth or falsity.[15] In a recent case, the Supreme Court unanimously reaffirmed this standard and extended it to claims by public figures that a publication caused them emotional distress.[16]

Other categories of speech that the Court has recognized with respect to the First Amendment include "fighting words," which may be punished,[17] and commercial speech, which, though not falling outside the First Amendment, may be substantially regulated.[18] Except for such categories, however, the Court has taken a dim view of restrictions based on content. Government may have legitimate reason

12. Roth v. United States, 354 U.S. 476 (1957)
13. Miller v. California, 413 U.S. 15 (1973)
14. Id., (Brennan, J., dissenting)
15. New York Times v. Sullivan, 376 U.S. 254 (1964)
16. Hustler v. Falwell, 108 S.Ct. 876 (1988)
17. Chaplinsky v. New Hampshire, 315 U.S. 568 (1942); but see Erznoznik v. Jacksonville, 422 U.S. 205 (1975); Gooding v. Wilson, 405 U.S. 518 (1972)
18. Virginia State Board of Pharmacy v. Virginia Citizens Consumer Council, Inc., 425 U.S. 748 (1976)

to restrict the time, place, or manner of expression—for example, in requiring permits to demonstrate—and courts accept such regulation provided the limits on expression are relatively minor and are outweighed by legitimate considerations such as maintaining public order.[19] Restrictions based on what speakers wish to express, however, are more suspect; in such cases government must demonstrate a compelling reason for the restriction and must convince the court that it is using the least restrictive means available.[20] In other words, content-based restrictions must be narrowly tailored to achieve a compelling purpose.

Freedom of association

The final major section of the First Amendment guarantees the right to demonstrate against the government. It makes it clear that one has a right to express one's views not only alone but in association with others who wish to express the same ideas. It also makes it explicit that freedom of expression includes the expression of ideas contrary to government policy.

The placement of the right to assemble within the First Amendment is consistent with the view that intellectual freedom, the unifying thread underlying the various clauses of the First Amendment, requires freedom of association. Government abridgment of association could dramatically limit meaningful expression of one's ideas, genuine exercise of one's religion via group prayers and activities, and access to the ideas of others. In fact, even without the freedom of assembly clause, it seems clear that freedom of association is implicit in the freedom-of-expression and free-exercise-of-religion clauses of the First Amendment (Haiman, 1981).[21]

Strict scrutiny

A basic principle of democracy is that laws should be made and executed by those elected for this purpose. Any time a judge strikes down a law or other government action, that judge is potentially

19. Perry Education Association v. Perry Local Educators' Association, 460 U.S. 37 (1983)
20. Brandenburg v. Ohio, 395 U.S. 444 (1969)
21. N.A.A.C.P. v. Alabama, 357 U.S. 449 (1958)

frustrating the will of the majority. Courts are highly sensitive to the anti-democratic nature of their power to declare laws and other government actions unconstitutional and properly show substantial deference to legislators and other government officials.

Nevertheless, even properly elected and highly popular government officials must act in accord with the Constitution and it is a responsibility of the courts to see that they do. When it appears that government has acted in violation of the Constitution, the normal attitude of judicial deference to other branches of government is replaced by strict scrutiny of the government's motives and the consequences of its actions. In particular, when a fundamental right, such as one of those protected by the First Amendment, is seriously abridged, a court will generally require government to show that its actions have a constitutionally acceptable purpose, that the purpose is sufficiently compelling to justify infringing on a fundamental right, and that any such infringement is no greater than absolutely necessary for government to achieve its compelling purpose (Tribe, 1988).

The Fourteenth Amendment
I have presented the First Amendment as limiting actions by government. The actual language of the Amendment specifically limits the legislative branch of the federal government ("Congress shall make no law . . ."). It has been established since 1803 that the judicial branch of the federal government has the power and responsibility to nullify any federal law that violates the Constitution (Brink, 1988).[22] It is clear, moreover, that the entire federal government, not just Congress, must operate within the constraints of the First Amendment (Oakes, 1987).[23] As ratified in 1791, however, the First Amendment set no limits on state or local governments.

The rights of individuals vis-à-vis state governments became a matter of sharp concern during the mid-1800s in connection with issues and events that eventually culminated in the Civil War. This led in 1868 to ratification of the Fourteenth Amendment, the first section of which reads as follows:

22. Marbury v. Madison, 5 U.S. 137 (1803)
23. New York Times v. Sullivan, 376 U.S. 254 (1964)

All persons born or naturalized in the United States, and subject to the jurisdiction thereof, are citizens of the United States and of the State wherein they reside. No State shall make or enforce any law which shall abridge the privileges or immunities of citizens of the United States; nor shall any State deprive any person of life, liberty, or property, without due process of law; nor deny to any person within its jurisdiction the equal protection of the laws.

The Fourteenth Amendment thus explicitly prohibited states from violating the rights of U.S. citizens—and, in fact, people in general—though it did not specify what rights were thus protected. It seems clear, however, that any accounting of the fundamental rights of U.S. citizens would have to include the intellectual liberties guaranteed by the First Amendment. Since the 1920s, the U.S. Supreme Court has consistently held that First Amendment rights are among those incorporated into the Fourteenth Amendment and thus applicable to the states (Haiman, 1981; Tribe, 1988).[24] It is, in fact, well established that agencies of government at all levels, from federal to local, and all government officials, "high or petty,"[25] are constitutionally required to respect the intellectual freedoms guaranteed by the First Amendment. The First Amendment does not, however, limit the actions of private individuals or voluntary groups, except when those parties act pursuant to state authority (Tribe, 1988).[26] With respect to the issues of specific concern in this book, the First Amendment thus applies to public schools, but generally not to private schools (unless they receive government support) or to parents acting in a personal capacity vis-à-vis their own children (van Geel, 1986, 1987).

Children, Education, and the First Amendment

The classic case for children's First Amendment rights is *Tinker v.*

24. Gitlow v. New York, 268 U.S. 652 (1925) (free expression); Cantwell v. Connecticut, 310 U.S. 296 (1940) (free exercise of religion); Everson v. Board of Education, 330 U.S. 1 (1947) (nonestablishment of religion)
25. West Virginia State Board of Education v. Barnette, 319 U.S. 624, 642 (1943)
26. Blum v. Yaretsky, 457 U.S. 991 (1982); Lugar v. Edmondson Oil Company, 457 U.S. 922 (1982)

Des Moines (1969),[27] in which the Supreme Court for the first time declared a government action unconstitutional on the ground that it violated minors' rights to freedom of expression. To fully appreciate the meaning and significance of *Tinker*, however, one must consider it in a broader historical context extending from the 1920s through the present time. Applications of the First Amendment to children are multifaceted and I will reserve differentiating and discussing the specific domains of application until Chapter 4. For present purposes, my intent is to highlight some of the most important cases, focusing on those that illustrate the major general themes and historical trends.

Basic principles

A good starting point is a pair of education cases from the 1920s in which the First Amendment was not yet invoked. In 1919 the state of Nebraska passed a law specifying that

> [n]o person, individually or as a teacher, shall, in any private, denominational, parochial or public school, teach any subject to any person in any language [other] than the English language. . . . Languages, other than the English language, may be taught as languages only after a pupil shall have attained and successfully passed the eighth grade. . . .[28]

In *Meyer v. Nebraska* (1923), the U.S. Supreme Court held that the law violated the Fourteenth Amendment's guarantee of liberty. Without questioning "[t]he power of the state to compel attendance at some school and to make reasonable regulations for all schools,"[29] the Court highlighted the right of teachers to teach and of parents to direct their children's education.

Two years later, in *Pierce v. Society of Sisters* (1925),[30] the Court addressed a related issue. Concerned about unorthodox education yielding unorthodox citizens, the state of Oregon had passed a law requiring that all children be educated in public schools. In striking down

27. Tinker v. Des Moines Independent Community School District, 393 U.S. 503 (1969)
28. Meyer v. Nebraska, 262 U.S. 390, 397 (1923)
29. *Id*. at 402
30. 268 U.S. 510

that law, the Court was clear that it did not doubt "the power of the State reasonably to regulate all schools" and "to require that all children of proper age attend some school."[31] Government could not, however, completely forbid private education. "The child," insisted the Court, "is not the mere creature of the State."[32]

Nearly two decades later, the Court struck down a West Virginia law requiring all public school students to salute the United States flag and pledge their allegiance. In *West Virginia v. Barnette* (1943),[33] the Court readily acknowledged that government may legitimately present ideas and attempt to convince students "by persuasion and example"[34] to share American values. Government may not, however, *require* belief. That is, government may inculcate up to a point, but may not coercively indoctrinate.

"We set up government by consent of the governed," argued the Court, "and the Bill of Rights denies those in power any legal opportunity to coerce that consent."[35] Noting the potential of government schools to "strangle the free mind at its source,"[36] the Court forbid school officials to "prescribe what shall be orthodox."[37] Of all government institutions, public schools must be especially careful to respect constitutional liberties lest they "teach youth to discount important principles of our government as mere platitudes."[38]

Barnette extended the *Pierce* mandate that children not be construed as "mere creature[s] of the State" to conclude that not only may they not be required to attend public schools but that, if they do, such schools must respect their intellectual liberties. Although the argument, like those of *Meyer* and *Pierce*, invoked broad constitutional considerations, *Barnette* highlighted the centrality of the First Amendment to the issues in question.

In the early 1960s, the Court turned specifically to the issue of public

31. *Id.* at 534
32. *Id.* at 535
33. West Virginia State Board of Education v. Barnette, 319 U.S. 624 (1943)
34. *Id.* at 640
35. *Id.* at 641
36. *Id.* at 637
37. *Id.* at 642
38. *Id.* at 637

school establishment of religion. In *Engel v. Vitale* (1962)[39] it ruled that public school teachers may not lead students in prayer and in *Abington v. Schempp* (1963)[40] it ruled out devotional Bible readings as well. The Court made it clear that, in addition to its general First Amendment concern about unlimited government inculcation, it would be especially stringent, on the basis of the establishment clause, in scrutinizing religious inculcation.

The Court elaborated on the more general significance of the First Amendment for public education in *Keyishian v. Board of Regents* (1967),[41] a New York case involving teacher loyalty oaths. "There can be no doubt," indicated the Court, "of the legitimacy of New York's interest in protecting its education system from subversion." But "the First Amendment," it added, ruling against the State, "does not tolerate laws that cast a pall of orthodoxy over the classroom."[42]

What remained unclear as late as 1969 was exactly how children were involved in all this. *Keyishian* most directly involved the rights of teachers. *Engel* and *Schempp* raised questions about who gets to decide what religion to inculcate and about the rights of parents whose religion is not the one inculcated. *Barnette* focused on the interests of a democratic society in the education of the next generation. *Meyer* and *Pierce* emphasized the childrearing rights of parents and the economic interests of teachers and private schools. Although all of these decisions were consistent with the idea that children have intellectual rights under the First Amendment, none of them was decided on that basis.

Tinker, involving the right of children to wear black armbands to school in order to protest the war in Vietnam, clarified that children have First Amendment rights not simply because government respect for their intellectual freedoms is in the best interests of their parents, their teachers, the educational system, or society as a whole but, more fundamentally, because they are persons under the Constitution. Stu-

39. 370 U.S. 421
40. School District of Abington v. Schempp, 374 U.S. 203 (1963)
41. Keyishian v. Board of Regents of the University of the State of New York, 385 U.S. 589 (1967)
42. *Id.* at 602, 603

dents, ruled the Court, "may not be confined to the expression of those sentiments that are officially approved."[43]

Once again, the Court was highly sensitive to "the special characteristics of the school environment."[44] It reaffirmed "the comprehensive authority of the States and of school officials . . . to prescribe and control conduct in the schools."[45] School officials, it was clear, had the authority to censor and punish students when necessary to prevent disruption of education or to protect the rights of others.

The Court indicated, however, that disagreeing with the views of the school is not in itself a disruption of education. The school may present its message, but students have a right to communicate ideas of their own. The school may express its disagreement with alternative views and values, but may not actively restrict exposure to them. "Students may not be regarded as closed-circuit recipients of only that which the State chooses to communicate."[46]

Tinker thus integrated the tradition of *Pierce, Barnette, Engel, Schempp,* and *Keyishian*—all recognizing the special dangers of government indoctrination via public schools—with the more general First Amendment regard for freedom of belief and expression as a fundamental right. Consistent with both the education cases and with established First Amendment law, it acknowledged government's compelling interest in education, and thus in regulating the public school environment, but put the burden of proof on the government to show that any restrictions on fundamental intellectual liberties directly serve that compelling interest and are the least restrictive way of doing so.

Tinker, then, carefully struck a delicate balance intended to maximally protect both liberty and learning. School officials may maintain order but they "do not possess absolute authority over their students."[47] Educators may teach what they deem appropriate but "state-operated schools may not be enclaves of totalitarianism."[48]

43. Tinker v. Des Moines Independent Community School District, 393 U.S. 503, 511 (1969)
44. *Id.* at 506
45. *Id.* at 507
46. *Id.* at 511
47. *Id.* at 511
48. *Id.* at 511

The retreat from principle

If the historical trend from the 1920s through the 1960s shows a recognition and elaboration of basic principles, the 1980s shows mostly ambivalence and confusion. In *Board of Education v. Pico* (1982),[49] the Supreme Court faced the thorny and much-litigated issue of schoolbook selection and removal. In the specific case in question, a school board had ordered the removal of 11 books from the school library. Despite a number of unusual and suspicious circumstances, the district court had issued a summary judgment in favor of the school. The appeals court remanded the case for trial and it was this decision that was appealed to the Supreme Court.

The nine justices issued seven distinct opinions, none of which commanded a majority. Four viewed the school's authority to inculcate as central and, considering this to include broad authority to select and remove books, voted to overturn the appeals court decision and thus uphold the summary judgment for the school. Four other justices argued that, although school boards may indeed select and remove books in keeping with the authority to inculcate, some inculcation oversteps First Amendment limits on indoctrination. Thus, they voted to uphold the decision to remand for a full trial that would determine whether the school had, in this case, overstepped its authority. The deciding vote to remand for trial was cast on procedural grounds. Although there was unanimous agreement that public schools may inculcate, there was mass confusion as to what limits, if any, the Constitution sets on such inculcation and how such limits are best specified and justified.

In *Bethel v. Fraser* (1986),[50] the Court found itself confronted with an amusing one-minute speech, given by a high school student in a school assembly, that drew repeatedly on a sexual metaphor. The Court ruled that, even in the absence of any disruption, school officials could punish the speaker for violating standards of "civility."[51] It provided no indication of how incivility was to be defined or recognized or where in its case law it found a basis for such an exception to

49. Board of Education, Island Trees Union Free School District No. 26 v. Pico, 457 U.S. 853 (1982)

50. Bethel School District No. 403 v. Fraser, 478 U.S. 675 (1986)

51. *Id.* at 681

the First Amendment. Its confusion was highlighted by reference in the majority opinion to Fraser's speech as "obscene."[52] Less than two years later, the Court acknowledged that Fraser's speech was obviously not obscene.[53] People make casual charges of obscenity all the time, of course. One does not, however, expect this sort of careless usage from the Supreme Court.

The Court's most recent encounter with children's First Amendment rights was *Hazelwood v. Kuhlmeier* (1988),[54] involving censorship by a principal of articles scheduled to appear in the school newspaper. Choosing to address the issue on broad grounds, the Court ruled that *Tinker* only applies to student speech outside of the curriculum. It ruled that schools may construe a wide variety of activities, outside as well as inside the classroom, as curriculum-related and that they have broad authority to censor student speech in all such contexts. Acknowledging that this limitation of students' First Amendment rights could not be justified on the basis of general First Amendment principles, the majority cited precedent that children's constitutional rights are not necessarily coextensive with those of adults.

But that begs the question. The question is, "Why the difference?" Rather than justify the specific limitations imposed by the present decision, the Court provided several ad hoc lists of educational circumstances that supposedly could not be addressed within the confines of *Tinker* and, more generally, with the principles of current First Amendment law. The dissent argued that the majority did not justify its decision on the basis of First Amendment precedent because it could not do so, and aptly characterized the list of special considerations as "an obscure tangle of . . . excuses."[55]

It has been a generation since *Tinker* established that children have First Amendment rights, two generations since *Barnette* explored the real and broad dangers to democracy of government indoctrination via public schools, and three generations since *Meyer* and *Pierce* set the

52. *Id.* at 680
53. Hazelwood School District v. Kuhlmeier, 108 S.Ct. 562, 567 (1988)
54. Hazelwood School District v. Kuhlmeier, 108 S.Ct. 562 (1988)
55. Hazelwood School District v. Kuhlmeier (Brennan, J., dissenting), 108 S.Ct. 562, 576 (1988)

fundamental context for everything since in specifying that children are not simply "creature[s] of the State." It appears that, in the 1980s, the Supreme Court has lost its way. It doesn't have the heart to reject the basic principles of these earlier decisions, but lacks the nerve to commit itself to them and work out their implications. The pervasively ad hoc, intuitive approach of its recent decisions suggests that the Court, as an institution, no longer recalls the rationale for applying the First Amendment to children and public education and fails to understand the profound dangers of failing to do so.

Why does the First Amendment apply to children and public education? To address this question, it will be necessary to look more deeply at the specifics of the above cases and many more. First, however, and more fundamentally, we must consider children's First Amendment rights with respect to general issues concerning constitutional interpretation, the meaning and purpose of the First Amendment, and the nature of children.

Construing the First Amendment

There is substantial disagreement about how the First Amendment should be interpreted. This is not only a matter of the proper interpretation of its various clauses. More broadly, disputes about how to construe and apply the First Amendment reflect broader differences of opinion about the general approach one should take in interpreting the Constitution and applying it to current issues. The broader disagreements reflect different philosophies of constitutional interpretation; that is, they raise questions of constitutional jurisprudence (cf. Brink, 1988; Lyons, 1987).

Constitutional interpretation generally draws on five major categories of relevant considerations: (a) *text*, the language of the relevant section of the Constitution; (b) *intent*, the purpose of the relevant section; (c) *constitutional theory*, the role of the Constitution as a whole; (d) *precedent*, consistency with relevant prior decisions; and (e) *values*, consistency with ethical considerations (Fallon, 1987). In this section I consider the First Amendment with respect to each of these five considerations.

Arguments from text

There can be no doubt that a major—perhaps *the* major—consideration in interpreting and applying the First Amendment must be its actual language. First Amendment decisions obviously must be consistent with the language of the First Amendment. A judge who decides the constitutionality of laws affecting freedom of religion, expression, and association without attending to what the First Amendment says is simply not doing his or her job.

The view that judges should do nothing more than mechanically apply the language of the Constitution, however, is clearly untenable. Linguists and psycholinguists agree that language is not a transparent vehicle of ideas (Brink, 1988; Clark, 1983; Piattelli-Palmarini, 1980). The interpretation of language always requires some degree of judgment; meanings are a function not only of words and syntax but of a variety of pragmatic and contextual factors. This is particularly true in the case of a statement such as the First Amendment, which was written two centuries ago in extremely broad language. It forbids laws "respecting an establishment of religion," for example, but provides no criteria for when religion has been established; similarly, it guarantees "free exercise" of religion and "freedom of speech" but does not define *freedom*.

This is not to suggest that interpretation of language is arbitrary. We can, of course, reasonably construe the First Amendment by considering its role in the Constitution as a whole; analyzing the political views of James Madison and Thomas Jefferson, who were primarily responsible for its language; and examining the historical and social circumstances in which it was ultimately adopted. But such interpretation necessarily involves some degree of judgment and leaves substantial room for reasonable and sincere people to disagree on meaning.

Arguments from intent

The suggestion that ambiguities in language can be resolved by considering the intent of the writer leads to the second general category of considerations—appeal to historical intent. Interpretation of language is more likely to be appropriate if it is done against a background understanding of what the writer was trying to communicate. To the extent that historical investigations can inform us about how the framers of the First Amendment construed its language, our own construal of it should be consistent with their intent.

Supplementing textual considerations with analysis of original intent, however, still does not suffice for constitutional decision-making (Bogen, 1983; Brink, 1988; Cox, 1987; Dworkin, 1986; Powell, 1985). For one thing, it is not always clear who was primarily responsible for a particular clause or section of the Constitution or what that individual's intention was. The framers of the Constitution did not even attempt to clarify the source and purpose of each of its specific provisions. On the contrary, they took great pains to enshroud their deliberations in a cloak of secrecy (Rotunda, 1987, 1988) and did not view their specific intentions, even if these could be ascertained, as controlling (Powell, 1985). Furthermore, the original Constitution and each subsequent amendment have legal force only because they were approved by a very large number of people, each of whom may have interpreted the language differently and given approval for different reasons.

Moreover, judges commonly must apply the Constitution to issues and circumstances that did not exist at the time the relevant sections were approved and about which those who formulated and approved the language can hardly be said to have had any intent whatsoever. Most of the legal issues addressed in this book, for example, concern the First Amendment rights of students in public schools. No schools in the late eighteenth century, however, were public in anything like the modern sense; the system of mass public education that we take for granted simply did not exist. It is highly implausible that those responsible for the First Amendment had any ideas *at all* about its implications for public schools.

Finally, it is worth noting that, whereas portions of the Constitution are quite precise—the President must "have attained to the Age of thirty five Years;" thirty-four will not do—the language of the Bill of Rights is extremely broad. If the writers intended the Bill of Rights to apply only to specific matters they had in mind, they could have written it that way. If, for example, they wished to ban certain penal practices that they found objectionable and to limit the ban to only those practices, they could have listed them in the Eighth Amendment. The fact that they instead forbid "cruel and unusual punishment" suggests that they intended the meaning of "cruel and unusual" to be flexible (Brink, 1988). Interpretation of the Eighth Amendment in terms of what punishments Americans of that time considered cruel and unusual, far from respecting the intent of its framers, would in fact violate their broader intent of protecting a general right by formulating an abstract principle whose meaning would have to be worked out (Dworkin, 1978, Chapter 5). Parallel arguments are easily made with respect to the broad language of the First Amendment, as well as the ban on "unreasonable searches and seizures" in the Fourth Amendment, the guarantee of "due process of law" in the Fifth, and the guarantee of "equal protection of the laws" in the Fourteenth (Reinstein, 1988). Paradoxically, then, an overly narrow appeal to the framers' intent violates the framers' intent of providing for broad construction on the basis of purposely general principles.

Arguments from constitutional theory
The last argument against overreliance on original intent suggests that the language and intent of specific sections of the Constitution should be construed not in isolation but against a background understanding of how the constitutional provision in question fits within the Constitution as a whole. This entails an appeal to the general purpose of the Constitution.

It is generally agreed, for example, that the Constitution was intended to provide for democratic self-government. It is difficult to see how meaningful self-government could proceed, however, if the public were not free to discuss current political issues and to criticize government policies. The free expression clauses of the First Amendment may thus be construed as forbidding government to interfere with such communication. This line of reasoning, for example, underlies the Supreme Court's special concern with political speech (Haiman, 1981; Lyons, 1987; Zacharias, 1987).[56] Although the language of the First Amendment makes no distinctions among various domains of expression, the Supreme Court has interpreted it, in the context of the Constitution as a whole, as requiring especially strict scrutiny of any

56. New York Times v. Sullivan, 376 U.S. 254 (1964)

government action that serves to inhibit freedom of expression on political issues.

Arguments from precedent

It seems clear that the text of the First Amendment, as well as other constitutional provisions, must be interpreted in the context of broader considerations concerning its specific purposes and its more general role within the Constitution as a whole. Obviously, however, there is room for many different theories about what the Constitution was intended to do and about the role of its various specific provisions. Reasonable people may reach different conclusions about the constitutionality of various government actions. Even if all judges were highly competent and showed perfect integrity, one would expect rather diverse reasoning and results with respect to the First Amendment and many other constitutional provisions.

The potential for such inconsistency is a serious problem. Not only is it desireable that judicial decisions be "correct," it is important for them to be as consistent and predictable as possible (Stevens, 1987). An important contributor to judicial consistency is that lower court judges are expected to decide constitutional cases not on the basis of completely original analyses of text, intent, and constitutional theory but on the basis of higher court rulings. That is, their rulings must be consistent with precedent.

Although this is a genuine and important constraint, it does not render the other factors superfluous. New cases are never absolutely identical to those already decided. There is always room for judgment as to what similarities and differences are constitutionally relevant. Inevitably, then, judges have substantial leeway in deciding whether there is a direct and binding precedent that applies to the present case and, if not, which prior decisions are relevant and how they should be applied. It is inevitable and appropriate that in making such judgments they will be influenced by the language of relevant constitutional provisions, by their own analysis of the intent of those provisions, and by their own general understanding of the Constitution. Precedent, then, although highly important, is rarely an independent and controlling factor.

Moreover, the Supreme Court is not bound by precedents from any higher court and is free to overrule its own precedents. This does not mean that precedent is unimportant at this level. In general the Supreme Court does follow, or at least claim to follow, its own precedents. The Court perceives consistency and stability in constitutional law as valuable in their own right and, except in the rare cases where a prior decision is deemed clearly wrong, it attempts to decide new cases in a manner consistent with previous decisions. As in the case of lower courts, however, this is less of a constraint than it may initially appear. Cases that reach the Supreme Court are likely to differ substantially from any case that has previously been decided and there is thus substantial room for judgment in deciding what precedent is controlling or how to reconcile a variety of relevant precedents. In making such judgments, considerations of text, purpose, and constitutional theory are inevitable and appropriate.

Value considerations
Appeal to value considerations is somewhat more controversial than any of the above factors as a legitimate aspect of constitutional interpretation. Many conservatives are genuinely—and correctly—concerned about the power of the judiciary to strike down laws or actions of a democratically elected legislature or school board. There is real danger in a situation in which unelected judges, in office for life and accountable to no one, can overturn legitimate acts of elected officials, perhaps supported by the vast majority of voters, on the basis of the judges' personal ethics or values.

Liberals are more often concerned about cases where judges fail to uphold genuine constitutional rights because they share the social values that led the majority to infringe on those rights in the first place. A recent example is *Bethel v. Fraser*, in which the Supreme Court construed the right to freedom of speech narrowly in its determination that this does not apply, at least in the case of students, to speech that is "offensive," that violates "the habits and manners of civility," or that goes outside "the boundaries of socially appropriate behavior." [57] Obviously, there is nothing whatsoever in the First Amendment about

57. Bethel School District No. 403 v. Fraser, 478 U.S. 675, 681, 683 (1986)

an exception for speech deemed offensive or outside the boundaries of socially appropriate behavior. The First Amendment explicitly and without qualification gives free expression a central place; it accords civility no status at all. Considerations of intent, constitutional theory, and precedent likewise provide little or no support for an incivility exception to the First Amendment. The decision in *Fraser* appears to reflect the Court's extraconstitutional determination that, at least for children in public schools, civility is more valuable than freedom of expression.

Notwithstanding the dangers of judicial value judgments, it would be naive to suggest that judges should make constitutional determinations independent of all value considerations. Psychologically, for one thing, this is probably impossible. Moreover, philosophically, it is far from obvious that, if value-neutral decisions were possible, they would be desireable. For one thing, the Constitution itself clearly rests on a variety of values (Brink, 1988; Oakes, 1987; Reinstein, 1988). The First Amendment, for example, was based on the view that intellectual freedom is a central value for a democratic society, partially because it serves specific democratic purposes such as permitting criticism of the government and meaningful elections, partially because freedoms of belief and expression are important for social progress, and partially because denial of liberty violates the dignity of the individual (Bogen, 1983).

One might suggest, then, that judges should consider constitutional values in making decisions—that is, they should consider the values underlying the language and intent of specific constitutional directives, the values underlying the Constitution as a whole, and the values underlying relevant precedents. Further, it is difficult to see how such analysis could proceed without considering the values of the society that generated the Constitution. Moreover, if judges may consider such values, they may—and perhaps should—consider developments in the field of ethics that shed light on relevant values— for example, current work on the nature and significance of liberty (Brink, 1988).

It appears, then, that consideration of values, though potentially dangerous, is unavoidable and proper. Judges try to avoid decisions based purely on their personal morality but may consider values implicit in the Constitution—or in the society that generated it—and apply ethical theories that illuminate the meaning of those values. Ideally, consideration of values takes place in the broader context of attention to language, intent, constitutional theory, and precedent, not as a substitute for such analysis (Fallon, 1987).

Conclusions

It is clear that judges cannot reach conclusions about current issues —including those involving children and education—solely on the basis of the literal text or specific intent of the First Amendment. They have no choice but to interpret and extend the Constitution, applying it to circumstances it does not directly address and to issues the framers could not possibly have foreseen. Such applications should not be ad hoc value or policy judgments. Rather, they should rest on clearly articulated principles derived from, and defensible in terms of, the language and intent of the Constitution and a long history of constitutional interpretation. It is clear, however, that derivation of such principles from the Constitution and their application to actual cases require genuine judgments—interpretations and extensions that, though not arbitrary, are not simply an objective, mechanical application of clearcut constitutional directives (Brink, 1988). Judging involves a creative effort to construct a line of reasoning as consistent as possible with text, intent, constitutional theory, precedent, and ethical considerations (Fallon, 1987). In complex cases there may be more than one defensible conclusion, but this does not mean that all conclusions are equally defensible and that judicial decisions are thus inherently arbitrary or "political" (Dworkin, 1986).

The approach urged here has judges functioning, in some respects, in a manner similar to ethical philosophers. They must formulate abstract principles, apply them to complex situations, and be willing to reformulate the principles whenever they turn out to be inconsistent with each other or lead to patently inappropriate results. They must aim toward a "reflective equilibrium" (Rawls, 1971). In this respect the present approach requires active formulation by judges.

In contrast to ethical philosophers, however, judges are not free to completely reconsider any and all assumptions. Unlike the ethical philosopher, the judge is constrained by a specific document, the Constitution, and a long history of judicial interpretation and application of that document. The constraints are not absolute, in the sense of leading mechanically to particular answers in every case, but they are real in the sense of limiting the possibilities (Dworkin, 1986; Fallon, 1987). The judge, like the philosopher, must attempt to reformulate principles to relieve internal inconsistencies and avoid patently absurd conclusions but, unlike the philosopher, is constrained by a concrete document and a history of interpretation in pursuing such reformulations. The judge's aim is not to formulate principles embodying the best possible moral philosophy but rather to formulate principles most justifiable in terms of the Constitution and legal precedent.

Construing Children

Having examined the sorts of considerations relevant in applying the First Amendment, we now turn to the more specific question of how it should be applied to children. Given that the Supreme Court has been applying the Constitution to issues involving children for many decades, this is by no means a new question. Nevertheless, as the review earlier in this chapter indicated, it is far from clearly settled. In fact, I argued that in the past decade the Court has been particularly confused about children. It knows there is something special about them, but it doesn't remember what.

Applying the First Amendment to children

It may be helpful to consider the relevance of the First Amendment to children with respect to the five aspects of constitutional interpretation distinguished in the previous section.

Text. The First Amendment prohibits Congress from restricting freedoms of religion, expression, and assembly. It makes no distinction between children and adults. Thus, the language of the First Amendment provides no indication that it applies only—or even more strongly—to adults.

Intent. It might nevertheless be argued that the framers of the Bill of Rights only had adults in mind and that, the language notwithstanding, it would be contrary to their intent to apply the First Amendment to children. It is equally arguable, however, that, although the Bill of

Rights refers generally to "people" and "persons," the framers had only white males in mind. Given the later Fourteenth Amendment guarantee of equal protection of the laws, it is clear that, whatever the framers' intent, the Constitution applies to women and nonwhites. Distinctions based on age may be less suspect than those based on gender or race but, whatever the framers' intent, children cannot arbitrarily be considered not to qualify as people.

It is worth adding, moreover, that even if the framers did not intend the First Amendment to apply to children, this does not mean they believed government should be free to control children's religious beliefs and behavior and to restrict their expression. On the contrary, if they thought about the matter at all, the framers undoubtedly assumed that children would be under the control of their parents and would have little or no direct contact with government. It is only with the later rise of public schools that government control of children's beliefs and expression became an issue. In other words, even if the framers did not specifically intend children to have First Amendment rights, this was not because they believed government should have the power to restrict children's intellectual freedom but rather because they implicitly assumed it would have no occasion to do so. Given the rise of public education, the relation between government and children is so fundamentally altered that any specific intent the framers may have had about children is of dubious relevance.

Constitutional theory. It may nevertheless be relevant to consider the more general intent of the framers with respect to the Constitution as a whole. As noted earlier, for example, it might be argued that the Constitution was intended to provide for democratic self-government and that the role of the free expression clause of the First Amendment was thus to guarantee voters the right to criticize the present government and to participate in political discussions leading to the possible election of a new government. Superficially, at least, a case might thus be made that the free expression clause of the First Amendment only applies to those old enough to vote.

Even if one accepts the dubious premise that only political expression is constitutionally protected, however, it does not follow that only adults have a First Amendment right to free expression. Adolescents and even younger children study political issues in school and many are at least as aware of such matters as many adults. Even if minors are not permitted to vote, their views may constitute a relevant contribution to political debate. Moreover, even if political speech lies at the core of the First Amendment, it is not the only form of speech that is constitutionally protected. It is widely recognized that no sharp line can be drawn between political and nonpolitical expression. Any restriction on free expression is thus likely to have a chilling effect on political speech. As discussed earlier, current precedents clearly indicate that speech on virtually all topics, including many relevant to young children, falls within the scope of the First Amendment (Haiman, 1981).

Precedent. As we have seen and will continue to see throughout this book, precedents with respect to application of the First Amendment to children are at best highly complex and multifaceted and at worst mutually contradictory. One key consideration is whether First Amendment issues involving minors should be settled on the basis of general First Amendment law, with due allowance for the special characteristics of children where appropriate, or on the basis of a view of minors as fundamentally different from adults (Rush, 1985). *Tinker*[58] is a good example of the first approach and *Hazelwood*[59] of the second. This book takes the first approach. There is no reason to believe that children and adolescents—right up to the age of majority—are so fundamentally different from adults that the First Amendment either does not apply to them or that its applications must involve a body of case law completely distinct from general First Amendment law. On the contrary, it is argued throughout the book that deviations from general First Amendment law in addressing issues involving minors should be based on specific evidence that children or adolescents of the age in question are different from adults in ways that justify those distinctions. Such an approach has the advantage of settling First Amendment issues involving children on the basis of well worked out First Amendment precedents except where there is specific reason to make new distinctions or exceptions.

Values. Finally, one might argue that in deciding whether and how

58. Tinker v. Des Moines Independent Community School District, 393 U.S. 503 (1969)
59. Hazelwood School District v. Kuhlmeier, 108 S.Ct. 562 (1988)

to apply the First Amendment to children we should consider the values underlying the First Amendment in general and determine their applicability to children. It might be argued, for example, that the point of intellectual freedom is to recognize and protect the dignity of the rational individual. Children, having not yet attained rationality, have no moral stake in freedom of belief or expression. This analysis, however, overlooks the possibility (to be assessed in detail in chapter 3) that many adolescents, who legally are minors, may be at least as rational as many adults. Moreover, children of all ages, even those who are indeed rather irrational, have things they want to express. Even if their observations are childish and their opinions unjustified, it is a moral affront to their dignity not to permit them to have their say. Furthermore, their very irrationality provides greater reason to be vigilant with respect to certain First Amendment concerns, specifically government inculcation of religious, political, or other ideological doctrines.

Alternatively, it might be argued that the purpose of the First Amendment is to promote truth by permitting criticism of current ideas and maximum presentation and consideration of alternatives (cf. Mill, 1859). Since children have not yet attained the level of rationality that allows them to be useful participants in intellectual discourse, their intellectual freedom is of limited significance. Once again, however, it must be recalled that older children and adolescents may indeed be sufficiently rational for there to be social value in protecting their freedoms of belief and expression. Moreover, even in the case of children who are indeed irrational, the First Amendment may be relevant in protecting them from programs of government indoctrination that would hinder their later contributions. Furthermore, as we will see in Chapter 3, even if rationality is in some ways prerequisite to making the best use of intellectual freedom, intellectual freedom is important to the development of rationality. To limit intellectual freedom on the basis of limited rationality is to restrict the development of rationality itself. Ethical considerations, then, suggest that children have a vital stake in the First Amendment and that society as a whole has a compelling interest in including them within its scope.

Finally, although the Constitution nowhere deals explicitly with family rights, the autonomy and privacy of families may be postulated as values that have undergirded our society for centuries and that have achieved constitutional stature as a result of decisions dating back to *Meyer v. Nebraska* (1923)[60] and *Pierce v. Society of Sisters* (1925).[61] Such values, then, may provide an important additional context for First Amendment decisions concerning to what extent government may intervene in children's lives and minds.

The psychology of children

Underlying much of the above discussion are assumptions about the nature of children. Should 16-year-olds have the same First Amendment rights as adults? What about 10-year-olds? What about 4-year-olds? The answers seem to depend on what characteristics we see as the constitutional basis for adult rights and whether children at various ages have those characteristics.

But what children are like at various ages is an empirical question. It cannot be answered by scrutinizing the Constitution. It can only be answered on the basis of empirical evidence about children—that is, through psychological research. This is not to say, of course, that empirical evidence is ever sufficient to resolve questions about constitutional rights. A legal framework is always necessary to determine what evidence is relevant and how it should be applied. The framework should, however, identify the key empirical questions, recognize their empirical nature, and require that they be resolved on the basis of relevant evidence, rather than by appeal to myths, speculations, or unjustified intuitions (Houlgate, 1980; G. B. Melton, 1987b).

For example, children are often denied liberties on the grounds of intellectual incompetence (Mill, 1859). A legal framework based on this rationale must specify that intellectual incompetence is the basis for the distinction between children and adults, identify the nature and level of the skills necessary for minimal competence, and explain their relevance to the liberties in question. Moreover, it must recognize that intellectual incompetence is not an *a priori*, defining characteristic of children but rather a postulated trait subject to empirical investigation. Children of the age in question must be shown

60. 262 U.S. 390
61. 268 U.S. 510

to be incompetent in the relevant respects on the basis of psychological research. It should be clear in this example that neither the legal framework alone nor the psychological research alone can resolve the question of children's rights: each is necessary and neither alone is sufficient.

Although few object in principle to the concept of identifying empirical questions in legal contexts and resolving them through appeal to relevant evidence, there are serious ambiguities and disputes within the law about when research is relevant, what research is relevant, and how research should be used (Black, 1988; Monahan & Walker, 1988). It is frequently and persuasively argued that data from the social and behavioral sciences are insufficiently considered in many areas of the law (Bersoff, 1987; Melton & Russo, 1987). The issue is particularly serious, however, with respect to children (G. B. Melton, 1987a).

Almost everyone has some experience with children and intuitive ideas about them. It is, of course, important not to discount the value of intuition or to suggest that research on children has yielded final, indisputable truths. Nevertheless, there has been systematic research on children for more than a century and the field is sufficiently advanced that the conclusions to be drawn from research, though not final, are often worthy of far greater weight than the intuitions of casual observers. It is critical to scrutinize applications of the First Amendment to children for underlying assumptions about the nature of children's intellects and intellectual development. Empirical matters should be resolved through appeal to relevant evidence. If available evidence is inadequate, this suggests a starting point for further research. Better communication between psychologists and the legal profession can be expected to provide a more solid basis for legal decisions concerning children and better guidance for psychologists who wish to do research with direct relevance for child policy.

The educational context
Given that applications of the First Amendment to children generally arise in the context of public education, it is important to consider the nature of children not just in the abstract but with respect to their behavior and experience in public schools. One might even theorize

that the Supreme Court's approach to children's First Amendment rights derives at least as much from its conception of education as from its conception of children.

Hazelwood provides some support for this view. For expression outside the educational curriculum, it reaffirms the standards of *Tinker*, which do not distinguish children from adults. Within the curriculum, by contrast, it provides greater leeway for censorship, for reasons that refer less to the age of the students than to what the Court perceives as the legitimate goals and needs of an educational institution. Similarly, in *Fraser*, the censorship was justified on the basis of a curricular intent to foster civility. This analysis is consistent with other cases concluding that children have due process and privacy rights but that, within public schools, these rights are less extensive than elsewhere.[62] There is no doubt, then, that the present Court, unlike that of *Barnette*, views public education as a special context in which many fundamental constitutional rights have only limited application. Far from applying strict scrutiny, it seems increasingly disposed to accept any action by school officials that is arguably "reasonable" (Rose, 1988).

It would be a mistake, however, to conclude that childhood status is not a factor in these decisions. *Hazelwood* and *Fraser* both refer explicitly to the age and immaturity of the students in question. Moreover, if the educational context were the only consideration, one would expect the Court's analysis to apply to public colleges and universities as well. But this is not generally the case. In *Widmar v. Vincent* (1981), for example, the University of Missouri argued that it should be permitted to restrict meetings by student religious groups in the student union in order to prevent a perceived establishment of religion.[63] This is not only a reasonable consideration but one that the Supreme Court has taken extremely seriously in cases involving public elementary and secondary schools. Nevertheless, the Court carefully scrutinized this restriction on freedom of expression. Emphasizing that college students are young adults and would understand the university's non-

62. New Jersey v. T.L.O., 469 U.S. 325 (1985); see also Goss v. Lopez, 419 U.S. 565 (1975)
63. 454 U.S. 263

endorsement of religion, it concluded that the university's interest was not sufficient to override the free speech rights of the students.

Unless one takes age into account, this rationale appears inconsistent with the *Hazelwood* conclusion that public high schools may censor expression of political views in order to avoid those views being incorrectly construed as the views of the school itself.[64] More broadly, the Court has not seemed inclined to extend its analysis of constitutional rights in public elementary and secondary schools to the level of college education, even where such education is also public. It appears that the Court's analysis in cases involving students in public elementary and secondary schools, though substantially based on what it perceives as the special goals and requirements of education, is also based on what the Court perceives to be the immaturity of the students in question.

Although empirical evidence provides grounds to question the Supreme Court's intuitions about both children and education, the Court is surely correct about the potential relevance of both factors. To understand children's First Amendment rights, we must consider not only the psychology of children but the purpose and nature of public education, since it is largely within the educational context that children's First Amendment rights become an issue. As we shall see in Chapter 3, much evidence concerning children directly concerns the processes by which they learn and develop and thus is relevant to understanding both the nature of children and the nature of education.

Conclusion: Children as Persons

Personhood plays a central role in both law and ethics (Moore, 1984). To a large extent one can trace the legal and ethical progress of humanity over the centuries in terms of the increasing accordance of full personhood to individuals regardless of race, religion, or sex. Many of the major lapses in law and ethics are similarly understandable in these terms. In the United States, the *Dred Scott* decision, denying blacks the constitutional status of persons,[65] remains justly infamous.

64. 108 S.Ct. 562, 570
65. Dred Scott v. Sandford, 60 U.S. 393 (1857)

The later determination that Native Americans are persons within the meaning of the law (Brown, 1970, Chap. 15: Standing Bear Becomes A Person) was a moral as well as a legal triumph. Similarly, the Holocaust did not emerge *ex nihilo* in the 1940s but was the endpoint of a systematic process beginning in the early 1930s by which Jews were gradually deprived of their legal status as German citizens and, ultimately, of their moral status as persons (Dawidowicz, 1975).

Considered in this context, the question of whether children are persons may be seen as an issue of fundamental significance. On one hand, denial of personhood has an appalling history. On the other hand, to consider the extreme case, it is clear that there are differences between newborn babies and adults far more dramatic in ways relevant to personhood than the differences among races, among religions, or between males and females. Babies are so different from adults that it is often not even clear what it would *mean* to accord them full human rights (e.g., free exercise of religion), much less whether this is a good idea.

The present approach suggests that, in considering restrictions on liberty, we should err on the side of personhood. We should assume that children are persons but recognize that, at least at early ages, they may be qualitatively different from adults in ways that relate to even the most basic rights of persons (cf. Rush, 1985, especially pp. 487–493). They should not have to earn the status of persons by meeting certain criteria, but they may be deprived of certain rights if—and only if—it is shown that they fail to meet criteria (such as rationality) directly relevant to the rights in question (such as free use of the intellect).

With children, as with adults, however, the burden should be on the government to show on the basis of relevant empirical evidence that fundamental rights should be denied (Rush, 1985). Childhood status in itself should never be a basis for denial of personhood. As Horton the elephant says,

> After all
> A person's a person. No matter how small.
> (Seuss, 1954)

2 : Proposed First Amendment Principles

The conceptual distance from the 45 words of the First Amendment to the numerous, multifaceted issues of children and schools is very great. It is not surprising that application of the First Amendment to these issues is a matter of intense controversy.

There is obviously no mechanical procedure for objectively deriving definitive solutions to issues such as school prayer, textbook censorship, or teaching creationism. Nevertheless, we should aim for resolutions to such problems that, though necessarily involving subjective judgment, are sufficiently objective to allow substantial agreement —at least among relevant authorities—for all but a few genuinely borderline cases. What is needed is a level of analysis midway between, and thus linking, the First Amendment and the specific issues that bedevil us.

A Principled Approach to Children's First Amendment Rights

It is clearly praise to refer to someone as a man or woman of principle and criticism to label someone "unprincipled." But what exactly does it mean to be a principled person and why is this a good thing?

At the very least, the principled person distinguishes matters of personal choice ("Shall I have chocolate or vanilla ice cream?") from matters of principle, and recognizes that with respect to the latter his or her decisions must be in accord with moral obligations (Kant, 1785/ 1959). In the social/political realm, this means distinguishing issues of *principle* from issues of *policy* (Dworkin, 1978, 1985, 1986). Issues of policy involve a range of legally and morally legitimate choices. These choices are and should be made via negotiation, compromise, and democratic vote. If there are multiple competing interests, complex bargaining and compromising may be involved in cementing a majority. In the end, however, the majority rules.

On matters of principle, on the other hand, the will of the majority should make no difference and compromise is, if at all possible, to be scrupulously avoided. Matters of principle include fundamental moral or constitutional rights, such as the intellectual freedoms guaranteed by the First Amendment. On matters of this sort, the individual has not merely interests but fundamental rights that should not be compromised and should not be subject to majority preferences.

To be fully meaningful, however, commitment to *principle* must be translated into a commitment to a clearly articulated set of *principles*. The Constitution, especially the Bill of Rights and the Fourteenth Amendment, lays out some of the basic constitutional principles that are to guide American government and makes it clear that these are to be treated as principles in the sense just discussed: they involve individual rights that are not subject to majority vote (Oakes, 1987; Reinstein, 1988). The principles are so broad and abstract that their application to specific contemporary circumstances is often a matter of intense dispute. This does not render the principles meaningless, but it does complicate the question of what constitutes a principled approach.

The purpose of this chapter is to articulate the fundamental principles of intellectual freedom that underlie the First Amendment in such a way as to make them more directly and objectively applicable to current issues involving children. Needless to say, this does not eliminate the need for subjective judgment in applying the principles and the resulting potential for substantial controversy regarding their application. Principles are not concrete solutions to particular cases; they are necessarily abstract. Nevertheless, I have tried, through the elaboration of a set of principles, to somewhat narrow the conceptual gap between the First Amendment and contemporary issues of children's intellectual freedom.

This approach is consistent with the analysis of constitutional interpretation in Chapter 1. The focus on settling constitutional dilemmas by applying principles that go beyond the literal language of the First Amendment acknowledges that the First Amendment must be interpreted and extended rather than applied in a direct, mechanical fashion. At the same time, the requirement that the principles be derived from and defended in terms of the First Amendment acknowledges that constitutional issues should be settled on the basis of the Constitution rather than purely on the basis of judges' personal values.

The following section of this chapter proposes and defends a set of six principles. It is argued that these principles embody the implications of the First Amendment for children. Although they are thus necessarily abstract and general, they are sufficiently concrete and specific to yield clear solutions to a variety of current educational issues. These issues will be presented, and the principles applied to them, in Chapter Four.

The present chapter then proceeds beyond the First Amendment to formulate seven additional principles consistent with its underlying ethical philosophy. It is argued that, from a constitutional point of view, these principles are based on an unduly broad construction of the First Amendment and thus cannot be considered constitutional mandates. Nevertheless, it is suggested that they can serve as moral guidelines for parents and as a basis for policy decisions by government.

Children's First Amendment Rights:
Proposed Principles

Table 1 (p. xv) presents six principles addressing the First Amendment rights of children. The first five are expressed in terms of limitations on government action. They reflect the standard view (van Geel, 1986, 1987) that the First Amendment places restrictions on all levels of government, including public schools, but not on individuals acting in nongovernmental capacities (e.g., parents, private schools). The sixth principle restricts the extent to which childhood status may be used to limit application of the first five principles. This section will be devoted to clarifying and justifying the six principles.

It is important to note in advance that these principles, though broadly consistent with established constitutional doctrine (cf. Chapter 1), represent a theory of the First Amendment, not a summary of current case law. That is, although I will argue that public schools should act in accord with these principles, the Supreme Court has not consistently required them to do so. Actual First Amendment decisions will be presented and analyzed in Chapter 4.

Free expression

The first principle reads as follows:

> Principle 1. *Free Expression*. (a) Government may not hinder children from forming or expressing any idea unless the abridgment of belief or expression serves a compelling purpose (e.g., to prevent disruption of education) that cannot be served in a less restrictive way. (b) *Freedom of Nonexpression*. Government may not require children to adopt or express a belief in any idea.

This principle follows directly from the First Amendment's mandate that government may not abridge freedom of speech or of the press. It includes the formation as well as the expression of ideas, since the right to express an idea is meaningless if you are prevented from forming or thinking about it (van Geel, 1983). In the words of federal judge Joseph Tauro,

> the First Amendment protects the communication of ideas. That protected right of communication presupposes a capacity to produce ideas. As a practical matter, therefore, the power to produce ideas is fundamental to our cherished right to communicate and is entitled to comparable constitutional protection.[1]

Government does not, however, have a First Amendment obligation to *facilitate* the formation or expression of ideas; it is merely forbidden to hinder the child. The First Amendment does not create an entitlement to government assistance but rather protects a liberty against government infringement.

The principle does allow for exceptions. If there is a compelling reason to restrict expression of certain ideas, limits may be imposed.

---

1. Rogers v. Okin, U.S.L.W., CA 75-1601-T, District Court of Massachusetts, slip opinion, p. 68

A math teacher may, for example, limit a student's expression of political opinions during class time in order to protect the right of other students to learn algebra. Even statements relevant to the course may be limited in order to guide discussion in a direction that, in the teacher's professional judgment, will be most educational (Strike, 1982b). Within the public school classroom, time is finite and the school has a compelling interest in using it for educational purposes. Even in this context, however, if it appears that certain students or certain views are systematically censored, the government should be expected to demonstrate that it had reason for the limitation, that the reason was sufficiently compelling to justify abridging a First Amendment right, and that there was no way to solve the problem that would have been less restrictive of children's rights.

The second part of Principle 1 (*Freedom of Nonexpression*) is closely related to the first. Freedom of expression implies not only freedom to form and express one's own ideas but freedom not to adopt or express ideas of which one has not been convinced. Freedom of expression would mean little if one could be required to contradict one's own views or statements. Requiring a child to make a pledge or sing a song that expresses views contrary to his or her own clearly would be an abridgment of freedom of speech. Children may, of course, be required to show they *understand* course material (e.g., 2 + 2 = 4; species evolve), but may not be required to say they believe what they in fact do not. This principle is stated in absolute terms. In the oft-quoted words of Justice Jackson:

> If there is any fixed star in our constitutional constellation, it is that no official, high or petty, can prescribe what shall be orthodox in politics, nationalism, religion, or other matters of opinion or force citizens to confess by word or act their faith therein. If there are any circumstances which permit an exception, they do not now occur to us.[2]

Free exercise of religion
The second principle follows the First Amendment in noting that in the area of religion one not only has the right to hold and express

2. West Virginia State Board of Education v. Barnette, 319 U.S. 624, 642 (1943)

certain beliefs but the right to act on them—that is, to behave as one's religion requires.

Principle 2. *Free Exercise of Religion*. Government may not restrict children from acting in accord with their religious beliefs unless the restriction serves a compelling purpose (e.g., to prevent a perceived establishment of religion in a public school) that cannot be served in a less restrictive way.

Since behavior, more than speech, has the potential to interfere with the rights of others, the right to free exercise is necessarily far from absolute. One might need to limit it in a public school setting, for example, if a child is doing things that interfere with the education of others, such as praying aloud during class. To limit a child's free exercise of religion, however, the government must show that there is a compelling reason to do so and that the limitation is the least restrictive available.

Consider, for example, a case where voluntary religious activities by students on school premises create the impression that the school has endorsed a particular religion. This may have the effect of inculcating those religious views in other children, thus violating Principle 5b. Cases of this sort pit Principle 2, based on the free exercise clause of the First Amendment, against Principle 5b, based more directly on the establishment clause. Because the First Amendment provides no ranking of these clauses in overall importance, one must attempt to respect both to the extent that this can be achieved. Although the best solution would depend on the specific circumstances, it is conceivable that some limitation on free exercise by the religious students might be necessary to achieve the government's compelling interest in avoiding perceived establishment of religion in the public school and thus protecting the rights of the other children. Government could be required, however, to justify its solution by showing that alternative solutions less restrictive with respect to free exercise by the religious students fail to resolve the establishment problem with respect to the nonreligious students.

Freedom of access

The third principle also raises complex issues. It relates to what is often termed a *right to know*.

Principle 3. *Freedom of Access.* Government may not restrict a child's access to ideas and sources of information unless the restriction serves a compelling purpose (e.g., to prevent demonstrable harm to the child) that cannot be served in a less restrictive way.

Access to a variety of sources of information and to a diversity of opinions and perspectives plays an important role in formulating one's own ideas, which in turn is necessary in order to have anything to express. Moreover, freedom of expression obviously becomes meaningless if government can prevent access by others to one's ideas. Thus, although the First Amendment refers to expression rather than receipt of ideas, it directly entails a right to receive as well (for a summary of Supreme Court decisions recognizing this right, see Bowers, 1983, pp. 566–568).

It would go too far, however, to say that people have a positive First Amendment right to express or right to know. In forbidding abridgment of expression, the First Amendment does not generally require government to *facilitate* expression (e.g., by providing financial support for publication). Similarly, with respect to receipt of ideas, government is not affirmatively obligated to provide a child with every idea anyone has expressed. It simply may not take action to restrict his or her access.

Although the right to know is thus limited, the Freedom of Access principle nevertheless accords it a meaningful status. Government may (actively) restrict a child's access to ideas or materials only when it can demonstrate a compelling reason for doing so.

Freedom of association

Principle 4. *Freedom of Association.* Government may not hinder children from associating with others of their own choice, nor require undesired associations, unless the abridgment of free association or nonassociation serves a compelling purpose (e.g., to enable education) that cannot be served in a less restrictive way.

The First Amendment (as extended to the states by the Fourteenth) requires that government take no action "abridging . . . the right of the people peaceably to assemble. . . ." As noted in Chapter 1, freedom of association is critical to genuine freedom of expression and to the free exercise of religion (Haiman, 1981).

Limited inculcation

Extending the first four principles, one is tempted to suggest that genuine respect for a child's freedom of belief and expression forbids government to inculcate any ideas whatsoever. The ideal of government by the will of the people, after all, becomes meaningless if government is free to mold the will of the next generation via the public schools (Arons, 1983; Garvey, 1979; Gottlieb, 1987; Harpaz, 1986; Kamiat, 1983; van Geel, 1983, 1986; Yudof, 1987). As Justice Jackson put it in *West Virginia v. Barnette* (1943),

> [w]e set up government by consent of the governed, and the Bill of Rights denies those in power any legal opportunity to coerce that consent. Authority here is to be controlled by public opinion, not public opinion by authority.[3]

Government, one might argue, should be strictly content-neutral, leaving all judgments of truth or falsity up to children and/or their parents. Public education should present all ideas and facts but take no stand, thus avoiding inculcation.

Any realistic consideration of the nature of education immediately raises serious problems for this view (Arons, 1983; Freeman, 1984; Strike, 1982b). It is difficult to see how public education would be possible at all if government inculcation—that is, systematic efforts by public school teachers to get students to believe certain things without fully exploring reasons and options—were strictly forbidden. There simply isn't time for full exploration of all topics, arguments, and alternatives.

One might propose as a solution that topic selection and inculcation of facts should be permitted but not inculcation of values. This would allow a public school to decide to devote more time to mathematics than to music, for example, and would allow a teacher to inculcate the idea that $2 + 2 = 4$. But this doesn't solve the problem. If a teacher be-

3. *Id.* at 641

lieves that math is a valuable skill and students perceive and adopt this view, the teacher is inculcating a value. Even within the "purely" cognitive (as opposed to the affective, social, or moral) realm, inculcation of values is unavoidable (Raven, 1987).

Consideration of the nature of children compounds the problem. Children, especially at very early ages, show powerful inclinations to imitate what they observe and believe what they are told, particularly when the models or authorities are prestigious adults such as teachers (Maccoby & Martin, 1983; Minuchin & Shapiro, 1983). It would be virtually impossible to be around a young child for any length of time and *not* inculcate ideas and values to some degree. Again, inculcation is simply unavoidable.

Moreover, even if inculcation could be avoided, it is not clear that it should be. Society has accumulated an immense store of knowledge and values over thousands of years. The transmission of this social wisdom is widely viewed as a major—if not *the* major—purpose of education. Unless we expect each child to reinvent the wheel, it is hard to see how such transmission could occur without some degree of inculcation (Strike, 1982b). Provided the ideas and values inculcated are potentially subject to later critical analysis, they need not constrain intellectual freedom. On the contrary, they may serve as a springboard for intellectual development.

Accordingly, the fifth principle does not view inculcation as an inherent infringement on any fundamental liberty and does not, in general, require a compelling justification for it. Nevertheless, as discussed earlier, there are constitutional reasons for deep concern about government inculcation, especially—given compulsory education laws—in the public school context. The principle therefore includes three limitations.

> Principle 5. *Limited Inculcation*. (a) *Legitimate Purpose*. Government may inculcate ideas and values, but only when it has a legitimate purpose for doing so (e.g., to produce educated citizens). (b) *Religious Neutrality*. Government inculcation may not have, as its purpose or principal effect, the advancement or hindrance of any religion or of religion in general. (c) *Nonindoctrination*. Government may not indoctrinate—that is, it may not inculcate ideas

or values in a way that unnecessarily limits the possibility of critical or rational analysis.

Legitimate purpose. Government must have a legitimate basis for inculcation. It may be expected to show, for example, that there is educational worth for the individual in the ideas it is inculcating or general benefit to society in the inculcation of certain values. Obviously, this is not as strict a standard as requiring a "compelling reason." It allows state legislatures and school boards substantial leeway to promote whatever they define as education.

Nevertheless, Principle 5a does set real (though very broad) limits on government authority to transmit ideas and values. For example, there can be no legitimate reason for systematically inculcating or refuting the platform of a particular political party. Similarly, if the intent of the First Amendment is, in part, to foster genuine self-government, there can be no justification for inculcating particular answers to current or potential political controversies (e.g., by fostering support for or opposition to controversial laws, bills, or court decisions). Finally, there can be no educational purpose for teaching ideas (e.g., that the earth is young, flat, or the center of the universe) that are justifiably rejected by virtually all professionals in the relevant discipline.

Religious neutrality. Given the First Amendment's explicit concern about religious liberty, a much stronger limit on inculcation of religious ideas seems called for (McCarthy, 1983; Melton, 1986). Although Principle 5b derives from the religion clauses of the First Amendment, its inclusion within Principle 5 makes it a special case of a broader concern with government inculcation. In general, inculcation is permitted to a substantial degree, but Principle 5b severely restricts government inculcation with respect to religion.

The religion clauses of the First Amendment are commonly interpreted as requiring a wall of separation between church and state (Pfeffer, 1984). This view, however, presents a number of difficulties (Beschle, 1987, McConnell, 1987), especially with respect to public education (Laycock, 1986; McConnell, 1986). If church is to be strictly separated from state, must students with strong religious beliefs be excluded from public schools? Should they be admitted but forbidden to express their views or visibly associate with like-minded students?

Must textbooks concerning history and culture avoid addressing the role of religion? Must value inculcation be limited to values with no religious connections (assuming any such values can be found)? Affirmative answers to these questions would seriously compromise free speech, free association, and free exercise of religion for religious students, would mandate highly distorted treatments of American and world history and culture, and might even inculcate an anti-religious worldview.

One possible solution is to relax the wall of separation. Perhaps it need not be high and impregnable. Perhaps the wall between church and state should be of moderate height or slightly porous. But how high and how porous should it be? There is no clear, principled way to answer these questions.

Principle 5b avoids such questions by relying not on the wall-of-separation metaphor but on the analytically more useful concept of government neutrality with respect to religion (Beschle, 1987; Freed, 1986; Laycock, 1986). Rather than banning religion from public schools, it constrains government action against religion as much as government action supporting religion. The two religion clauses are together interpreted as requiring that government neither support nor oppose any particular religion or religion in general. The intent and main effect of all government action must be religiously neutral. In order to achieve such neutrality, it is often wise to minimize contacts between government and religion. Separation of church and state may thus be an appropriate solution to many issues. Even in such cases, however, the analysis favored by Principle 5b views it as a means to an end, not an end in itself.

Principle 5b thus requires religious neutrality in purpose and principal effect. With respect to purpose, application of the principle is of course complicated by the fact that government actions often have several purposes. The key consideration in cases of multifaceted intent, it seems to me, should be whether a religious purpose was decisive. With respect to actual litigation, the initial burden would be on the plaintiff to show a religious purpose. Given a successful showing by the plaintiff, the burden would shift to the government to demonstrate that it had a secular purpose for its action and would have taken the action for that reason in the absence of any religious intent. In other words, whenever a religious motive can be demonstrated, government must show that the religious purpose did not affect the actual decision (Simson, 1987).

In the absence of a decisive religious purpose, government action may still violate Principle 5b on the basis of its effects. Effects of a government action, however, are likely to be even more multifaceted than its purposes. Principle 5b indicates that a government action with no religious intent nevertheless may be unconstitutional if its primary effect is to advance or hinder religion. The principle does not, however, rule out government actions in which there is some incidental advancement or hindrance of religion provided this is an unavoidable side effect of government's secular purpose and primary effect.

Principle 5b is generally consistent with the first two prongs of the *Lemon* test[4] (see Chapter 1). It does not, however, include *Lemon*'s ban on "excessive" entanglement between government and religion. This omission does not constitute an endorsement of church/state entanglement but rather reflects my view that some entanglement is unavoidable and that entanglement is excessive precisely when it unnecessarily threatens government neutrality toward religion. Entanglement, then, is not a separate concern but a consideration already implicit in Principle 5b. Church/state entanglement violates Principle 5b when its purpose or primary effect is not religiously neutral.

Nonindoctrination. Finally, Principle 5c recognizes a continuum extending from (relatively) non-inculcative teaching through inculcation to indoctrination (cf. Gottlieb, 1987; Kilpatrick, 1972; Siegel, 1986, 1988). In non-inculcative teaching, a wide diversity of views and a range of information are presented. Students are encouraged to pursue their interests and ideas and to express and justify their opinions. In inculcation, the teacher does not present students with the full range of reasons for believing something or a full range of alternative ideas because the time available is limited or because the students' cognitive abilities are too immature for them to grasp certain justifications or to grapple with competing points of view. In *indoctrination*, by contrast, reasons and alternatives are omitted because the school (or

---

4. Lemon v. Kurtzman, 403 U.S. 602 (1971)

other indoctrinator) does not want the views it favors to be subjected to critical analysis or rational evaluation. Viewpoints are presented, for example, as if no alternative could possibly be defensible, with the intention that students not only will adopt certain beliefs but will continue to believe them regardless of relevant evidence (Snook, 1972). In other words, although inculcation involves transmission of ideas and values without full appeal to the learner's critical rationality, indoctrination unnecessarily goes beyond this to short-circuit the possibility of rational analysis.

Principle 5c absolutely forbids governmental indoctrination. It recognizes that schools often must inculcate ideas in a way that limits —or at least fails to encourage—questioning. Public school teachers must decide what topics, views, arguments, and information to teach and what to omit on the basis of professional judgments about what is important for children to learn and what they are intellectually capable of understanding. In presenting ideas, however, they may not withhold contradictory evidence, alternative ideas, or relevant contrary arguments, or discourage questions or critical observations, simply in order to direct students' minds toward certain beliefs.

With respect to specific litigation, the initial burden should be on the plaintiff to make a *prima facie* case that indoctrination is taking place. Such a case might be made by showing a pervasively non-objective presentation of ideas, systematic exclusion of major relevant points of view, inclusion of clearly discredited viewpoints, or frequent omission of important relevant evidence. Thus, for example, the plaintiff might show that a curriculum or major textbook systematically ridicules or omits a perspective that has strong support in the scholarly literature. A *prima facie* case for indoctrination might also consist of evidence of unbalanced or questionable input in the preparation or selection of a curriculum or text. There would be grounds for suspicion, for example, if a state adopted a state history text that was developed and donated by a particular ethnic, religious, or political group, especially if the text unduly emphasized the positive role of that group, or the negative role of its adversaries, in the history of the state.

Given a successful showing by the plaintiff, the burden would shift to the school system, school board, or state to show that the demonstrated substantial deviations from full presentation and objective treatment are justified on the basis of educational goals, practical constraints, and/or empirical evidence concerning the intellectual competence of the students in question. A public school need not provide an open marketplace of ideas, but when its deviations from that ideal are sufficiently substantial and systematic to raise a spectre of indoctrination, it may be expected to justify its choices.

In sum, government restrictions on critical analysis go beyond inculcation to indoctrination when they cannot be justified on educational grounds. Public school teachers must recognize limitations in students' critical thinking abilities but must not systematically educate them in such a way as to hinder the development of their rational competencies and, thus, their abilities to exercise First Amendment freedoms of belief and expression. The intent of inculcation should be to instill rebuttable presumptions that may serve as a starting point for reasoning, not unquestionable absolutes that will inhibit rational analysis. Government may not "cast a pall of orthodoxy over the classroom."[5]

Nonarbitrary distinction of child from adult
The first five principles are stated in terms of limitations on government action. It is specified, however, that most of these limitations are not absolute. The principles suggest that government may inculcate ideas and values to a considerable extent and may limit children's freedom of expression, free exercise of religion, access to ideas, and freedom of association to the extent that it can demonstrate a compelling interest in doing so. The compelling interest standard, routinely applied by the courts when constitutional rights are at stake, is a stiff but not insurmountable one. In proposing that such a standard should be met to justify denying children First Amendment protections, it is implied that childhood status itself is not a compelling reason for denial of rights.

The issue of childhood status as a basis for denying rights is sufficiently important to merit a principle of its own.

5. Keyishian v. Board of Regents of the University of the State of New York, 385 U.S. 589, 603 (1967)

Principle 6. *Nonarbitrary Distinction of Child from Adult*. Protection of children from harm due to their limited rationality may be a compelling reason for limiting their First Amendment rights provided it can be shown that (a) the children in question are less rational than a minimally normal adult; (b) the difference in rationality is of a nature and extent such that substantial harm is likely unless First Amendment freedoms are abridged; and (c) the potential harm outweighs countervailing parental and First Amendment interests.

The usual justification for restricting children's freedom is that children are irrational (Garvey, 1979). Judicial decisions, as well as legal and philosophical analyses, do not always make this explicit. They often suggest or assume a wide variety of limitations related to children's cognitive or emotional immaturity. The central concern, however, is not with superficial lapses in perception or memory, specific gaps in concepts or vocabulary, or distraction due to momentarily disturbing feelings. Adults as well as children are subject to such difficulties. Rather, the focus in distinguishing children from adults is on deeper problems in understanding, reasoning, and decision making that appear to relate to a systematic deficit in basic rationality.

Even adults, of course, may be patently irrational without immediately forfeiting their basic human rights (Moshman, 1985c). Nevertheless, there is no doubt that irrational individuals are likely not to act in their own best interests, and are thus likely to suffer harm unless their freedoms are limited. More specifically, with respect to the First Amendment, they may dangerously misconstrue or fail to evaluate ideas. Principle 6 acknowledges the relevance of this argument to children but requires an empirical basis for invoking it (cf. Houlgate, 1980). It puts the burden of proof on the government to show that any asserted difference in rationality between children and adults does exist and does result in sufficiently serious risk to justify abridging fundamental rights. That demonstration must be based on empirical evidence rather than speculative intuitions about children.

This analysis views children as—in a legal sense—persons. It assumes that the First Amendment applies to all people and then proceeds, with caution, to the recognition of exceptions. This approach can be justified on the ground that the Bill of Rights nowhere distinguishes children from adults—it refers only to "people" and "persons." The literal language of the First Amendment constrains *all* government interference with freedoms of religion and expression. A clear intent of the Amendment—and one relevant to children as well as adults—was to protect the intellectual autonomy necessary for self-government (Harpaz, 1986).

Criterion 6a sets the rationality of a normal adult as the constitutionally relevant standard. It is, of course, possible to propose standards of perfect rationality that few adults ever meet and no adults meet consistently. Clearly, we do not deny adults fundamental rights on the basis of whether they meet such a rational ideal. Rather, we deny them fundamental rights (e.g., by restricting them to psychiatric wards and subjecting them to mandatory treatments) only if they fall demonstrably so far below the typical level of rationality that they are judged to be dangerously outside the normal range. Presumably, as we consider younger and younger children, the proportion who fall below the normal adult range increases, and the case for restricting fundamental liberties becomes correspondingly stronger. The central point here is that the appropriate standard is not some rational ideal, nor even the rationality of an average or typical adult, but rather the rationality of a minimally normal adult. The question of what constitutes normal adult rationality is, of course, an empirical issue; it will be treated in detail in Chapter 3.

Criterion 6b specifies that although subnormal rationality is necessary for denial of First Amendment rights it is not sufficient. The criterion requires inquiry into the nature and extent of the irrationality and a demonstration that substantial harm is likely unless First Amendment freedoms of religion and expression are abridged.

It might be argued that, in case of doubt, government should err on the side of protecting children from any risk of harm (cf. Wringe, 1986). Criterion 6b requires a more stringent standard in mandating that the harm be likely and substantial. Obviously, there is room for considerable difference of opinion in making evaluations of degree of risk and harm. Criterion 6c suggests the rationale for requiring likelihood of substantial harm and provides some basis for evaluation. Government restriction of children must be weighed against (1) parental rights to raise their own children, (2) children's First Amendment interests, and (3) the First Amendment interests of the community. I will consider each of these points in turn.

Government protection is not the only, or even the major, protection children have. On the contrary, our society relies primarily on parents to protect their children from reading harmful materials or forming dangerous beliefs. For government to step in and play a role in this seriously threatens not only children's rights but the rights of their parents as well (Garvey, 1981). As Justice Fortas wrote,

> It begs the question to present . . . undefined, unlimited censorship as an aid to parents in the rearing of their children. . . . [U]ndefined and unlimited approval of state censorship . . . denies to children free access to books and works of art to which many parents may wish their children to have uninhibited access.[6]

Government should indeed have the power to limit children's access to harmful materials, but should be required to demonstrate a strong likelihood of substantial harm to prove its compelling interest in any particular case.

Government protection is also a threat to children's First Amendment liberties. Child or adult, liberty is important to the individual in permitting her to pursue her own ends. Such freedom is valued not only in that it presumably enables one to attain those ends but for its symbolic recognition of one's personhood. Being accorded intellectual freedom may not immediately lead children to better understanding but, even when it fails to do so, may be important for their conception of themselves as autonomous agents. For children as well as adults, external constraints on what one may see, say, or believe go right to the heart of one's personal sense of human dignity.

Furthermore, even if one is concerned only with adult liberties, it is critical to keep in mind that children turn into adults and that what they can think and express as adults depends in large part on their experiences as children (Feinberg, 1980; Garvey, 1979; Kilpatrick, 1972). A strong case can be made that, as future adults, children have

6. Ginsberg v. New York, 390 U.S. 629, 674 (1968) (Fortas, J., dissenting)

First Amendment interests at least as great as those of present adults. There is substantial evidence that exposure to diverse points of view and encouragement to form, express, and discuss one's opinions are crucial to intellectual development (Bearison, Magzamen, & Filardo, 1986; Berkowitz, 1985; Johnson & Johnson, 1985; Walker, 1983). When government denies an adult access to diverse ideas, it is restricting available input; in denying such access to a child, however, it is also restricting development of the ability to coordinate differing views. Similarly, when government denies an adult free expression, it is denying the opportunity to communicate; in denying free expression to a child, however, it is also restricting development of the ability to form his or her own ideas. In short, denying First Amendment rights to a child restricts not merely the present exercise of those rights but also the further development of precisely those rational competencies that make the First Amendment meaningful. Contrary to the suggestion that children have limited First Amendment interests, then, it appears that, as future adults, they may have *more* to lose than present adults from government restriction of their intellectual freedoms.

An equally strong case can be made that the community as a whole has a compelling interest in children's First Amendment rights. Self-government requires a substantial degree of intellectual competence and autonomy in its citizens; to the extent that the First Amendment promotes these it prepares children for their civic responsibilities as adults (Garvey, 1979; Kilpatrick, 1972; Siegel, 1986, 1988).

Moreover, denial of First Amendment rights in public schools raises a special problem of its own. One of the major rationales for compulsory education is the need to develop good citizenship. Presumably, good citizenship in the United States includes understanding of and respect for the Bill of Rights. But students can hardly be expected to learn this if the school itself demonstrates by its actions that it sees the First Amendment primarily as a threat to public order and civility. We must not "teach youth to discount important principles of our government as mere platitudes."[7] The community has a strong interest in public schools that, rather than applying the First Amendment in as

7. West Virginia State Board of Education v. Barnette, 319 U.S. 624, 637 (1943)

restrictive a fashion as they can get away with, instead take particular care to demonstrate government respect for freedoms of religion and expression (Franks, 1986).

In sum, although allowing children too much freedom may put them at risk, there is also profound risk in restricting them too much. The Bill of Rights embodies the philosophy that government restriction poses dangers of its own that may be greater than the harms it is intended to avoid. It is not obvious that in doubtful cases the State should err on the side of protecting children from dangerous options and harmful ideas. It may in fact be (a) imposing on parental discretion; (b) jeopardizing children's dignity and autonomy; (c) shielding children from perspectives and possibilities that would, in the long run, be intellectually liberating; (d) subverting community interests by producing a generation incapable of or indisposed toward independent thinking; and perhaps even (e) fostering contempt for the constitutional value of individual liberty. When evidence is lacking or ambiguous, the Bill of Rights requires government to err on the side of too much freedom, rather than on the side of unnecessary restriction.

Children's Intellectual Rights: Proposed Principles

It would be historically inaccurate and ethically obtuse to view the First Amendment as an arbitrary legalism that just happened to find its way into the Constitution. On the contrary, the First Amendment was based on philosophical conceptions of fundamental intellectual rights considered to have a moral basis prior to government (Bogen, 1983). Moral rights not derived from any particular governmental, legal, or social system were commonly referred to as "natural rights"; today they are usually labeled "human rights." They are the sorts of rights codified in the Universal Declaration of Human Rights (adopted by the General Assembly of the United Nations on December 10, 1948) that governments of any form or ideology are widely considered obligated to respect.

This section focuses on seven principles concerning children's intellectual rights. These are consistent with the six First Amendment principles but go beyond them in that they are derived not from the First Amendment itself but from what I have taken to be the broader philosophy of intellectual freedom underlying the First Amendment. Accordingly, I will argue that there is no constitutional obligation to respect these rights. I will, however, argue that governments, private schools, and parents are *morally* obligated to act in accord with these principles. I will support this claim by showing that the principles are consistent with other ethical standards and with both of the major contemporary philosophical approaches to ethics.

Seven principles of children's intellectual rights

Table 2 (p. xvii) presents seven principles concerning the intellectual rights of children. These are derived from the six principles that were in turn derived from the First Amendment. Although the new principles are thus consistent with the general philosophy of intellectual freedom underlying the First Amendment, they go too far beyond the actual language of the First Amendment to be considered constitutional guarantees. They do, however, correspond to the sorts of intellectual rights that philosophers (e.g., Siegel, 1986, 1988; Snook, 1972; Strike, 1982a, 1982b; Strike & Soltis, 1985; Tucker, 1985; Wilson, 1972) justify on moral grounds. They may thus be considered moral rather than legal rights.

Principles 7 through 11 correspond respectively to the First Amendment requirements of Principles 1 through 5. They differ in three major respects. First, they take the form "Children have a right . . ." rather than "Government may not . . ." Although the First Amendment merely sets limits on government actions, its moral intent is clearly to prevent people from being limited in the exercise of freedoms to which they are morally entitled. Whether a child is indoctrinated by the government or by his or her parents may be a constitutionally significant distinction but, from the point of view of the child's access to the intellectual world, is irrelevant. We should thus construe the underlying moral philosophy of the First Amendment as providing for certain intellectual rights. Only the government is *constitutionally* required to respect these rights (van Geel, 1986) but private individuals, including parents, have corresponding moral obligations.

A second difference between the rights in the two sets is that those in the second set are expressed more absolutely, with fewer qualifications. There are, of course, limitations on rights in the latter set corresponding to those noted in the former set, and it would have been possible to write these into the principles. Not doing so, however, has the advantage of reminding us that, even when denial of a certain right is justifiable, it is nonetheless regrettable. It may be appropriate to forbid a 9-year-old to read certain things but it is unfortunate when this is necessary. It follows that in limiting children's intellectual rights on the basis of lack of rationality, we incur a moral obligation to facilitate the development of rationality to an extent that would make such denial of rights unnecessary (Principle 13, *Right to Education*).

A third distinction between the rights in the two sets is that, whereas those in the first set are entirely negative rights–that is, rights not to have certain things done to you—the second set of principles includes an affirmative obligation to expose children to diverse perspectives and sources of information (Principle 9). This reflects a broader "right to know." Parents have moral obligations to children's intellectual development that go beyond anything either they or the government are constitutionally required to do.

Principle 12 (*Distinction of Child from Adult II*) differs from its counterpart in the first set (Principle 6) primarily in its greater emphasis on individualized determination. To the extent that the government limits rights on the basis of intellectual competence it would typically do this for groups of children (e.g., remove a book from an elementary school library on the basis of evidence that it is harmful to children under age 12). Parents, on the other hand, should be more sensitive to the individual characteristics of their own children, who may be more or less advanced than their peers in their ability to deal with conflicting opinions or make sense of certain types of issues.

Relation to other ethical guidelines

A variety of basic rights are widely considered to be fundamental, are included in the Universal Declaration of Human Rights, and are contained in the U.S. Bill of Rights and subsequent Amendments. These include the right not to be searched or seized without specific cause; to be informed of charges against one; to receive a prompt, public, and fair trial; not to be enslaved, tortured, or subjected to cruel or degrading punishment; and to be accorded equal protection of the law.

Fundamental rights are always considered to include the sorts of intellectual rights that, in the United States, appear in the First Amendment. Articles 18 and 19 of the Universal Declaration of Human Rights, for example, read as follows:

18. Everyone has the right to freedom of thought, conscience, and religion; this right includes freedom to change his religion or belief, and freedom, either alone or in community with others and in public or private, to manifest his religion or belief in teaching, practice, worship, or observance.

19. Everyone has the right to freedom of opinion and expression; this right includes freedom to hold opinions without interference and to seek, receive, and impart information and ideas through any media and regardless of frontiers.

The conformity of these guidelines and the principles of intellectual rights just discussed is clear. Although the Universal Declaration does not specify that it applies to children, the term "everyone" certainly does not exclude them. In fact, it is noteworthy that Article 16, concerning the right to marry, limits itself to "men and women of full age." Given that Articles 18 and 19 provide no such limits, they may be taken to apply to children.

With respect to the rights of students, the Code of Ethics of the Education Profession (adopted by the 1975 National Education Association Representative Assembly) is explicit about the moral obligation of the educator to the intellectual freedom of students (Strike & Soltis, 1985). Principle I provides that the educator

1. Shall not unreasonably restrain the student from independent action in the pursuit of learning.

2. Shall not unreasonably deny the student access to varying points of view.

3. Shall not deliberately suppress or distort subject matter relevant to the student's progress.

The language here is closer to the negative rights language of my First Amendment principles than to the broader and more affirmative rights of my Intellectual Rights principles. Nevertheless, it is clear that the NEA principles are consistent with the philosophy of the First Amendment. In proposing these principles as ethical, not legal, guidelines, the NEA is proposing that educators, independent of their legal obligations, have a moral obligation to respect the sorts of intellectual freedoms underlying the First Amendment and that these freedoms apply to children as well as adults.

The Library Bill of Rights, adopted as official policy by the American Library Association, also includes guidelines for freedom of access and expression consistent with the Principles developed in this chapter (Office for Intellectual Freedom, American Library Association, 1983). Of particular interest for our purposes is the ALA's Principle 5, which maintains that "a person's right to use a library should not be denied or abridged because of origin, *age*, background, or views" (p. 14, my italics).

The meaning of this Principle with respect to age is explicated in a document entitled *Free Access to Libraries for Minors: An Interpretation of the Library Bill of Rights*, adopted by the ALA in 1972 and amended in 1981. It holds that

> Some library procedures and practices effectively deny minors access to certain services and materials available to adults. Such procedures and practices are not in accord with the Library Bill of Rights and are opposed by the American Library Association. . . .
>
> Material selection decisions are often made and restrictions are often initiated under the assumption that certain materials may be "harmful" to minors, or in an effort to avoid controversy with parents. Libraries or library boards which would restrict the access of minors to materials and services because of actual or suspected parental objections should bear in mind that they do not serve in loco parentis. Varied levels of intellectual development among young people and differing family background and child-rearing philosophies are significant factors not accommodated by a uniform policy based upon age.
>
> In today's world, children are exposed to adult life much earlier than in the past. They read materials and view a variety of media on the adult level at home and elsewhere. Current emphasis upon

early childhood education has also increased opportunities for young people to learn and to have access to materials, and has decreased the validity of using chronological age as an index to the use of libraries. The period of time during which children are interested in reading materials specifically designed for them grows steadily shorter, and librarians must recognize and adjust to this change if they wish to serve young people effectively. Librarians have a responsibility to ensure that young people have access to a wide range of informational and recreational materials and services that reflects sufficient diversity to meet the young person's needs.

The American Library Association opposes libraries restricting access to library materials and services for minors and holds that it is the parents—and only parents—who may restrict their children —and only their children—from access to library materials and services. Parents who would rather their children did not have access to certain materials should so advise their children. The library and its staff are responsible for providing equal access to library materials and services for all library users. . . . (Office for Intellectual Freedom, American Library Association, pp. 22–23).

It is clear in this statement that, consistent with the general perspective of Principles 7 through 11, the ethical and professional obligation of the librarian to respect the intellectual freedom of the library user is considered by the ALA to hold for children as well as adults. Without denying that minors may sometimes require protection from harm, it is argued that constraints based purely on chronological age are inadequate (cf. my Principle 12) and that, in any event, it is the role of parents, not librarians, to set such constraints. The role of the librarian is to promote access and diversity.

It appears, then, that educators and librarians acknowledge a moral obligation to respect the intellectual rights of children. No matter how many groups propose ethical guidelines consistent with those I have derived from the First Amendment, however, this would not show that those guidelines are ethically sound. What is needed is a philosophical defense of those principles. Although the philosophy of ethics is complex and multifaceted, there are two major approaches—teleological and deontological (Frankena, 1973; Houlgate, 1980; O'Neill, 1988; Strike & Soltis, 1985; Tucker, 1985). I will briefly defend my principles of children's intellectual rights with respect to each in turn.

The moral basis for children's intellectual rights

A teleological perspective. The teleological perspective on ethics focuses on consequences. Its best-known example is utilitarianism, which posits that the ethical choice in any situation is that which optimizes the amount of pleasure or happiness, summed across all affected individuals (Mill, 1861/1957). In more general terms, the moral criterion is the greatest overall good. Not surprisingly, there are many variations of this, depending on how one defines and measures pleasure, happiness, or "the good" (Frankena, 1973).

J. S. Mill (1859/1974) provided what is still considered the definitive utilitarian justification of intellectual freedom. He argued that liberty should be absolute except to the extent that it infringes on the rights of others and that this entails virtually unlimited rights to receive, form, and express ideas. His utilitarian defense focused on the role of intellectual freedom in fostering important new ideas and challenging old ones. Accepted opinion has commonly turned out to be wrong, he argued, and there must thus be freedom to deviate from it in order for truth, an important good, to triumph. Even when accepted opinion is correct, it is likely only a part of the greater truth. Moreover, even if accepted opinion is the absolute and total truth, freedom to express alternative views remains important to society in making it necessary for truth to be continually defended, thus ensuring that it will remain vital rather than hardening into dogma.

Mill was clear, however, that his arguments applied only to adults in well-developed societies:

> It is, perhaps, hardly necessary to say that this doctrine is meant to apply only to human beings in the maturity of their faculties. We are not speaking of children or of young persons below the age which the law may fix as that of manhood or womanhood. Those who are still in a state to require being taken care of by others must be protected against their own actions as well as against external injury. For the same reason we may leave out of

consideration those backward states of society in which the race itself may be considered as in its nonage. . . . Despotism is a legitimate mode of government in dealing with barbarians, provided the end be their improvement and the means justified by actually affecting that end. Liberty, as a principle, has no application to any state of things anterior to the time when mankind have become capable of being improved by free and equal discussion (1859, p. 69).

Few today would accept Mill's view that individuals in less developed societies are inherently irrational in such a way and to such an extent that freedom of expression should not be permitted. Contemporary anthropology suggests that his views of non-European societies reflected considerable ethnocentrism.

On the basis of current psychological research (see Chapter 3), there is reason to be equally skeptical of his views of children. Children do not suddenly and spontaneously become rational upon attaining chronological adulthood. On the contrary, development of rationality is a gradual process. To the extent that children are relatively rational, Mill's utilitarian argument for intellectual freedom applies to them as well as adults. Moreover, the development of rationality appears to be greatly facilitated by intellectual freedom itself (see Chapter 3). Thus intellectual freedom for children is defensible in utilitarian terms on the grounds that it facilitates the development of rationality, which in turn facilitates the progress of truth, which is either good in itself or an important contributor to other goods.

A deontological perspective. The deontological approach to ethics traces its roots to John Locke (1690/1960) and Immanuel Kant (1785/ 1959) and is reflected in the modern work of John Rawls (1971) and Ronald Dworkin (1978, 1985, 1986). In its Kantian variants, it analyzes moral correctness not in terms of the consequences of an action for society as a whole but in terms of respect for persons (Kilpatrick, 1972; Siegel, 1986, 1988; Tucker, 1985). To qualify as moral, a principle must focus on persons as ends rather than means. This includes showing respect for the dignity and autonomy of individuals. Moreover, the principle must be universalizable—that is, it must be a principle one would want everyone to follow.

Clearly, infringements on intellectual freedom would rarely satisfy these criteria. To prevent someone from expressing what she or he thinks because one believes the ideas will have bad consequences is to treat the person as a means rather than an end. To restrict someone's right to believe or express something, or to require expression of ideas not genuinely believed, attacks his or her dignity and autonomy. To indoctrinate someone or restrict access to, and thus independent judgment of, ideas you oppose, is to treat that person in a way you yourself would not want to be treated.

To the extent that a person is seriously deficient in rationality it may be possible to justify limiting intellectual freedoms on the grounds that intellectual autonomy is not possible for this person, dignity is thus not at stake, and the person should be protected in a way that we ourselves, in his or her cognitively vulnerable position, would wish to be protected. We might be expected to show, however, that in restricting access to ideas in order to protect a child from harm we are simultaneously treating her as an end and respecting her dignity by facilitating her intellectual development so as to make our paternalistic restrictions unnecessary, just as we would wish others to do for us.

A more systematic ethical analysis of children's intellectual rights would, unfortunately, be beyond the scope of this book. It will suffice for present purposes if I have shown that the principles proposed in this chapter are defensible in terms of each of the two major approaches to ethics in contemporary philosophy.

Conclusion

Moving beyond the six First Amendment principles presented earlier in this chapter, I have proposed in this section a set of seven additional principles that are consistent with the philosophy underlying the First Amendment. These latter principles go sufficiently beyond the language of the First Amendment that the government, in my view, is not constitutionally required to respect them. They do, however, correspond to other ethical and professional guidelines concerning intellectual rights and can be justified on the basis of both teleological and deontological ethics. They may thus serve as appropriate moral guidelines for parents and private schools.

Even if government is not constitutionally obligated to follow the ethical guidelines of Principles 7 through 13, it may choose to do so. There is a broad range of possibilities between what government is constitutionally required to do and what it is constitutionally forbidden to do. Government may, and should, use First Amendment values of intellectual freedom as a basis for choosing educational policies in the optional area. In other words, it is wise social policy for it to go further than required in actively promoting freedoms of religion and expression. In fact, government may sometimes be justified in asserting that it has a compelling interest in furthering children's intellectual opportunities and should thus be permitted to do so even at the expense of parental rights to direct the development of their own children. Compulsory education, for example, may require a rationale of this sort. This is an issue to which we will return in Chapter 4 in the discussion of the extent to which government may regulate private and home schools.

Conclusion: Intellectual Freedom as a Moral Ideal

The fact that judges may strike down public school actions that violate the First Amendment can, unfortunately, lead school officials to view the First Amendment primarily as a legal threat. But the First Amendment should not be viewed as a legal formality that one must consider in order to avoid irritating or costly litigation. Underlying the First Amendment is a commitment to intellectual freedom as essential to the pursuit of truth, a critical prerequisite for democratic self-government, and a fundamental moral right of every individual (Principles 7–13). The First Amendment thus provides more than legal constraints on what government (including public schools) may do. More broadly interpreted, it embodies a general value of intellectual freedom. Public schools, and private schools as well, should use it as a guide in setting educational policy within the broad range of constitutionally acceptable possibilities. Further, in deciding what values to inculcate, First Amendment values of respect for intellectual freedom and tolerance of diverse ideas should be prime candidates for inclusion.

3 : The Emergence of Rationality

All of us are less rational on occasions of high stress, fatigue, or carelessness than we are when reasoning at our best, and some people are, in general, less rational than others. To the extent that we are irrational, we may inadequately evaluate ideas we are exposed to, accept false or unjustified assertions as true, or reach new conclusions unsupported by the information at our disposal. Such reasoning may put us at serious risk to the extent that we express or act on dangerously false ideas or inadequate information.

There is also risk, however, in too lightly granting government the power to protect us from our irrationality by limiting the intellectual freedoms guaranteed by the First Amendment. If government had the power to limit access to or expression of any idea it judged irrational, to forbid the practice of religions it deemed irrational, or to establish religions it considered rational, the First Amendment would be meaningless (Moshman, 1985c). Similarly, we would not want government to have extensive power to deny certain people or certain groups of people First Amendment protection by simply asserting that they are irrational and thus need governmental protection from their own irrationality.

Chapter 2 argued that children should not be dismissed as inherently irrational and thus falling, as a group, outside the scope of the First Amendment. Principle 6 nevertheless recognizes that in some situations some children may indeed be less rational than adults in ways that put them at substantial risk and that do justify abridgment of First Amendment liberties. It was argued that such abridgment must be justified on the basis of empirical evidence that the children in question are indeed irrational in the manner and to the extent claimed by the government and that this irrationality yields a likelihood of harm sufficient to justify abridging a fundamental right. The present chapter will consider empirical research on children's rationality and its development.

The Nature and Relevance of Rationality

Arguments for abridging fundamental liberties commonly propose the capacity for choice as a prerequisite for freedom of choice (Garvey, 1979; Moore, 1984). With respect to children's First Amendment rights, Justice Stewart's analysis in *Ginsberg v. New York* is typical:

> The Constitution guarantees . . . a society of free choice. Such a society presupposes the capacity of its members to choose. . . . I think a State may permissibly determine that, at least in some precisely delineated areas, a child—like someone in a captive audience—is not possessed of that full capacity for individual choice which is the presupposition of First Amendment guarantees.[1]

The cogency of this analysis depends on the definition of "choice." If we define choice broadly, this approach can hardly justify any limits on children at all. Even very young children have a capacity for choice —they choose to eat candy, they choose not to eat spinach, they choose which toy to play with and which to drop over the side of the crib. If we define choice too restrictively, however, granting liberty only to those who make correct choices and allowing government to decide which choices are correct, we would obviously render the Bill of Rights meaningless. It appears that we should interpret Justice Stewart's "full capacity for individual choice" as requiring, not some sort of absolute correctness, but a level of rationality comparable to that of adults (Houlgate, 1980).

This does not get us very far, however, unless we can define what we mean by rationality. At the very least, it seems clear that rationality has to do with reasons (Moore, 1984; Rescher, 1987; Siegel, 1986, 1988;

---

1. Ginsberg v. New York, 390 U.S. 629, 649–50 (1968) (Stewart, J., concurring in the result)

Snook, 1972; Strike, 1982a; Wilson, 1972). Rational individuals not only make choices but have reasons for their choices. This includes both their choices of what to do and—especially important with respect to intellectual freedom and the First Amendment—their choices of what to believe. Moreover, their use of reasons is not limited to post hoc justifications (which one might skeptically label "rationalizations") but is central to the actual generation of actions and ideas. As a first approximation, then, we may define rationality as *the use of reasons in generating and justifying beliefs and behavior*.

It is clear, however, that the belief system of a rational person would not consist of a finite set of ideas and a distinct reason for each one. Similarly, it is clear that human behavior cannot be reduced to individual acts with a particular reason for each. On the contrary, beliefs and behavior are typically generated and justified on the basis of complex lines of reasoning that integrate multiple reasons (Baron, 1985). Moreover, the reasons for one's beliefs and behavior must be somewhat consistent with each other. No one's actions, ideas, and reasons form a completely coherent system, of course, but to the extent that one deviates from this ideal one is less than fully rational. In addition, rationality must include a tendency to combine beliefs in such a way as to generate defensible new ideas and actions. We can expand the definition to capture these considerations of integration, coherence, and combination of ideas by defining rationality as the *coordination and use of reasons in generating and justifying beliefs and behavior*.

This is still inadequate, however. Imagine a computer that has been programmed in such a way that it tests the truth of various propositions, derives new propositions from them, and generates output from these new propositions. If its procedures are sufficiently systematic and rigorous we might be tempted to say that it is coordinating and using propositions in generating and justifying other propositions and actions. If it can respond to questions about the basis for its output we might even perceive something like "beliefs" and "reasons."

We would be rightly hesitant, however, to call the computer rational. There may be beliefs involved and reasons for what the computer does, but they are not the computer's beliefs or reasons. It is simply following mechanistic directives. The computer is not *purposeful* in its appeal to or coordination of reasons. It does not *understand* that it is justifying current ideas or generating new ones. It links various propositions but it does not have *beliefs*, nor does it see propositions as *reasons* for, or *conclusions* based on, other propositions.

In short, the computer does not decide to reason or know it is reasoning. If there is rationality involved here, it is on the part of the programmer. Although the computer does, in a weak sense, coordinate and use (what *we* see as) reasons, only the programmer reflects on the process of reasoning or on the use of reasons *as reasons*. The definition of rationality should thus be restricted to include only the *self-reflective and intentional* coordination and use of reasons in generating and justifying beliefs and behavior.

The revised definition is still open to criticism on the grounds of epistemological relativism (Siegel, 1987). It does not face the fact that some reasons are better than others and that not all coordinations of reasons are equally justifiable. It is not enough that a person provide what she or he *considers* to be a reason; the reason must provide a genuine basis for the belief or behavior. Similarly, not any coordination and use of reasons is rational; some standard of acceptability must be met.

For First Amendment purposes, of course, it would be dangerous to give government too much power to decide the normative standards. On the contrary, when government seeks to deny liberty on the grounds of irrationality, the burden should be on the government to show clear deviation from any arguably justifiable standard. Nevertheless, a normative component in the definition, though dangerous, is unavoidable. Adding the requirement that reasons be genuine and their coordination and use appropriate, we may define rationality as *the self-reflective, intentional, and appropriate coordination and use of genuine reasons in generating and justifying beliefs and behavior* (Moshman & Hoover, 1989).

On the basis of this definition it seems clear that an irrational person permitted broad intellectual freedoms would be at risk. To the extent that one fails to use reasons one's ideas and behavior are unjustified and may be unjustifiable. One is at risk of expressing foolish ideas that harm one's reputation or behaving in ways harmful to oneself or others. Moreover, one will continue to generate new ideas and engage in further behaviors without regard for the reason for these ideas and behaviors, thus exacerbating the risk and harm. To the extent that one fails to coordinate one's various reasons, one's reasoning is incoherent and may lead to emotional trauma and self-defeating sequences of behavior. Even if one does coordinate and use reasons, to the extent that the reasons are not genuine they are merely rationalizations and thus provide only an illusion of solving the above problems. To the extent that the coordination and use of reasons is not in accord with appropriate norms of reasoning one will reach and act on unjustified conclusions. Finally, to the extent that one is not self-reflective about one's reasons and intentional in one's reasoning, one will fail to aim for greater rationality and to recognize and correct irrationality and its ensuing harms.

All of this sounds—and is—serious, especially given the extensive evidence that even adults deviate substantially from standards of rationality (Evans, 1982, 1983; but see Cohen, 1981). Nevertheless, it does not justify massive abridgments of the First Amendment. There is no reason to believe that government can identify irrationality with sufficient precision to justify routinely abridging the First Amendment for certain ideas, religions, individuals, or groups. Even if irrationality could be precisely identified, it is not clear that such abridgment would decrease the risks in question without yielding far greater risks in their place.

It may be suggested, however, that this argument does not hold for children. Perhaps children, at least below some ascertainable age, are so clearly less rational than any normal adult and so clearly subject to avoidable harms as a result, that there is compelling reason for abridging their First Amendment liberties. The task of this chapter is to explore the empirical evidence relevant to this possibility. The next three sections of the chapter will trace the development of rationality in three critical areas: deductive reasoning, inductive reasoning, and moral reasoning.

Development of Deductive Reasoning

A key aspect of rationality is the ability to make deductive inferences. When a conclusion is deduced properly from a set of premises that are themselves defensible, the premises provide reason for believing in the conclusion; commitment to the conclusion is thus rational. Improper deductions, or inadequate understanding of the nature of premises, conclusions, and deductive inferences, may result in beliefs that are not rationally defensible.

There have been thousands of studies of deductive reasoning in children and adults and there is much controversy over what changes take place over the course of development and how such changes are best explained. Fortunately, without getting into the more technical disputes, it is possible to provide a useful overview of four stages in the development of deductive reasoning that is consistent with available evidence. Although the stages can be interpreted in theoretical terms that raise controversial issues (Moshman, 1989), they are presented here as a descriptive summary of development in the area of deductive reasoning.

On the basis of available evidence, four important points should be made about these developmental stages. First, the transition from stage to stage is a gradual process. People do not jump suddenly from one stage to the next. Second, the age of transition varies from person to person. Thus the ages associated with each stage are only approximate. Third, depending on the task and context, people may not use their most sophisticated reasoning. An individual who shows Stage 3 reasoning on a familiar task may use Stage 2 reasoning on a different problem, in a different situation, or under conditions of fatigue, low motivation, high stress, and so forth. Finally, people differ substantially in how far they progress. Not everyone achieves the highest stage.

Stage 1: focus on content

There is extensive evidence that even preschool children can make correct inferences from a wide variety of premises (Braine & Rumain, 1983; Hawkins, Pea, Glick, & Scribner, 1984; Thayer & Collyer, 1978). In fact, if we defined rationality simply as a matter of correct inference, one could make a case that even five-year-olds, though prone to error in complex situations, are not qualitatively less rational than adults.

The earlier definition of rationality as inherently self-reflective, however, highlights the fundamental deficiency of young children. Stage 1 children, typically preschoolers, think about content rather than about the process of making inferences. Even when they correctly infer conclusions from premises, they do not grasp the fundamental distinction between premises as given information and conclusions as deduced propositions. That is, they *use* inference but do not think *about* inference.

Consider, for example, the following argument:

> 1. Sprognoids are either animals or plants.
>   Sprognoids are not animals.
>   Therefore, sprognoids are plants.

Stage 1 children, given the two premises, will correctly reach the conclusion that sprognoids are plants. They see the conclusion, however, not as a conclusion but as a new fact. They are not thinking about deducing a conclusion from premises; they are thinking about sprognoids, animals, and plants. We as psychologists, of course, can determine that they have engaged in deductive inference. The process of inference is merely implicit in their thinking, however. What they are explicitly aware of is not inference but content.

Stage 2: focus on inference
Children at this stage, typically in the elementary school years, can think about the process of inference and grasp the distinction between premises and conclusions. In other words, they recognize their conclusions *as* conclusions, as resulting from inference. This can be seen in the fact that they, unlike Stage 1 children, distinguish conclusions that are logically necessary from those that are merely reasonable, plausible, probable, or conventional (Fabricius, Sophian, & Wellman, 1987; Moshman, 1989; Moshman & Timmons, 1982; Pieraut-Le Bonniec, 1980; Somerville, Hadkinson, & Greenberg, 1979). Stage 2 children also grasp the idea that one may gain knowledge via inference, as distinct from direct observation (Sodian & Wimmer, 1987).

Consider, for example, the following argument:

> 2. Sprognoids are animals or plants or machines.
>   Sprognoids are not animals.
>   Therefore, sprognoids are plants.

Stage 2 children recognize that this argument differs from the previous one in that, although the conclusion has some basis in the premises, it is not logically required by the premises. It can be argued that in distinguishing necessary inferences from merely plausible ones, Stage 2 children are making use of logical form. Argument 1 differs from argument 2, for example, in that, given X *is p or q* and X *is not p*, it follows necessarily that X *is q*; the alternative, X *is not q*, yields a logical contradiction. Although Stage 2 children are explicitly aware of making inferences, however, the form of the argument, which is the basis for judgments of necessity, is merely implicit in their thinking, rather than an object of explicit awareness.

Stage 3: explicit logic
Consider another argument:

> 3. Elephants are either animals or plants.
>   Elephants are not animals.
>   Therefore, elephants are plants.

Children at Stages 1 and 2 would reject this argument. Elephants, they would note, are *not* plants, so the argument is clearly illogical. Stage 3 individuals, on the other hand, would respond differently. Because they are expressly aware of logical form and understand its distinction from empirical truth, they can appreciate that the form of Argument 3 is identical to the form of Argument 1, even though the conclusion to Argument 3 is empirically false. They not only distinguish logical form from empirical truth but understand their subtle interrelationship. Given the form of arguments 1 and 3, the conclusion in each case necessarily follows from the premises. This does not guarantee that the conclusion *is* empirically true but shows that it *would be* true if the premises were true. The Stage 3 explicit understanding of the necessity of the relationship between premises and conclusion allows the individual to appreciate the validity of the argument form: An argument is valid if, regardless of the empirical truth of its premises and conclusions, it has a logical form such that, *if* the premises were true, the conclusion would have to be true as well.

The explicit grasp of the interrelated concepts of logical form and necessity, and of their subtle relation to the concept of truth, thus is summed up in comprehension of the concept of inferential validity. Express awareness of the form of propositions and arguments allows the Stage 3 individual systematically to distinguish internal logical structure from the truth or falsity of content.

Research by Moshman and Franks (1986) indicates that Stage 3 thinking begins to appear about age 11. They found that 9- to 10-year-olds had great difficulty with argument 3 and others of this sort. On a variety of tasks involving several different forms of argument, children that age sorted and ranked arguments on the basis of the empirical truth or falsity of the content and appeared to ignore validity of argument form. Even after careful definition of validity, examples distinguishing validity from truth, instructions to use the concept of validity to evaluate arguments, and up to 40 trials with systematic feedback, very few 9- to 10-year-olds seemed to grasp the concept of inferential validity as distinct from empirical truth. In sharp contrast, many 12- to 13-year-olds in the same series of studies spontaneously distinguished arguments on the basis of validity. With appropriate definition, examples, instructions, and/or feedback, most were quite consistent in evaluating arguments on the basis of validity rather than on the basis of empirical truth.

It appears that although children between ages 6 and 10 have sufficient metalogical understanding to recognize when a conclusion is logically necessary, they are still strongly influenced by content. Only beginning about age 11 or 12 is there sufficient attention to the form of arguments to recognize explicitly that certain forms are inherently valid—their conclusions necessarily follow from their premises regardless of the content. Of course, the Stage 2 child's ability to distinguish necessary from merely plausible conclusions does show an implicit awareness of logical form and the associated quality of logical necessity. Only at Stage 3, however, is awareness of form and necessity sufficiently explicit to distinguish valid from invalid arguments independent of the empirical truth or falsity of their content (Moshman & Timmons, 1982).

Achievement of stage 3 metalogical understanding has implications not only for deductive reasoning but, more broadly, for the development of natural epistemologies—that is, conceptions about the nature of knowledge. An explicit grasp of necessity allows one to distinguish logical from empirical domains. Logical knowledge includes propositions that are necessarily true (tautologies) or necessarily false (self-contradictions), whereas the truth or falsity of empirical propositions can only be determined on the basis of evidence external to those propositions.

Osherson and Markman (1975) investigated reactions to a variety of propositions, including tautologies (e.g., *either the chip in my hand is not red or it is red*), self-contradictions (e.g., *the chip in my hand is white and it is not white*), and empirical statements (e.g., *the chip in my hand is yellow*). Subjects were asked whether they could decide the truth or falsity of the statements without seeing the chip. Children ranging in age from 6 through 11 years typically saw a need for empirical information in all cases, whereas most adults distinguished logical propositions (which were necessarily true or false) from empirical propositions (which could not be evaluated without seeing the chip). Cummins (1978) and Russell and Haworth (1987), replicating the study with various methodological refinements, confirmed the difficulty elementary-age children have in distinguishing empirical from nonempirical propositions.

Komatsu and Galotti (1986) used a different methodology in which children (ages 6, 8, and 10) were asked about various social conventions (e.g., the school year begins in September), empirical regularities (e.g., banging on a pot makes a loud noise), and logical necessities (e.g., there cannot be more apples than fruit). The questions focused on whether each of the various truths could be changed by consensus or could fail to hold in a different culture or on a different planet. They found distinctions between social conventions and other phenomena even in the youngest participants and increasing grasp of these distinctions with age. Children at all three ages, however, had trouble with the distinction between empirical regularities (which cannot be changed by consensus but might fail to hold on another planet) and logical necessities (which must hold in any conceivable world). A comparison group of college students appeared to grasp the distinction between empirical and logical knowledge.

Evidence from diverse sources thus suggests that Stage 3 understanding is not seen in children before the age of about 11 but is fairly common in adolescents and adults.

Stage 4: explicit metalogic
The explicit logic of Stage 3 may be postulated to require implicit metalogical knowledge about the nature of logical systems. Explicit formalization of logical systems involving reflection on the nature of such systems and on their relations with each other and with natural languages may be defined as Stage 4 (Moshman, 1989). Although there is evidence of such reasoning in some college undergraduates (Politzer, 1986), it does not appear to be a widely achieved stage of development.

Conclusions about the development of deductive reasoning
Each of the four stages of deductive reasoning may be construed as a systematic reflection on the previous stage and thus as a higher level of rationality. Stage 1 reasoning deals with content through the use of inference. Stage 2 involves reflection on inference from the perspective of logical form. Stage 3 reasoning involves reflection on form from the viewpoint of metalogic, and Stage 4 involves reflection on metalogic itself. Although there is no upper limit in principle, it appears that even Stage 4 is relatively rare. If, in accord with Principle 6, we take the rationality of the minimally normal adult as the appropriate constitutional standard, it appears that Stage 3 should be considered a mature level of rationality in the area of deductive reasoning. It is clear that Stage 3 is indeed a relatively sophisticated level of reasoning involving a subtle grasp of the nature of arguments, the purpose of inference, and the interrelations of premises and conclusions.

The evidence reviewed above suggests that Stage 3 understanding of deduction begins to appear about age 11. Although young adolescents may not apply Stage 3 reasoning as well as many adults, they cannot be distinguished from a minimally normal adult in this area. Moreover, children as young as age 6 show a significant degree of rationality in reasoning at Stage 2. In general, then, research on deductive reasoning suggests genuine, though limited, rationality in most elementary-age children and provides little or no basis for distinguishing adolescents from adults.

Deductive reasoning, however, is limited to relations between premises and conclusions. Rationality also includes the ability to induce generalizations from empirical evidence and to test them against reality. We must therefore turn to the development of inductive reasoning.

Development of Inductive Reasoning

Inductive reasoning is an even broader domain than deductive reasoning. It includes forming generalizations, dealing with uncertainties and probabilities, testing hypotheses, and understanding the nature of reality, knowledge, and the relation between these. One might argue for restricting the information available to children and strictly guiding their conclusions on the grounds that they cannot adequately test the truth of ideas they are exposed to or conclusions they reach themselves; that they cannot distinguish facts from opinions; that they are incapable of dealing with uncertainties, probabilities, or diverse points of view; or that they are simply naive about the nature of knowledge.

Although detailed coverage of the various aspects of inductive reasoning would be beyond the scope of this chapter, the following account, based on empirical research on a wide variety of topics, provides a broad overview of development in this area. As with deductive reasoning, it should be emphasized that development is gradual and individual differences are substantial. Thus actual children will often be in transition between stages rather than fitting neatly into a particular stage. Moreover, the age at which they begin to move to a new stage and the speed of transition may vary substantially depending on intra-individual and social/environmental factors.

Stage 1: focus on content

Probably the most impressive and extensively documented ability of very young children is the ease and rapidity with which they learn language. There is no doubt that, at least in this area, even two-year-olds form proper generalizations, apply them to new situations, test them against evidence, and modify them as necessary. In fact, given the extraordinary complexity of language, the remarkable ability of young children to learn it has led theorists such as Noam Chomsky to suggest that such learning must be guided by some sort of innate language-acquisition program (Piattelli-Palmarini, 1980). Extensive evidence of effective inductive learning in other areas has led to similar proposals of innate inductive abilities functioning at very early ages (e.g., Keil, 1981). For our purposes, the question of to what extent there is an innate basis for the impressive abilities of young children and to what extent such abilities are learned is not critical. What is important is that highly effective inductive learning is common at very early ages (cf. Donaldson, 1978; Gelman & Baillargeon, 1983).

Although preschool children reason effectively in many situations, they are surprisingly naive about their own reasoning. In fact, it appears that they usually do not even realize they are reasoning: They think about content rather than about the process of knowing. Three- and four-year-olds have great difficulty, for example, distinguishing what something "looks like" from what it "really and truly" is, even when researchers make systematic efforts to use familiar items and circumstances, to ask simple questions, and to teach the relevant concepts (Flavell, 1985, 1986; Flavell, Green, & Flavell, 1986; Flavell, Green, Wahl, & Flavell, 1987). Young children can mentally represent reality but lack the "metarepresentational" ability to consciously consider and compare their own representations (Gopnik & Astington, 1988). They view knowledge as something directly absorbed from the world and fail to grasp the role of subjective construction in creating ideas that do not directly reflect reality and may, in fact, differ from person to person (Broughton, 1978; Clinchy & Mansfield, 1986). In short, the Stage 1 child, typically a preschooler, engages in much effective reasoning but thinks about the *content* of reasoning rather than about the *process* of reasoning. Although the existence of a subjective perspective is implicit in all reasoning, Stage 1 children have little or no awareness of their own subjectivity.

Stage 2: awareness of subjectivity
Stage 2 children expressly distinguish knowledge and appearance from reality. Reflecting on the nature of mental representation, they

realize the world may be different from what one sees or thinks. They recognize that one's ideas may differ from those of other people and are not simply absolute truths based on raw observation of reality. Although even 3- and 4-year-olds have a preliminary awareness of thoughts and feelings as distinct from physical entities (Wellman & Estes, 1986; Harris, Donnelly, Guz, & Pitt-Watson, 1986), understanding of subjectivity and its implications appears to be sporadic before age 5 or 6 (Astington, Harris, & Olson, 1988; Clinchy & Mansfield, 1986; Flavell, 1985, 1986; Flavell et al., 1986, 1987; Gopnik & Astington, 1988; Hogrefe, Wimmer, & Perner, 1986; Sodian, 1988; Taylor, 1988; Wimmer, Hogrefe, & Perner, 1988). Stage 2 reasoning is typical in elementary school children.

Stage 2 awareness of one's own subjectivity constitutes a higher level of rationality in that it involves the conception that ideas must be supported on the basis of reasons. If challenged, for example, the Stage 2 child may defend his or her ideas by citing evidence consistent with them or seeking more such evidence—a *verification strategy*. In a sense, the child is forming and testing theories about his or her world and is far more aware of doing this than was the case at Stage 1. Awareness of theories *as theories*, however, is still limited. As will become apparent in the following discussion of Stage 3, the Stage 2 child, though actively *using* theories, has no clear grasp of the nature of theory and is thus unsystematic in testing and modifying his or her ideas.

Stage 3: explicit theory

Stage 3 individuals, typically adolescents and adults, have a more explicit grasp of theory and its relation to data. Consider, for example, the hypothesis *If a person uses fluoridated toothpaste he or she will have healthy teeth* (Moshman, 1979a). Would it be better to test this by studying (a) patients with healthy teeth (to see whether or not they use fluoridated toothpaste), or (b) patients with unhealthy teeth (to see whether or not they use fluoridated toothpaste)? One's natural response is *a*: Study patients with healthy teeth; if they use fluoride they will support the hypothesis. This response reflects the Stage 2 orientation toward verification and thus reflects some degree of rationality. The proposition that people who use fluoridated toothpaste have healthy teeth is construed as a generalization based on having observed fluoride users with healthy teeth in the past and supportable by finding more such people.

Given sufficient chance to think through the issues, however, the Stage 3 reasoner recognizes the inadequacy of this response (Moshman, 1979a). Although patients with healthy teeth who use fluoride are indeed consistent with the hypothesis, patients with healthy teeth who do not use fluoride would not disconfirm it. The only sort of person who would disconfirm the hypothesis *If a person uses fluoridated toothpaste he or she will have healthy teeth* is one who uses fluoridated toothpaste and does *not* have healthy teeth. Thus the proper answer is *b*. In order to genuinely test the hypothesis one must study people who do not have healthy teeth, since only such people could possibly disconfirm the hypothesis.

The Stage 3 reasoner recognizes that theories are not merely more general than data but exist on a different plane, a plane of possibilities as opposed to the plane of realities (Inhelder & Piaget, 1958). The theoretical status of theories and the need to rigorously test—rather than merely support—them is now understood. It is recognized that, in an infinite world, theories can never be proven true but can be disproved by a single disconfirming datum. The Stage 3 thinker understands that the key to genuinely testing a theory is not to accumulate supportive data but rather to seek potentially disconfirming data—a *falsification strategy*. Evidence from a variety of sources indicates that Stage 3 conceptions are difficult even for adults (Evans, 1982, 1983; Skov & Sherman, 1986). Nevertheless, under favorable circumstances, adolescents and adults, but not preadolescent children, often do show Stage 3 competence (Moshman, 1979a; O'Brien, 1987; O'Brien, Costa, & Overton, 1986; O'Brien & Overton, 1980, 1982; Overton, Ward, Noveck, Black, & O'Brien, 1987).

Stage 3 reasoning involves what may be labeled metatheoretical competence (Moshman, 1979b)—an ability not merely to generate theories and use data but to think explicitly about the nature of theories and data and the complex interrelations between them. Such an ability constitutes a higher level of rationality in that it permits more sophisticated understanding of the sorts of reasons relevant to inductive knowledge, more rigorous evaluation of such reasons, and more systematic efforts to strengthen them (Kuhn, Amsel, & O'Loughlin, 1988).

Stage 4: explicit metatheory

Research on the development of people's conceptions of knowledge and reality (Broughton, 1978; Kitchener & King, 1981; Kitchener & Wood, 1987; Welfel & Davison, 1986) indicates that the metatheoretical competence implicit in Stage 3 reflection on theories and data can itself become an object of reflection, thus generating a higher level of rationality. Some individuals begin to think about the metatheoretical assumptions underlying their theories and about their approach to testing those theories, thus yielding an increasingly explicit philosophy of science. Recognition that all data are theory-laden and that apparent falsifications of theory can always be explained away through additional assumptions may lead to epistemological relativism, a transitional phase between Stages 3 and 4 in which the possibility of rationally comparing and testing theories is rejected. Further reflection, however, leads to recognition that even if the Stage 3 falsification strategy is less than fully adequate, rational coordination of theory and data leading to genuine progress in understanding reality is nevertheless possible (cf. Siegel, 1987).

Research on development beyond Stage 3 has focused on college undergraduates and graduate students and thus does not give clear indication of the generality of Stage 4 understanding. It appears, however, that Stage 4 thinking, though not uncommon, is far from universal even in highly educated populations. Stage 3 is probably the norm for adults, and even intelligent adults may fail to reason beyond Stage 2 when functioning under less than optimal conditions.

Conclusions about the development of inductive reasoning

In general, research on inductive reasoning provides a picture of development comparable to what we saw in the case of deductive reasoning. Although there is evidence for development during adolescence and perhaps even extending into adulthood, this appears to be limited to consolidation of Stage 3 understanding and emergence of a sophisticated Stage 4 rationality that many normal individuals never reach.

It is difficult to make a case that adolescents beyond the age of about 11 are fundamentally less rational than the normal adult. Children as young as age 5 or 6 show impressive rationality in reflecting on the subjectivity of their own reasoning, though they do appear limited in their ability to effectively test hypotheses. Preschool children, though capable of correct inferences, are even more limited in their rationality in that they seem to have no sense of the subjectivity of knowledge and the consequent role of reasons in generating and justifying ideas.

Deductive and inductive reasoning are both very general modes of cognition applicable to any content area. It would be useful at this point to look at the development of reasoning in a specific domain that has been the source of intense educational controversy.

Development of Moral Reasoning

Moral rationality

One rationale for limiting the First Amendment rights of children to express and be exposed to ideas about morality might be that children have little or no sense of morality and, as a result, must be protected from morally wrong ideas and ideologies until they are old enough to recognize the immorality of these and reject them. Otherwise they are likely to develop immoral beliefs and may harm themselves or others by acting on such beliefs.

Available evidence does not support the view that children have no conception of morality. Although they may not have adult conceptions (a point to be considered in detail below), even preschoolers know and use the terms "right" and "wrong" in moral contexts and have clear ideas about what fits in each category (Kurtines & Gewirtz, 1984; Piaget, 1932/1965; Rest, 1983; Shultz, Wright, & Schleifer, 1986; Smetana, 1985; Turiel, 1983; Wimmer, Gruber, & Perner, 1985). There is no doubt that children have moral ideas well before the school years and construe what they perceive in terms of these ideas.

One might respond that although children do have moral ideas, their ideas are often wrong and thus do not shield them from moral error. This rejoinder does not get us very far, however. Clearly, we would not accept the view that government may shield adults from harmful ideas and abridge expression of their own ideas if it disapproves their moral views. There appears to be no reason for granting it greater authority to restrict the First Amendment rights of children on the basis of its disapproval of their morality.

A more satisfactory rejoinder is to argue that children's First Amendment liberties with respect to morality should be limited not because they have *no* moral ideas or *wrong* moral ideas but because their reasoning about moral issues is demonstrably less rational than that of the normal adult and, as a result, they are subject to harm unless their liberties are abridged. To pursue this line of argument, of course, we need to be clear on what is meant by moral rationality. Obviously, this approach would be merely a subterfuge if we were to define moral rationality as agreement with the moral values of the government. If, however, we focus not on absolutist notions of right and wrong but on the extent to which one can provide reasons for one's moral views and systematically reflect on and coordinate those reasons to generate an internally coherent moral philosophy, we may find a principled basis for distinguishing children from adults with respect to First Amendment rights in the moral domain.

The first effort to get beyond children's *ideas* about right and wrong and explore their *reasoning* about moral dilemmas was a classic series of studies by Jean Piaget (1932/1965). His research indicated that older children differ from younger children not so much in the content of their moral beliefs but in the sophistication of their moral reasoning. The most systematic effort to pursue this insight has been the extensive research and theorizing of the late Lawrence Kohlberg and his associates over the past three decades.

Kohlberg's theory
Kohlberg (1984) proposed that moral reasoning develops through a sequence of six stages, each demonstrably more rational than the preceding one. Progress through the stages is very gradual and individuals may show a mixture of reasoning from two or more adjacent stages. Moreover, people differ greatly in how far through the sequence they develop. The order of the stages does appear to be invariant, however, not only for Americans but for individuals in a wide variety of cultures (Boyes & Walker, 1988; Snarey, 1985; Snarey, Reimer, & Kohlberg, 1985; Vasudev & Hummel, 1987). The six stages are as follows.

Stage 1: heteronomous morality. The Stage 1 child perceives moral behavior as what does not get punished. Obedience is right for its own
sake. Immoral actions are punished because they are immoral and
immoral because they are punished. Although there is respect for the
superior power of authorities, the child does not distinguish the authorities' perspective from his or her own. Goodness or badness are
inherent in acts. Tattling is wrong, for example, in the same sense that
the sky is blue. If asked why it is wrong to tell on someone, the child
is likely to reply, "Because it's tattling" and see that as a definitive and
sufficient reason. Available evidence suggests that Stage 1 reasoning
predominates in young children and declines over the course of the
elementary school years.

Stage 2: individualism and exchange. Moral behavior is acting to further
one's interests and letting others do the same. There is recognition
that others have their own interests that differ from and may even conflict with yours. To get what you want from other people, you must
recognize and respond to their needs. Morality includes arranging fair
deals and equal exchanges with others. This stage constitutes a higher
level of moral rationality in that moral rules ("Don't steal; don't hit;
don't tattle") can be justified on the basis of the needs and perspectives of others and the advantage to self and others of making deals
on the basis of fairness and equality. Stage 2 reasoning is predominant
in elementary school children and typically declines over the course
of adolescence, though remaining influential in the reasoning of some
adults.

Stage 3: mutual expectations. Stage 3 involves recognition that other
people are not there merely to serve your purposes. Relationships
with others, based on mutual trust and loyalty, are important for their
own sake. You should live up to the expectations of those close to
you and fulfill your roles (e.g., be a good student). You are moral
because you genuinely care about others, want them to think of you as
a good person, and want to consider yourself a good person. Mutual
expectations and shared moral norms take primacy over individual
interests. In a sense that transcends the tit-for-tat deals of Stage 2,
you genuinely put yourself in the other's shoes. The Stage 3 thinker
can not only defend moral rules on the basis of considering other

perspectives (Stage 2) but can justify the coordination of perspectives and the value of fairness and equality by appeal to the inherent value of relationships. There is thus greater social rationality in the sense of a deeper appeal to and reflection on moral reasons. Evidence indicates that Stage 3 reasoning is typical of American adolescents and remains common in adults.

Stage 4: social system. At this level, one's acceptance of moral conventions is based not on immediate interactions with others but on an abstract understanding of society as a whole. The social system defines appropriate roles and rules. Individual relations are still important, of course, but they are now understood and justified from the point of view of the entire social, legal, or religious system. Morality means upholding the law, fulfilling one's social and/or religious duties, and contributing to society and its institutions. You should do what is right in order to meet your obligations and preserve the social structure. Antisocial behavior is wrong because it potentially contributes to the breakdown of the system. Stage 4 individuals may differ dramatically in the nature of the system they appeal to and thus in their specific moral conclusions. What marks Stage 4 rationality is not the content of one's conclusions but the possibility of justifying relationships themselves at a deeper level on the basis of their place in a coherent social system. Stage 4 reasoning can be seen in adolescence and is predominant in most, though not all, American adults.

Stage 5: social contract. We have seen that each stage in Kohlberg's system can be construed as a higher level of moral rationality than the stage before in that it constitutes a source of reasons for the morality of the previous stage. Stage 1 rules may be justified on the basis of Stage 2 attention to other people's perspectives, which may be justified on the basis of a Stage 3 commitment to relationships, which may be justified by appeal to a Stage 4 sense of the social system. But why should one be committed to the social system? Most people, according to Kohlberg, never fully face this question.

Those who do, however, may move to a new level of reasoning based on a conception of social contract. The stage 5 thinker adopts a prior-to-society perspective. Rational individuals existing with no social arrangements (if this were possible) would set up a society because this would benefit all of them (through mutual protection, division of labor, and so on). They would agree on procedures for deciding on laws and would agree to abide by those laws.

The Stage 5 thinker believes that, because law is the result of a social contract, one should usually follow it. As an autonomous individual, one understands the basis for social commitments and freely accepts them. Laws and social duties should, however, be based on rational calculation of the greatest overall good (a utilitarian conception) and should respect individual rights such as life and liberty (a deontological conception). Thus, although laws are generally to be obeyed, a given law or even an entire social structure or religious system may be rejected as violating the intrinsic worth and dignity of individuals or failing as a rational social contract. The social system, though highly important, is not the last word. From a prior-to-society perspective, societies themselves can be evaluated morally. This deeper search for moral reasons in prior-to-society considerations of social contract constitutes a highly sophisticated moral orientation that is rare even in adults.

Stage 6: universal ethical principles. Stage 6 involves justification of Stage 5 reasoning on the basis of explicit ethical principles that form a formal moral philosophy. Kohlberg suggests this stage as an ideal endpoint to moral development that may be achieved by a small number of individuals with intense experience in ethical evaluation (e.g., some judges, theologians, and moral philosophers). He does not find any evidence of such reasoning, however, in the normal populations he has studied.

Implications of Kohlberg's theory

It would obviously be inappropriate to argue that, since children do not show the ideal moral rationality of Kohlberg's Stage 6, their access to moral ideas and freedom to form and express such ideas should be limited. This same rationale would apply to virtually all adults. In accord with Principle 6, we should evaluate children with respect to the moral rationality of a minimally normal adult.

Using this criterion, there appears to be no basis for distinguishing adolescents from adults. Although Kohlberg did find that moral reasoning continues to develop in at least some adolescents and adults, such development is moving toward increasingly rarified levels of understanding. Given that Stage 3 reasoning is already predominant in adolescence and that many adults never move beyond this, it is difficult to imagine a case in which one could argue that adolescents as a group are sufficiently less rational than adults in conceptualizing moral issues that they will be at much greater risk than adults unless their First Amendment rights are restricted.

With respect to elementary school children, the situation is less clear. There is overlap even here in that some Stage 3 reasoning is found at this age and some Stage 2 reasoning is still seen in adults. Nevertheless the typical elementary school child does relatively little Stage 3 reasoning whereas the vast majority of adults reason mostly at this level or beyond. This does not justify any sort of blanket restriction but may justify restrictions in specific cases. The burden of proof would be on the government to show, for example, that as a result of their fundamentally less rational understanding of human relationships as the basis for morality, elementary-age children would dangerously misconstrue certain books or ideas in ways that a normal adult would not.

With respect to preschool children, the difference in rationality from adults is more striking. According to Kohlberg's theory and data, such children think in terms of absolute rules rather than moral reasons. Even this may not put them at risk, of course, but it does appear to be a difference worth considering in anticipating and understanding their reactions to what they experience.

Critiques of Kohlberg and their implications

Although there is no major theoretical alternative to Kohlberg's theory that is comparable in theoretical scope or extent of empirical support, there have been numerous critiques, many of them thoughtful and important. Most relevant for our purposes are those that question Kohlberg's views about the competence of children at various ages. Almost without exception, critics raising this issue have argued, on the basis of diverse data, that Kohlberg (and Piaget before him) systematically underestimated the moral competence of children (Coles,

1986; Kurtines & Gewirtz, 1984; Radke-Yarrow, Zahn-Waxler, & Chapman, 1983; Rest, 1983; Shultz, Wright, & Schleifer, 1986; Smetana, 1985; Turiel, 1983; Wimmer, Gruber, & Perner, 1985).

With respect to the above conclusions about adolescents, such research, if anything, strengthens the conclusion that there is little empirical reason to judge them less rational than adults with respect to moral issues. With respect to children, especially very young children, recent research suggests that even when they appear morally deficient this may reflect problems in our assessment rather than actual deficiencies in their reasoning. Thus, young children may be more like adults than is initially apparent; in restricting them on the basis of empirical evidence of moral inadequacy, we must be careful to appeal to evidence that is methodologically suited to revealing actual competence with respect to the issues in question.

Kohlberg's view of moral development has also been questioned by Gilligan (1982), who claims that Kohlberg's conception of morality stresses abstract rights and justice and overlooks issues of care, compassion, and responsibility that are equally fundamental. Moreover, Gilligan suggests that these latter moral conceptions are more central to females than to males and that Kohlbergian research, as a result of defining morality along masculine lines, underestimates the moral sophistication of girls and women.

Gilligan's analysis raises important questions about the definition of morality and the scope of the moral domain. In support of her specific claims that males and females differ in their moral orientations, however, she provides only anecdotal evidence. Recent research and systematic reviews of the existing literature generally fail to support Gilligan's claims of sex differences in moral development or sex bias in Kohlbergian theory or research (Brabeck, 1983; Broughton, 1983; Gibbs, Arnold, & Burkhart, 1984; Kohlberg, 1984; Nunner-Winkler, 1984; Pratt, Golding, & Hunter, 1984; Smetana, 1984; Snarey, 1985; Snarey et al., 1985; Thoma, 1986; Vasudev & Hummel, 1987; Walker, 1984, 1986a, 1986b; but see Baumrind, 1986; Gilligan, 1987).

In sum, the various critiques of Kohlberg indicate, not surprisingly, that morality is a complex, multifaceted domain and that its measurement is difficult and controversial. It does seem clear from the evidence, however, that even young children have genuine moral understanding and that by early adolescence, if not before, there is no clear basis for distinguishing minors from adults.

Development of Socioemotional Autonomy

Rationality has thus far been addressed as a cognitive rather than an emotional matter, a question of how one reasons rather than how one feels. Although this focus is defensible (Moshman & Hoover, 1989), it is important to keep in mind that cognition and emotion are intricately interdependent (Moshman, Glover, and Bruning, 1987, Chap. 13). With respect to rationality in particular, in order to operate on the basis of appropriate reasons one must have some degree of emotional autonomy. Otherwise, one is likely to overlook or misconstrue reasons as a result of being unduly influenced by people, organizations, or ideologies to which one is emotionally committed.

Strong emotional commitments can, of course, be psychologically healthy (Gilligan, 1982; Kegan, 1982). To the extent that one's social and ideological commitments are carefully considered and based on appropriate reasons, they may be considered rational commitments and may be a positive influence on one's further reasoning. Nevertheless, there is no doubt that all of us have emotional commitments that are not adequately justified and that interfere with our rationality in some aspects of our lives. The question here is whether children have substantially less socioemotional autonomy than adults and are thus less likely to think rationally.

Available evidence indicates that young children do indeed show a degree of socioemotional dependence on others that raises serious questions about their ability to consider, and act in accord with, genuine reasons. In general, there appears to be an initial dependence on parents that expands over the course of childhood to include other adults and then gives way in early adolescence to a strong dependence on peers (Hartup, 1983; Maccoby & Martin, 1983). That dependence typically peaks at about age 13 or 14 and then declines to adult levels in later adolescence (Coleman, 1980; Steinberg & Silverberg, 1986).

Although the developmental increase in autonomy is real, it should not be overemphasized. Attachment to others and susceptibility to social influence are characteristic of all normal individuals from very early childhood through late adulthood (Hill & Holmbeck, 1986; Kegan, 1982). Even young children show some degree of independence and self-governance; even adults are significantly constrained by their developmental histories and social environments. Genuine autonomy begins to develop in early childhood (Erikson, 1963, 1968) and the typical adolescent is no more dependent or vulnerable to social influence than are many adults (Hill & Holmbeck, 1986; C. C. Lewis, 1987). Thus, although developmental trends in self-governance are worthy of serious consideration, evidence does not support flat assertions that children are so lacking in socioemotional autonomy as to be inherently irrational or that adolescents are qualitatively different from adults in this respect.

The Construction of Rationality

The process of development

The discussion of rationality to this point has focused on the levels of rationality through which children pass over the course of development and the typical ages of transition. Evidence describing the degree of rationality typical of children in various age ranges can be useful in considering the extent to which government is constitutionally required, permitted, or forbidden to engage in certain activities vis-à-vis children. It would be a mistake, however, to assume that development simply proceeds on a preprogrammed course independent of environmental circumstances or that certain levels of rationality simply appear when the time is right. On the contrary, evidence indicates that development is very much a function of the environment and that the progress of rationality can be substantially facilitated or hindered. This has important implications and is a phenomenon worthy of detailed consideration. In order to pursue it, we must move beyond the earlier focus on describing levels of development and turn to the question of explaining the developmental process.

The most influential general theory of the process of development has, for several decades, been Jean Piaget's theory of equilibration (Campbell & Bickhard, 1986; Furth, 1981; Ginsburg & Opper, 1988; Kegan, 1982; Piaget, 1985). Piaget proposed that cognitive development is neither the maturation of innate capabilities nor the internalization of knowledge and skills from the environment. Rather, he argued that the intellect develops by actively constructing new modes of understanding out of earlier capabilities during the course of interaction with the physical and social environment. Efforts to deal with one's environment inevitably create conflicts and ambiguities (disequilibrium) that can only be resolved via the construction of more adequate modes of understanding, a process Piaget referred to as equilibration.

Although other theorists have disagreed with Piaget on many specifics, his general analysis has become increasingly influential over the years. Nativists, who emphasize a genetically guided process of maturation, increasingly acknowledge the critical importance of interaction with the environment in fulfilling one's genetic potential (Lerner, 1986; Piattelli-Palmarini, 1980). Learning theorists, who emphasize internalization from the environment, have increasingly moved toward information processing views in which the environment does not simply mold the individual but rather provides a basis for active processing by the person, leading to the construction of new knowledge (Resnick, 1980; Sternberg, 1984). Although important theoretical differences remain, the view that individuals actively construct their own knowledge and development during the course of their interaction with the environment is virtually universal among modern developmental psychologists (Flavell, 1985; Moshman, 1982; Moshman, Glover, & Bruning, 1987).

Support for the constructivist view of development and more detailed knowledge of what factors facilitate cognitive development have come from a wide variety of empirical studies. It seems clear that interacting with (rather than being passively molded by) one's physical and social environment—including the opportunity to confront multiple views, to reflect on one's own thinking, to make choices, and to work at resolving social conflicts and cognitive contradictions—plays a critical role in learning and development. Provision of such opportunities, moreover, can facilitate the developmental process and thus play a major role in education (Adams, 1985; Amigues, 1988; Bearison, Magzamen, & Filardo, 1986; Berkowitz, 1985; Doise & Mugny,

1984; Haan, 1985; Johnson & Johnson, 1985; Kurtines & Gewirtz, 1987; Nemeth, 1986; Rogan and MacDonald, 1983; Tremper & Kelly, 1987; Walker, 1983).

Implications

With specific reference to the First Amendment, research and theory on the process of development is thus consistent with what one might intuitively suppose. To the extent that one provides or restricts access to diverse ideas one facilitates or hinders development of the ability to coordinate different points of view. To the extent that one encourages or restricts expression of views, one facilitates or hinders the ability and inclination to form and express one's own ideas. In short, there is much parents and schools can do to facilitate or hinder development of precisely those intellectual competencies that make the First Amendment meaningful and important.

In some cases, evidence to this effect may, it seems to me, be cited by critics of government to show that certain government actions are unconstitutional. Principle 6 holds that even when government restrictions are necessary to prevent demonstrable harm to children and succeed in doing so, the alleviation of harm must be weighed against First Amendment interests. Children have an interest in not suffering government restrictions that hinder development of those intellectual competencies that will enable them to maximally exercise First Amendment freedoms as adults (Feinberg, 1980; Garvey, 1979). For example, although it is unlikely that removing a book or two from a school library will significantly impair long-term intellectual development, a systematic program of shielding students from conflicting or controversial views over the course of their schooling may plausibly have such impact. To the extent that this can be shown, there is a greater burden on the government to show that its restrictions are necessary to avoid sufficiently great harm to outweigh the First Amendment interest.

In other cases, government itself properly may invoke evidence concerning the facilitation of intellectual development to defend its activities. It may, for example, justify infringements on parental rights to regulate their own children's educations by arguing that it has a compelling interest in fostering development of those intellectual abilities that make the First Amendment meaningful and citing evidence that certain educational requirements can be expected to achieve that purpose. I will return to this point in Chapter 4 in discussions of whether government may require participation by children in public school activities to which their parents object and whether and to what extent the State may regulate private schools.

Conclusion: Rationality and Liberty

The First Amendment issue of when government may limit children's intellectual freedom is a subset of a much broader issue: the justifiability of restricting children's liberties. There is no doubt that people, in general, have a right to make their own decisions about getting medical treatment, seeking psychotherapy, participating in research, and other personal matters. Children's competence in making such decisions is of central relevance in determining the nature and extent of their rights in these areas (Melton, Koocher, & Saks, 1983; Urberg & Rosen, 1987).

Given the focus of this book on First Amendment issues of belief, expression, and access to ideas, the focus of this chapter has been research on general reasoning and understanding, rather than concrete decision-making. It is worth noting, however, that the conclusions reached in this chapter are fully consistent with the existing psycholegal literature. It is well established in a variety of legally relevant contexts that children have substantial ability to make rational choices and that the decision-making of adolescents is, in fact, rarely distinguishable from that of adults (Melton, 1983, 1983–84; Tremper & Kelly, 1987; Weithorn & Campbell, 1982).

The present conclusions are also consistent with the views of virtually all theorists of cognitive development. Stage theorists generally view the last major stage transition as beginning no later than age 11 or 12 and see no general, qualitative difference between the typical adolescent and the typical adult (Campbell & Bickhard, 1986; Case, 1985; Fischer, 1980; Inhelder & Piaget, 1958; Piaget & Inhelder, 1969; see also Byrnes, 1988; Ginsburg & Opper, 1988; Moshman, Glover, & Bruning, 1987, Chap. 8). Theorists dubious of developmental stages question whether even younger children are qualitatively different from adults (Donaldson, 1978; Gelman & Baillargeon, 1983; see also Flavell, 1985; Sternberg, 1984). Theorists postulating development beyond adolescence generally focus on relatively abstruse abilities that remain largely beyond the normal functioning of most adults (Basseches, 1984; Commons, Richards, & Armon, 1984; see also Rybash, Hoyer, & Roodin, 1986).

Principle 6 proposes that children's First Amendment rights may be restricted on the basis of limited rationality provided the government can demonstrate specific cognitive limitations (relative to a minimally normal adult) that are likely to result in substantial harm unless intellectual liberties are abridged. Implicit in this principle is an assumption that children are persons and that analysis of their constitutional rights thus must begin with a presumption in their favor. The burden of proof is on the government to justify treating them differently from adults.

As noted in Chapter 1, the trend of the 1980s has been toward decreasing respect for children's First Amendment rights and disinclination to seriously apply the First Amendment to public education. School officials regularly restrict students' intellectual freedom and judges increasingly evaluate such restrictions against an implicit background assumption that minors are inherently irrational in their decisions about what to believe and express and that governmental restrictions on their intellectual liberties therefore do not merit strict First Amendment scrutiny.

The evidence adduced in this chapter sharply counters such assumptions. Even preschool children show impressive competence in representing and processing information and children as young as 5 or 6 show substantial ability to reflect rationally on their mental representations and processes. Qualitative differences between children and adults in the sophistication of their reasoning, understanding, and decision making disappear no later than age 11 or 12. Moreover, research on the processes of learning and development indicates that children of all ages benefit substantially from intellectual freedom.

General evidence of this sort cannot itself resolve particular issues or cases. It does, however, suggest that a rather skeptical attitude toward governmental restrictions on children's intellectual liberty is highly justified. When public school officials assert that students' freedoms of belief, expression, association, or access to ideas should be restricted or that adolescents should be treated differently from college students or adults in this regard, they are taking a position difficult to reconcile with current research and theory in developmental psychology. The burden of proof should be on the government to show that there is a compelling purpose for its restrictions and that the restrictions infringe on First Amendment rights only to the extent that this is necessary for achieving that purpose. When the government's policy is based on assumptions about children's limited rationality (as is generally the case), it should be required to make these assumptions explicit and to justify them on the basis of relevant empirical evidence.

In general terms, then, substantial evidence from a wide variety of sources suggests that restrictions of liberty on the basis of limited rationality are often unjustifiable even in the case of elementary school children and are rarely justifiable in the case of adolescents. It is the burden of the government to show that a specific situation is so exceptional as to justify restrictions on children or adolescents greater than those that would apply to adults.

4 : Educational Applications

In this chapter, I apply the principles and research discussed in Chapters 2 and 3 to eight current educational issues: (a) students' freedom of expression, (b) students' freedom of association, (c) the selection and removal of textbooks and school library books, (d) religion in public schools, (e) secular humanism, (f) scientific creationism, (g) values and morality in public education, and (h) government regulation of private education. With respect to all but the last issue, the focus will be on public schools, since this is where government action is most commonly and clearly involved and the First Amendment is thus most directly applicable. Issues of intellectual freedom also come into play in children's relations with their parents and with private schools, however, a matter I will consider in the last section of the chapter.

With respect to each of the eight issues, the discussion will be organized in five sections. For each issue, I will provide an overview of the controversy, followed by a summary of its history and the current legal situation. I will then provide my own legal analysis, based on the principles discussed in Chapter 2, after which I will explore the relevant empirical considerations. Finally, I will reach a conclusion, involving critique of the current legal situation and specific suggestions.

Students' Freedom of Expression

Nature of the issue
A variety of issues fall under the heading of student expression. They can be divided, roughly, into five major categories: oral expression,

written expression, symbolic expression, dramatic expression, and forced expression.

Oral expression. Obviously, students speak in school, both in connection with the curriculum and independent of it. No one doubts that some restriction of student speech is permissible: For example, teachers must have authority to take action against students who speak during class on matters irrelevant to the topic at hand and thus prevent other students from learning the material. But to what extent and in what ways may school officials restrict when a student speaks, where she speaks, with whom she speaks, what she speaks about, what she says about that topic, and how she expresses herself?

Written expression. Students communicate through writing as well as orally. A central purpose of schooling in every state is, in fact, development of students' ability to do precisely that. May schools restrict students' writing? This issue usually comes up in connection with school newspapers, which are typically written and edited by students with the guidance of a faculty advisor. May the advisor forbid a reporter to pursue a certain topic or forbid the editor to publish certain articles? To what extent and in what ways may administrators restrict what is published in the school newspaper or limit the distribution of the paper? And what about nonofficial ("underground") newspapers published and/or distributed by students on or off school premises?

Symbolic expression. Expression need not be oral or written. Students may wish to express themselves by wearing political buttons or armbands. Even their clothing or hairstyle may be, for them, an important means of expressing themselves. What limitations may schools place on this?

Dramatic expression. Students may express themselves by participating in plays. To what extent may schools restrict what plays students choose to put on or what they include in those plays?

Forced expression. In some sense, the flip side of the above issues is where a school wants a student to express something the student does not believe or does not wish to express. May schools require students to salute the flag, recite the pledge of allegiance, or sing songs they object to? If a student disagrees with what is being taught, may she be required to express ideas she disagrees with in order to pass a test?

History and current status of the issue

Tinker v. Des Moines (1969). In 1965, John Tinker, Mary Beth Tinker, and Christopher Eckhardt, ages 15, 13, and 16, respectively, wore black armbands to school to symbolize their opposition to U.S. involvement in Vietnam. After they were suspended for this, they sued. Since it was not clear at the time that children had constitutional rights, the outcome of the case was anybody's guess. In 1967, however, the Supreme Court held in *In re Gault*, a due process case, that children are persons in a legal sense and do have constitutional rights.[1] The following year, in *Ginsberg v. New York*, the Court indicated that, although government may distinguish children from adults in regulating what they read, the First Amendment does apply to children, at least in principle.[2]

In 1969, the Supreme Court made it clear in *Tinker v. Des Moines* that children's constitutional rights include a meaningful First Amendment right to freedom of expression and that this holds in public schools.[3] The Court ruled that for a school to censor or punish expression it must demonstrate that the expression in question would seriously disrupt education or otherwise interfere with the rights of others. The Court did show considerable solicitude for the special purposes and characteristics of schools, including the need to maintain order. Nevertheless, its decision in favor of the students showed that it took the First Amendment issues seriously and that a school's burden in justifying abridgment of student expression would henceforth be substantial.

Although *Tinker* involved symbolic speech, it has had a dramatic impact in all areas of student expression. It would not be an overstatement to suggest that the history of student freedom of expression is usefully divided into two eras—pre-*Tinker* and post-*Tinker*. The language of the majority opinion was broad and stirring:

> In our system, state-operated schools may not be enclaves of totalitarianism. School officials do not possess absolute authority

1. In re Gault, 387 U.S. 1 (1967)
2. Ginsberg v. New York, 390 U.S. 629 (1968)
3. Tinker v. Des Moines Independent Community School District, 393 U.S. 503 (1969)

over their students. Students in school as well as out of school are "persons" under the Constitution. They are possessed of fundamental rights which the State must respect, just as they themselves must respect their obligations to the State. In our system, students may not be regarded as closed-circuit recipients of only that which the State chooses to communicate. They may not be confined to the expression of those sentiments that are officially approved. In the absence of a specific showing of constitutionally valid reasons to regulate their speech, students are entitled to freedom of expression of their views.[4]

Bethel v. Fraser (1986). In 1983 high school student Matthew Fraser spoke at a school assembly to support a candidate for student government office. His speech was as follows:

> I know a man who is firm—he's firm in his pants, he's firm in his shirt, his character is firm—but most of all, his belief in you, the students of Bethel, is firm.
> Jeff Kuhlman is a man who takes his point and pounds it in. If necessary, he'll take an issue and nail it to the wall. He doesn't attack things in spurts—he drives hard, pushing and pushing until finally—he succeeds.
> Jeff is a man who will go to the very end—even the climax, for each and every one of you.
> So vote for Jeff for A.S.B. vice-president—he'll never come between you and the best our high school can be.[5]

The students reacted positively, electing Fraser's candidate by a wide margin. Bethel school officials were less enthusiastic; they responded to the one-minute speech by suspending him for two days and denying him the opportunity to speak at graduation.

Fraser, relying on *Tinker*, sued on the ground that the school had violated his First Amendment right to freedom of expression by punishing him for what he had said. A federal judge ruled in Fraser's favor

4. *Id.* at 511
5. Bethel School District No. 403 v. Fraser (Brennan, J., concurring), 478 U.S. 675, 687 (1986)

and this decision was upheld by the Ninth Circuit Court of Appeals. Given that there had been no disruption of education, the school had no authority to censor Fraser's speech or to punish him for it.

In 1986 the Supreme Court disagreed, ruling 7-2 in favor of the school. Writing for himself and for Justices Rehnquist, O'Connor, White, and Powell, Chief Justice Burger labeled Fraser a "confused boy" and argued that schools must have the authority to inculcate "the habits and manners of civility." He characterized the speech as "obscene," "plainly offensive to both teachers and students," and "acutely insulting to teen-age girl students."[6] Justice Brennan concurred in the result but wrote a separate opinion, arguing that the speech was neither obscene nor indecent but could be punished, under *Tinker*, as "disruptive."[7] Justice Blackman also concurred in the result but likewise declined to sign Chief Justice Burger's opinion.

Justice Marshall dissented, arguing that the speech was not even disruptive and was therefore protected by the First Amendment. Justice Stevens also dissented, questioning whether a determination about what was offensive to high school students could reasonably be made by "a group of judges who are at least two generations and 3,000 miles away from the scene of the crime."[8]

Fraser is best viewed as an exception to *Tinker* rather than a rejection of it. The majority explicitly declined to overturn *Tinker*, accepting the precedent that students have an "undoubted freedom to advocate unpopular and controversial views."[9] They did limit the scope of *Tinker*, however, ruling that this freedom must be "balanced against the society's countervailing interest in teaching students the boundaries of socially appropriate behavior."[10] It is not yet clear how broadly courts will construe this limitation on the principles set forth in *Tinker*.

Hazelwood v. Kuhlmeier (1988). In 1983, the same year as Fraser's speech, a Missouri high school principal blocked publication in the

6. Bethel School District No. 403 v. Fraser, 478 U.S. 675, 680, 683 (1986)

7. Bethel School District No. 403 v. Fraser (Brennan, J., concurring), 478 U.S. 675, 689 (1986)

8. Bethel School District No. 403 v. Fraser (Stevens, J., dissenting), 478 U.S. 675, 692 (1986)

9. Bethel School District No. 403 v. Fraser, 478 U.S. 675, 681 (1986)

10. *Id.* at 681

student newspaper of articles addressing pregnancy and divorce. After the Eighth Circuit Court of Appeals ruled in favor of the students (S. L. Melton, 1987),[11] the school board appealed to the Supreme Court, which, in 1988, overturned that decision.[12]

The majority opinion by Justice White, joined by Justices Rehnquist, O'Connor, Scalia, and Stevens, distinguished "expressive activities that . . . may fairly be characterized as part of the school curriculum, whether or not they occur in a traditional classroom setting"[13] from "a student's personal expression that happens to occur on the school premises."[14] *Tinker*, ruled the Court, governs only the latter. In the former category, the issue is not "whether the First Amendment requires a school to tolerate particular student speech" but whether it "requires a school affirmatively to promote particular student speech."[15] School officials "retain the authority to refuse to sponsor student speech" that

> is, for example, ungrammatical, poorly written, inadequately researched, biased or prejudiced, vulgar or profane, or unsuitable for immature audiences [or that] might reasonably be perceived to advocate drug or alcohol use, irresponsible sex, or conduct otherwise inconsistent with 'the shared values of a civilized social order,' [citation omitted] or to associate the school with any position other than neutrality on matters of political controversy.[16]

The Court concluded that the principal's decision to forbid publication of the articles in question was based on his determination that they invaded the privacy of individuals discussed in them, did not meet proper journalistic standards, and were inappropriate for younger readers. It ruled that these determinations were not unreasonable and were thus an adequate basis for his decision (Rose, 1988).

The side of the students was taken by the Court's three oldest members. In a sharply worded dissent, Justice Brennan, joined by Justices

11. Kuhlmeier v. Hazelwood School District, 795 F.2d 1368 (8th Cir. 1986)
12. Hazelwood School District v. Kuhlmeier, 108 S.Ct. 562 (1988)
13. *Id*. at 569–570
14. *Id*. at 569
15. *Id*. at 569
16. *Id*. at 570

Marshall and Blackmun, argued that the standards set forth in *Tinker* were fully adequate to deal with the issues of this case and that under those standards the principal had violated the students' First Amendment right to freedom of expression.

> The Court offers no more than an obscure tangle of three excuses to afford educators "greater control" over school-sponsored speech than the *Tinker* test would permit: the public educator's prerogative to control curriculum; the pedagogical interest in shielding the high-school audience from objectionable viewpoints and sensitive topics; and the school's need to disassociate itself from student expression [citation omitted]. None of the excuses, once disentangled, supports the distinction that the Court draws. *Tinker* fully addresses the first concern; the second is illegitimate; and the third is readily achievable through less oppressive means.[17]

Quoting from *Barnette*, the dissent argued that the majority opinion "teach[es] youth to discount important principles of our government as mere platitudes."[18] "The young men and women of Hazelwood East expected a civics lesson," concluded Justice Brennan, "but not the one the Court teaches them today."[19]

With this background in mind, it may be useful to go through the five categories of free expression distinguished earlier.

Oral expression. It is clear that the Supreme Court recognizes students' First Amendment right to freedom of expression in public schools. The Court has also been clear on several major categories of exception: Free speech may be abridged when there is a serious threat of disruption (*Tinker*), when it interferes with the rights of others (*Tinker*), when there is a violation of fundamental civility (*Fraser*), and, for a wide variety of reasons, when it occurs within a curriculum-related context (*Hazelwood*). Exactly what constitutes a disruption of education, a violation of rights, or a breach of civility is not well established; it is even less clear what constitutes a curriculum-related context or

17. Hazelwood School District v. Kuhlmeier (Brennan, J., dissenting), 108 S.Ct. 562, 576 (1988)
18. *Id.* at 580
19. *Id.* at 580

what limits there are on censorship in such contexts. There is thus ample basis for continuing litigation.

Written expression. Censorship of school newspapers is a highly litigated area. In the years after *Tinker,* high school newspapers were consistently held to have strong First Amendment rights, though schools could provide reasonable restrictions on the time, place, and manner of distribution and could regulate papers to the extent necessary to prevent genuine disruption of the school program and publication of libelous or obscene materials (Ingelhart, 1986). Although prior restraint on publication was often upheld in principle, specific programs and instances of prior restraint by school administrators were usually struck down as unconstitutional on the basis of vague criteria, undue delay, or inadequate opportunity for appeal (Huffman & Trauth, 1981).

In general, then, federal courts have been quite solicitous of high school freedom of the press. *Hazelwood* is already changing this. Moreover, regardless of case law, cases of censorship that get challenged in court are only the tip of the iceberg. A careful survey by Kristof (1983) of 500 randomly-selected public high schools around the United States (including schools in every state) suggested that, even before *Hazelwood,* censorship was pervasive and usually went unchallenged. Some editors reported blatant restrictions, many reported more subtle forms of control, and many indicated that a substantial degree of self-censorship was necessary to avoid trouble. "Censorship and self-censorship," concluded Kristof, "are institutionalized in most American public high schools (p. 36)." *Hazelwood* tips the balance even further toward school authorities.

Symbolic expression. Tinker, the first major student expression case, was in fact a symbolic expression case in that it involved the wearing of armbands. Given the decision in that case, there is no doubt that the Court includes symbolic expression within the First Amendment rights of students. Students have a First Amendment right to wear buttons or armbands to express specific political views.

With respect to choice of clothing or hairstyle, however, the situation is less clear. There were numerous such cases in the 1960s and 1970s and the decisions showed no consistent pattern (Friedman, 1986; van Geel, 1987). Some judges viewed the cases as frivolous and irritating, while others, especially after *Tinker*, saw them as raising a variety of genuine constitutional issues. With respect to hair cases, for example, the Third, Fifth, Sixth, Ninth, Tenth, and Eleventh Circuits ruled various hair regulations to be constitutionally valid, whereas the First, Second, Fourth, Seventh, and Eighth Circuits supported students' constitutional challenges (van Geel, 1987). The Supreme Court, despite the conflict among the circuits, was absolutely resolute in avoiding the issue: Appeals of ten different hair cases reached it in the late 1960s and early 1970s, and it declined to hear any of them (Friedman, 1986). Hair and dress code cases have largely disappeared not because the issue was ever settled but because, as a result of changing social norms, schools generally relaxed their standards and there was less reason to appeal their regulations.

Dramatic expression. Students' right to choose school plays is a much less litigated area and the legal status of the issue, prior to *Hazelwood*, was unclear (Faaborg, 1985). Nevertheless, the issue can, when it does arise, attract substantial attention. In 1987, for example, the Nebraska legislature overwhelmingly supported a resolution condemning the performance by junior high students in Omaha of a play they had written that was considered by the legislators to present a stereotyped view of Hispanics. An amendment to specifically condemn school officials for not canceling the play was defeated on the ground that the resolution was already sufficient to ensure strong action by school officials.

The only reported opinion on the issue of school plays is a Third Circuit ruling that an administrative decision to cancel a play was no different from other such decisions concerning allocation of school resources and selection of curriculum and that student First Amendment rights were not implicated.[20] The decision appears to be consistent with the Supreme Court's later reasoning in *Hazelwood*.

Forced expression. The classic case in the area of forced expression in public schools is *West Virginia v. Barnette* (1943).[21] Jehovah's Witnesses challenged a board of education resolution requiring that all public school students (and teachers) participate in a daily flag salute and

20. Seyfried v. Walton, 668 F.2d 214 (3d Cir. 1981)
21. West Virginia State Board of Education v. Barnette, 319 U.S. 624 (1943)

pledge of allegiance. Failure to participate could result in expulsion from the school, which in turn could lead to delinquency proceedings and prosecution of the child's parents. The challenge was based primarily on the infringement of religious liberty, since the salute and pledge were argued by the Jehovah's witnesses to be prohibited by their religious beliefs.

Although the court ruled in favor of the plaintiffs, the plurality opinion of Justice Jackson focused not on the religious claim but, more generally, on a right to intellectual individualism inherent in the right to freedom of expression (Harpaz, 1986): "[N]o official, high or petty, can prescribe what shall be orthodox . . . or force citizens to confess by word or act their faith therein."[22] There are thus limits on the extent to which a public school may require expression by students, though the extent of those limits is not clear.

Application of the principles

Principle 1a proposes that "government may not hinder children from forming or expressing any idea unless the abridgment of belief or expression serves a compelling purpose . . . that cannot be served in a less restrictive way." The most obvious compelling purpose a school might cite is its responsibility to educate students.

Oral and symbolic expression in the classroom. Within a classroom, expression is typically controlled by an understanding that students must raise their hands in order to gain permission to speak and that they may not speak unless recognized by the teacher. Such a system maintains a level of decorum necessary for education. It ensures that only one person will speak at a time, that the teacher will have adequate control of expression to ensure getting through the lesson, and that the teacher will be able to facilitate expression by quieter students and restrict domination of the classroom by a small number of vocal individuals. Although the expression of an individual student at a particular time may be restricted by such an arrangement, there is no doubt that a system of this sort is necessary for a teacher to maintain order in the classroom and, thus, for government to pursue its compelling interest in the education of students. Unless it can be shown

22. *Id.* at 642

that the teacher is abusing the system by unnecessarily limiting the speech of certain students or the expression of certain views, I see no First Amendment objection.

Restrictions on symbolic expression, even within the classroom, are more difficult to justify. Although there is no doubt that education would be seriously disrupted if students were free to speak at will and commonly interrupted other students or the teacher, it is not obvious there would be significant disruption if students were free to wear a variety of buttons, armbands, clothing styles, or hairstyles. The government's burden of proof in limiting symbolic expression in the classroom should be substantially harder to meet.

One might wonder whether a distinction should be made between buttons or armbands expressing a specific political view and clothing or hair styles with no obvious political content. It is important to note, however, that even clothing and hairstyles may express something the student considers important; the fact that a rather general sort of self-expression rather than a specific political view is involved in no way makes the expression less meaningful to the expressor or unworthy of constitutional protection. In the late 1960s and early 1970s, for example, hairstyle was very clearly a primary mode of self-expression:

> Almost cut my hair
> > It happened just the other day
> > It was gettin' kinda long
> > > I coulda said it was in my way
> But I didn't
> > and I wonder why
> > I feel like letting my freak flag fly
> (Crosby, 1970).

Oral, written, and dramatic expression outside the classroom. The school is not required to set up forums for students to address other students outside the classroom. Similarly, it is not required to provide for a school newspaper or a series of student plays. If it does set up such forums, it may limit them to certain topics, provided there is a clear educational rationale for doing so. For example, a school may arrange an assembly for students to present their views on candidates for student government and restrict presentations to this topic. Similarly, the science department may arrange for a student newsletter on current topics in science and refuse to publish content irrelevant to science. The key, it seems to me, is that the purpose of the forum and its main effect is to facilitate speech on certain education-related topics, not to hinder other categories of expression.

Principle 1 cannot, however, countenance ad hoc manipulations of existing forums that restrict certain ideas or categories of expression simply because the topics addressed are controversial or the particular views disfavored. Thus the school may not, in my view, restrict the use of a forum on the basis of the speaker's point of view or mode of expression unless it has a compelling reason to do so. Topic discrimination is acceptable if it can be justified on the basis of clear, *a priori* guidelines intended to limit a forum to certain topics (e.g., science) but not if it consists of ad hoc censorship of disfavored topics. Examples of reasons sufficiently compelling to justify censorship would be clear evidence that the view expressed or topic addressed is likely to spark uncontrollable violence, or to seriously harm the listeners, or to result in serious consequences for the speaker that she or he is incompetent to anticipate and evaluate.

Forced expression. There are surely situations in which government has a compelling interest in what someone knows and may require him or her to communicate it (e.g., by subpoenaing the person as a witness). It is difficult, however, to imagine any circumstance in which an individual may be required to express a view contrary to his or her actual beliefs. The indignity of being forbidden to speak pales beside the indignity of being required to misrepresent one's views. Moreover, even if there is occasionally such potential for harm from expression that government has a compelling reason to enforce silence, it is far more difficult to imagine a circumstance in which silence would be so harmful that government would have compelling reason to require expression, not of what one knows or believes, but of something one in fact does not believe. Students may, of course, be required to demonstrate that they are aware of and understand certain ideas in order to get adequate grades in their courses. It should be made clear to them, however, that they are only required to demonstrate understanding, not to profess belief.

Empirical considerations

In general, there is little evidence that children are commonly harmed by what they say or hear, or that free exchanges of views among them lead to uncontrollable violence. On the contrary, as discussed in Chapter 3, there is much evidence that intellectual development is facilitated by the opportunity to form and express one's own views and by exposure to the views of others. Government claims that specific cases are so exceptional as to merit censorship should be based on specific data. The general thrust of relevant evidence, especially at the secondary level, is strongly on the side of the students.

Conclusion

My analysis concludes that students should be construed as having a First Amendment right to express themselves through speeches, buttons, armbands, choice of clothing, hairstyle, publication of newspaper articles, performance in school plays, and so forth. Schools may limit expression in various ways, but Principle 1 suggests that the burden of proof should be on the school to show a compelling purpose for the restriction and to demonstrate that it has no less restrictive means available for achieving that purpose.

Bethel v. Fraser. In *Fraser*, for example, the school set up a forum for speeches about candidates for school government. It would have been legitimate to require that all speeches be relevant to this purpose. The punishment of Fraser, however, was based on what he proposed as reasons for supporting his candidate and his manner of expressing those reasons. Although there was no prior restraint, the punishment does constitute censorship in that the threat of punishment is clearly a restriction on future expression.

Bethel school officials apparently found Fraser's remarks deeply offensive, especially given the public high school context. But offensiveness has never been considered a legitimate basis for censorship: "[T]he Constitution does not permit our government to decide which types of otherwise protected speech are sufficiently offensive to require protection for the unwilling listener or viewer." [23]

There are, of course, categories of speech such as "obscenity" and

23. Erznoznik v. Jacksonville, 422 U.S. 205, 210 (1975)

"fighting words" that are not protected under current First Amendment law (see Chapter 1). Fraser's speech, however, fell into no such category. On the contrary, it was clearly, indisputably, political. It was intended to get people to feel positively disposed toward, and thus vote for, the candidate Fraser favored. It appears that it succeeded in achieving this legitimate political purpose. As noted in Chapter 1, such speech is not only within the scope of the First Amendment but, if anything, lies at its very core. Clearly, then, there is no precedent for the conclusion that government may censor political speech simply because it determines it to be "offensive."

Fraser's speech did, of course, take place in a public school. The censorship would have been justifiable under *Tinker* if the school had shown that the speech so disrupted normal activities that the school's compelling interest in educating students was seriously compromised. No evidence of such disruption was provided (Alpern, 1987; Schwetschenau, 1987).

Alternatively, it might be noted that Fraser was a minor speaking to other minors. The school would have been constitutionally correct, it seems to me, if it had been able to show that students in the audience were extremely innocent of sexual matters, that they were thus likely to be harmed by sixty seconds of sexual allusions, and that this harm was likely to be so serious as to justify infringing Fraser's First Amendment right to say what he pleased about the candidate he favored. Again, the school failed to demonstrate anything of this sort. Given that the students were all at least 14 years old, there is no reason to think it could have done so.

It might be argued that long-term harm is difficult to demonstrate and we must defer to the judgments of school authorities about their students. But *Fraser* shows clearly that, given authority to censor, school officials are likely to use that power on the basis of what they personally find offensive, not on the basis of any special insight into their students' psychological reactions. Even Justice Brennan, who ruled for the school, acknowledged that "there is no evidence in the record that any students . . . found the speech 'insulting'."[24] As for

24. Bethel School District No. 403 v. Fraser, 478 U.S. 675, 689n.2 (1986) (Brennan, J., concurring)

the majority's particular concern for the sensibilities of teenage girls, *New York Times* education reporter Fred Hechinger (1986) wrote:

> The Chief Justice may have been motivated by old-fashioned chivalry; but in the contemporary context, [his opinion] has a sexist ring. Should high-school girls be sent out of the room when Shakespeare's 'lewd' ways of dealing with male sexuality and his frequent sexual metaphors and innuendo appear in literature classes?

For children as for adults, then, there is reason to question the wisdom of censors. Content-based censorship of expression should trigger strict judicial scrutiny. It is clear that the punishment of Matthew Fraser could not have survived such scrutiny.

Hazelwood. Whereas the Supreme Court's analysis in *Fraser* focused on the content of Fraser's speech, its analysis in *Hazelwood* focused on the school's relation to the medium of expression. To understand and critique its analysis it is critical to distinguish three categories of newspapers.

The unofficial—or "underground"—newspaper is in no way sponsored by the school. It may be aimed at students in a particular school, and thus be considered in some sense a school newspaper, but it represents pure and simple expression by the students who write, edit, produce, and distribute it. If the paper is distributed on school grounds, of course, there is a potential for disruption of educational activities (e.g., if it is distributed during class). Such problems, however, are adequately addressed in *Tinker*.

The *official* school newspaper, by contrast, is largely set up and financially supported by the school itself. It is, however, typically run and edited by students and is intended, at least in part, to serve as a forum for student expression. Provision of such a forum is generally viewed as an important educational benefit to students.

It is possible, and instructive, to imagine a very different sort of publication that could also be called a school newspaper. Suppose the administrators of a school decide that, in order to better communicate with their various constituencies, they will publish a newspaper about the school. The paper typically includes articles by various school officials and, perhaps, an occasional article by a student. To distinguish this from the usual sort of school newspaper, let us label this an *administration newspaper*.

Suppose a student submits an article to this latter sort of school newspaper and school officials decide not to publish it. Although the student might charge censorship, she could not reasonably claim violation of her First Amendment rights. Those who publish a newspaper have, in general, the right to decide what to publish in it. It is the school, not any student, that is communicating via the administration newspaper, and it is up to school officials, not to students, to decide what the school wishes to say. Deciding to express certain ideas and not others does not, in itself, constitute censorship of those ideas one does not choose to communicate.

A central question in *Hazelwood*, then, is whether school newspapers of the usual sort—authorized and financed by the school but written and edited by students—are more like unofficial student newspapers or more like the sort of administration newspaper just described. There can be no doubt that government must and does have substantial freedom to express its own views (Haiman, 1981, Chapter 17; Yudof, 1983, 1987). A long history of judicial precedents makes it clear, however, that, having set up a forum for expression by nongovernmental sources, government must operate that forum in accord with strict constitutional constraints (Haiman, 1981, Chapter 14). As the Supreme Court itself has put it,

> under the Equal Protection Clause, not to mention the First Amendment itself, government may not grant the use of a forum to people whose views it finds acceptable, but deny use to those wishing to express less favored or more controversial views. And it may not select which issues are worth discussing or debating in public facilities. . . . Selective exclusions from a public forum may not be based on content alone, and may not be justified by reference to content alone.[25]

A public school is not, of course, constitutionally required to set up an official school newspaper written and edited by students.

25. Chicago Police Department v. Mosely, 408 U.S. 92, 96 (1972)

Nevertheless, such a newspaper is widely considered to provide students with important educational opportunities. This is precisely why schools establish them and why the Supreme Court deemed the Hazelwood East paper part of the school's curriculum. Public schools are constitutionally permitted to provide students with the educational opportunity of writing for and working on a school newspaper; they are also constitutionally permitted *not* to establish such an opportunity. *Hazelwood* breaks dangerous new ground, however, in suggesting that public schools are constitutionally permitted to provide this important educational opportunity to students who hold and wish to express ideas the school agrees with but withhold it from students who wish to express alternative views or to address controversial topics.

Is there something about children or public schools that justifies such an extraordinary deviation from clear precedent? The *Hazelwood* majority noted that a school might wish not to be associated with certain ideas or values and might thus be concerned about what is expressed in an official school newspaper. One may readily acknowledge that government has a legitimate interest—and a public school often has a *compelling* interest—in not having certain viewpoints incorrectly attributed to it (cf. Principle 1b). But even when this interest is compelling, censorship is an unnecessarily restrictive solution (cf. Principle 1a). It would almost always be adequate simply to have a general disclaimer published in the newspaper indicating that the student paper is a forum for student expression and that views expressed within it are not necessarily those of the school. If this is deemed insufficient, the school might insist on a more specific disclaimer appearing prominently with a particularly problematical article. It is difficult to imagine any circumstance, at least at the secondary school level, where this would not suffice to insure that the views of the school are not misconstrued.

The fact that a school newspaper, unlike most public forums, is related to an educational curriculum is a potentially important distinction, especially if production of the paper is an integral part of a particular journalism class, as was the case in *Hazelwood*. The standards of *Tinker*, however, suffice to address this. They allow government regulation to the extent necessary to achieve government's compelling educational purposes. Just as a history teacher may insist that a paper meet certain standards to be given a grade of A, the journalism teacher may insist that an article meet certain standards to merit inclusion in the newspaper. Provided there are legitimate professional grounds for the journalism teacher's judgment, withholding publication of low-quality work is no more censorship than withholding a high grade. We would be highly suspicious, however, if the school principal looked over a set of history papers and directed the teacher that two of them should not receive passing grades. We should be equally suspicious of publication decisions made not by the journalism teacher but by the principal. The specific circumstances of *Hazelwood* make it clear that the decision to exclude certain articles was not made by a professional with special competence in journalism and raise serious doubts as to whether it was made on educational grounds at all.

Tinker also permits the school to censor expression that violates the rights of others. The burden of proof, however, should be on the censor to show strong reason to expect substantial harm. Speculative assertions about possible reactions to an article are not sufficient to justify abridging a fundamental right. Moreover, even when there are legitimate concerns about an article, both educational and constitutional considerations demand a process of negotiation between censor and student to eliminate objectional aspects of the article with as little restriction as possible on expression of what the student wishes to express. No such process was offered in *Hazelwood*. The Court attempted to justify this by arguing that the principal was genuinely unaware of the options available to him because he misunderstood the publication process and timelines. But this only underscores the fact that the censor was not a knowledgeable journalist making professional judgments.

Although the facts of *Hazelwood* are complex, a number of factors suggest that the school's rationale for censorship was largely a pretext; the real intent was to prevent publication of articles that might lead to controversy. Even more disturbing than the specific outcome of the case, however, is the dangerously broad and vague language of the majority opinion. The Court unnecessarily reached the sweeping conclusion that "a school need not tolerate student speech that is inconsistent with its 'basic educational mission.' "[26]

What does this mean? A narrow construal would read it to mean that a school need not tolerate student speech that severely compromises its ability to educate its students. But this is simply another way of stating the *Tinker* rule that a school need not tolerate genuine disruption of education. The tone of the opinion and the conclusion reached suggest that the *Hazelwood* Court meant to provide broader limits on student expression than those countenanced by *Tinker*.

A very broad construal of the same phrase would read it to mean that a school not only may decide what ideas and values it wishes to communicate—a power that has never been in doubt—but may forbid the expression of any ideas or values inconsistent with those that define the school's educational mission. Students, in other words, may be limited to expressing and encountering those views—and only those views—that the school decides to inculcate. But this flatly contradicts *Tinker's* fundamental conclusion that students "may not be confined to the expression of those sentiments that are officially approved" and "may not be regarded as closed-circuit recipients of only that which the state chooses to communicate."[27] Given that the *Hazelwood* Court began its analysis with an explicit reaffirmation of *Tinker*, it is not obvious that it meant *Hazelwood* thus to cut the heart out of students' First Amendment rights.

What, then, does *Hazelwood* stand for? It is simply impossible to say. Justice White's welter of examples of when censorship might be justifiable were perhaps intended to clarify what the Court had in mind but do not bear close analysis. They seem to reflect his immediate intuitions about what sorts of things should be censorable rather than being derived from any ascertainable set of general, justifiable principles. They thus offer lower court judges limited guidance as to how to apply the vague language and loose reasoning of *Hazelwood* to the multifaceted issues they will undoubtedly face in coming years.

Conclusion. The status of student expression is, then, less clear after

26. Hazelwood School District v. Kuhlmeier, 108 S.Ct. 562, 567 (1988)
27. Tinker v. Des Moines Independent Community School District, 393 U.S. 503, 511 (1969)

Fraser and *Hazelwood* than it was before. In backing off from its own principles, the Court has sacrificed a substantial degree of clarity and predictability. On pragmatic as well as substantive grounds, there is good reason to wish it had not tinkered with *Tinker*.

What can we expect in the wake of the recent changes? School officials who don't wish to risk a lawsuit may hesitate to censor anything that is arguably still protected. Others will censor extensively, eager to test the limits of their newfound power to control what ideas are expressed in their schools. Similarly, some students may aggressively test the limits of their liberty and autonomy via purposely controversial speech and writing. Others will succumb to the chilling effect of the school's increased censorial powers, carefully avoiding any ideas and topics that might conceivably turn out to be sensitive or controversial. Parents, aware of schools' greater power to control the exchange of ideas, will apply a variety of political pressures to get schools to use those powers as the community—or some segment of it—deems appropriate. Judges faced with new cases will have to make difficult decisions about the state of constitutional law in this area.

Perhaps the most important conclusion for school officials is that, although they have broader power to censor than they did before, they are not obliged to use this power. They are free to continue acting in accord with the principles of *Tinker*, and both educational and constitutional considerations suggest they should do so. As discussed in Chapter 3, there is extensive evidence that exposure to diverse information and ideas, and encouragement to form and express one's own conclusions, play a positive role in development. Schools must have substantial leeway to choose what they wish to communicate, but restriction of the school's intellectual environment to only that which the school wishes to inculcate, by censoring students who wish to express contrary or alternative ideas, serves no valid educational purpose and is, in fact, generally contraindicated by psychological considerations.

With the exception of obvious rules of courtesy for maintaining order and permitting education within classrooms, then, limitations on student expression are rarely justified. *Tinker* laid out the appropriate principles in this area; *Fraser* was an unprincipled exception, and *Hazelwood* a dangerous step backward. Fraser's mode of expression may displease some adults and Kuhlmeier et al.'s topics may scare them. Limitations on a humorous speech may seem a trivial matter; publication of a potentially controversial article may seem dangerous. Except in the most extraordinary circumstances, however, it is not up to the government to distinguish the important from the trivial or the safe from the dangerous in deciding what speech to permit. There is no reason to disparage the First Amendment claim of a student who wishes to amuse, or chooses to address controversial matters, or objects to saluting the flag, or wears clothing carefully selected to "make a statement" to her peers, or who simply, and perhaps inarticulately, wants to let his freak flag fly.

Students' Freedom of Association

Public schools often allow students to use their facilities for a wide variety of voluntary activities (Holland & Andre, 1987). Especially at the secondary level, this may include regular meetings of formally organized student groups. In recent years, religious students have often requested permission to meet on the same basis as any other voluntary group. For public school administrators, this creates a serious legal quandary: If they allow access to religious groups they may be sued for permitting an unconstitutional establishment of religion, while if they deny equal access they may be sued for discriminating against religious groups on the basis of the content of their beliefs and expression, thus violating students' First Amendment rights to free exercise of religion, freedom of expression, and/or freedom of association. Thus, although student freedom of association is a potentially broad topic, the main focus of controversy, and thus of this section, is the free association of religious students.

History and current status of the issue

The courts. There have been a number of court cases concerning equal access for student religious groups to public secondary school facilities. Four U.S. Courts of Appeals have addressed the issue in recent years, and all four have ruled against equal access, viewing the establishment-of-religion problem as the predominant consideration (Laycock, 1986; Strossen, 1985, 1987; Thompson, 1985; van Geel,

1987). Although the Supreme Court did agree to hear one of these cases, it ultimately ruled that the plaintiff lacked standing to sue and thus did not settle the underlying issue.[28]

There is, however, an analogous Supreme Court case at the college level, in which the University of Missouri at Kansas City informed student religious groups that they would no longer be permitted to use the student Union for their activities. The University, as a public institution, maintained that to permit use of the Union by religious groups would be perceived as government endorsement, and thus an unconstitutional establishment, of religion. Several students sued, arguing that they were not asking for endorsement but merely equal treatment. To be singled out for exclusion, they maintained, violated constitutional guarantees of free speech and free exercise of religion.

In *Widmar v. Vincent* (1981), the Supreme Court ruled 8-1 in favor of the students, concluding that the University's exclusion of religious speech involved a content-based discrimination and thus violated the students' freedom of speech.[29] It rejected the University's argument that it needed to protect other students against perceiving government endorsement of religion. In a key footnote, it made it clear that its opinion was based, at least in part, on the maturity of college students:

> University students are, of course, young adults. They are less impressionable than younger students and should be able to appreciate that the University's policy is one of neutrality toward religion. . . . In light of the large number of groups meeting on campus . . . we doubt students could draw any reasonable inference of University support from the mere fact of a campus meeting place. The University's student handbook already notes that the University's name will not "be identified in any way with the aims, policies, programs, products, or opinions of any organization or its members."[30]

It appears from this rationale that, with young enough students, concerns about a perceived establishment of religion would be taken

28. Bender v. Williamsport Area School District, 475 U.S. 534 (1986).
29. Widmar v. Vincent, 454 U.S. 263 (1981).
30. *Id.*, Footnote 14.

more seriously and might lead to the opposite decision. The Court did not, however, indicate what it considered the proper age of demarcation. In the absence of clear judicial guidance, and the presence of intense political pressure, Congress leaped into the breach.

The Equal Access Act. In the early years of the Reagan administration, there were vigorous efforts in Congress to pass a constitutional amendment to permit prayer in public schools. When it became apparent that Congress would not pass such an amendment, supporters of school prayer began to push for a law guaranteeing that voluntary student religious groups would have the same access to school facilities as other voluntary student groups. Early versions of the bill specified only that public schools not discriminate against religious groups. Opponents argued that this singled out religion for special treatment in that discrimination against nonreligious student groups was not addressed. The final version of the law, passed in 1984 and known as the Equal Access Act[31], requires that if a public secondary school permits *any* noncurricular student group to meet on school premises it must permit *all* such groups regardless of the religious, political, or philosophical content of their speech or activities. The Act specifies that any religious group permitted must be genuinely student-run: It must not be led by a teacher or other adult, though a school official may be present to monitor discipline and maintain order.

The Equal Access Act was able to gather enough support to be passed into law because its original intent to permit more religion in public schools was pleasing to conservatives and the broad student rights language of the final version was attractive to liberals. Nevertheless, skepticism about its ultimate effects remained. The American Civil Liberties Union, for example, maintains that

> [t]he persistent, widespread, and continuing efforts to evade the Establishment Clause in public elementary and secondary schools, and the vulnerability of elementary and secondary school students to the consequences of official and unofficial attempts to promote religious activities and to divide and identify students on the basis of their religious beliefs and affiliations make virtually all so-called non-government sponsored religious activities

31. 20 U.S.C. Sec. 4071 (1984).

so suspect as to cause us to oppose such activities as violations of the Establishment Clause. . . . The Equal Access Act is in flagrant violation of the Establishment Clause. The ACLU calls upon Congress immediately to repeal the Act. (From ACLU Policy #99)

Mergens v. Westside. In 1985, Bridget Mergens approached Westside High School in Omaha, Nebraska for permission to form a voluntary student religious group that would meet after hours at the high school on the same basis as other student groups. The school refused and the students sued in federal court, arguing violation of their First Amendment rights and of the Equal Access Act. In 1988 federal judge C. Arlen Beam ruled for the school.[32] He concluded that the school could reasonably consider all of the currently-allowed groups—even the chess club, the photography club, "subserfers," and several service clubs—as curriculum-related. Since the school did not permit *any* noncurriculum-related groups, the Equal Access Act was not triggered and its constitutionality did not need to be assessed. As for the First Amendment claims, Judge Beam, relying on *Hazelwood*,[33] ruled that, not having established an open forum of any sort, the school had broad discretion to exclude groups, such as the student religious group in question, that it did not construe as relevant to its curriculum. The ruling was immediately appealed to the Eighth Circuit. Several other potential tests of the Equal Access Act are also currently in litigation (Boston, 1988).

Application of the principles
Principle 4 (*Freedom of Association*) holds that government may restrict free association only in cases where it has a compelling reason to do so. Government is not, of course, required to facilitate association. Thus a public school need not make its facilities available to student groups. If it chooses to do so, however, thus establishing a forum, it may not, consistent with Principle 4, discriminate against certain groups simply because it dislikes the individuals involved or the content of their beliefs or speech. In general, then, the Equal Access Act is on the

---

32. Mergens v. Board of Education of the Westside Community Schools, District 66. U.S.D.C. NE CV 85-0-426 (1988).
33. Hazelwood School District v. Kuhlmeier, 108 S.Ct. 562 (1988)

right track. Arbitrarily allowing certain student groups and not others violates my Principles 1 and 4.

With respect to religious groups, however, the issue is genuinely complex. The existence of religious groups on school property may lead students to infer government support for religion in general and/or for the specific religions represented. To the extent that government permits such perceptions, especially in the context of public education, it is indeed aiding religion. This obviously would violate Principle 5b (*Religious Neutrality*) and the Establishment Clause.

On the other hand, given the secular nature of most school activities, further exclusion of religion may lead students (rightly or wrongly) to perceive a systematically anti-religious ideology and, if they are sufficiently impressionable, may inculcate this ideology, thus also violating Principle 5b. Further, in addition to the general violation of free expression (Principle 1) and association (Principle 4), a case might be made on the basis of the free-exercise clause that, if anything, religious speech deserves more, not less, protection than other forms of speech. Exclusion of religious groups makes it more difficult for religious students to act on the basis of their religious beliefs in choosing after-school activities, thus arguably violating Principle 2 (*Free Exercise of Religion*).

On balance, it appears that if students will unavoidably perceive government establishment of religion, then public schools must forbid religious meetings of any sort. Although this does somewhat restrict religious students, they are still free to exercise their freedoms of religion, speech, and association away from the school. The restriction is real, but it is the minimum sufficient to achieve the compelling government interest in nonestablishment of religion. If, on the other hand, students can understand the voluntary nature of student groups and the nonendorsement of the school, then the establishment-of-religion problem is minimal. In that case, it seems to me, the constitutional mandates of free expression, free association, and free exercise of religion (cf. my Principles 1, 4, and 2, respectively) mandate that schools permit religious students to meet on the same basis as any other group.

The crux of the matter appears to be an empirical question (Note,

1983). Was the Supreme Court correct in its assumption that college students are capable of distinguishing voluntary activities on school premises from school-sponsored activities? Was it correct in its suggestion that young children might be too "impressionable" to make this distinction? At what age does the ability to make the relevant distinction emerge?

Empirical considerations

In the discussion of the development of deductive reasoning in Chapter 3, it was concluded that a relatively abstract distinction between form and content, including ability to dissociate the form of an argument from the truth or falsity of its component propositions, constituted Level 3 understanding, beginning at about age 11. The distinction in question in the equal access cases seems to be at this level. Students must comprehend the idea of a forum that is created by and physically included within the school but is open to all groups and ideas regardless of content. A student who systematically confuses form with content is likely to attribute the content of student activities to the school itself, whereas one who distinguishes form from content is likely to understand that the school merely creates the forum and is not responsible for the content within it.

These considerations support the Supreme Court's conclusion that most college students will understand the voluntary nature of student groups and will not perceive an establishment of religion. The evidence reviewed in Chapter 3 suggests that high school students, and probably junior high students as well, cannot be sharply distinguished from college students. There is no reason to think that secondary students will naively assume that all groups meeting in a school are thereby endorsed by the school or that they are encouraged to join all such groups. On the contrary, it seems likely that a prominent sign associated with notices of student activities would be sufficient for adolescents to grasp the voluntary nature of the activities.

On the other hand, the evidence reviewed in Chapter 3 suggests that children under 11 or 12 are qualitatively different from college students with respect to a variety of abstract abilities and concepts. There is reason to believe that elementary school students would not spontaneously comprehend the abstract distinction between voluntary and school-endorsed activities and would fail to fully grasp it even if it were carefully explained (Moshman, 1988).

Conclusion

It appears, then, that the Equal Access Act, which is limited to secondary students, is constitutionally acceptable in that secondary students, like the college students in *Widmar*, are capable of understanding a school's nonendorsement of religion. In fact, even in the absence of the Equal Access Act, public secondary schools should be constitutionally required to permit equal access for religious groups. Concerns about a perceived establishment of religion can be handled through announcements, notices on bulletin boards, etc., rather than through the more restrictive alternative of abridging freedom of speech, freedom of association, and the free exercise of religion.

In implementing and evaluating equal access, schools and courts will, of course, need to be attentive to various specifics (Note, 1983; Strossen, 1985, 1987). Schools may not create open forums specifically to permit or benefit religious groups, may not allow domination of their forums by religious groups, must not permit adults to initiate or lead the groups, must limit the role of teachers and other school personnel to nonsubstantive matters, and must be sure their disclaimers are adequately communicated and understood. All of this, however, is consistent with the Equal Access Act, which in fact includes detailed requirements to counter a perceived establishment of religion. Schools should not be permitted to undermine equal access by gerrymandering the definition of *curriculum-related* to include all groups they have traditionally accepted and exclude all those they do not wish to permit.

An elementary school analogue of the Equal Access Act would, it should be added, be unconstitutional. Most elementary school students are incapable of fully understanding abstract concepts. There is serious danger that, regardless of explanations and other precautions, elementary school students would perceive school endorsement of religion if they observed religious groups being granted use of the school. The government is required to avoid such a perception, even if this means restricting the free expression, free association, and religious exercise of young children.

School Book Selection and Removal

Even in a fairly small school system, thousands of decisions must be made each year concerning what books to assign in classrooms and what books to make available in school libraries. Those decisions, and the numerous challenges to those decisions from inside and outside the school system, have long been a source of substantial, and often bitter, controversy (Bogdan & Yeomans, 1986; Moffett, 1988).

A survey of school librarians conducted by the American Library Association, the Association of American Publishers, and the Association for Supervision and Curriculum Development revealed that hundreds of school library books were challenged in the period 1978–1980, and that about half of the challenged books were ultimately restricted or removed (*Limiting What Students May Read*, 1981). Periodic reports from People for the American Way suggest that over the course of the 1980s the frequency of such challenges, if anything, increased. One report (People for the American Way, 1987a) indicated that for the period 1982–1987 the most frequently challenged books were *The Chocolate War* (Robert Cormier), *The Catcher in the Rye* (J. D. Salinger), *Of Mice and Men* (John Steinbeck), *The Adventures of Huckleberry Finn* (Mark Twain), *Deenie* (Judy Blume), *Go Ask Alice* (anonymous), *A Light in the Attic* (Shel Silverstein), *Forever* (Judy Blume), *Blubber* (Judy Blume), *Cujo* (Stephen King), *The Diary of Anne Frank* (Anne Frank), *Finding My Way* (health textbook), *Then Again Maybe I Won't* (Judy Blume), and *To Kill a Mockingbird* (Harper Lee). Every issue of the *Newsletter on Intellectual Freedom*, published bimonthly by the Intellectual Freedom Committee of the American Library Association, reports dozens of new cases.

Book decisions and challenges are by no means limited to the library. Selection of textbooks, whether done by an individual school, a school system, or a state commission, frequently generates equally intense controversy (Gottlieb, 1987; Sewall, 1988). Texas and California have been the focus of national attention in this regard in that textbooks are selected on a statewide basis in those states; publishers, rather than lose such large markets, often revise their books to suit Texas or California. Thus the nature of the texts available for the entire country is often substantially affected by decisions made in one or two key states.

Nevertheless, library books, textbooks, and curricula are selected by a wide variety of individuals and committees on the basis of a variety of criteria. Similarly, there is no single theme that accounts for all the critiques of and challenges to these decisions. Since the 1970s, challenges by fundamentalist Christians have received much publicity; data on challenged books indicate that conservative moral and religious views are indeed the basis for most current book challenges. Challenges from the political left, however, are not uncommon. Textbooks have been criticized by feminists for stereotyped portrayals of women, Shakespeare's *The Merchant of Venice* has been challenged by Jews as anti-Semitic in its presentation of Shylock, and Mark Twain's *Huckleberry Finn*, criticized by blacks for its frequent use of the word "nigger," is one of the most-challenged books of the 1980s.

Those who challenge public schools' books and curricula are commonly labeled censors, an obviously pejorative term. But do we really wish to suggest that challenges to selection decisions are never justified? Who should have the authority to make selection decisions in the first place: Teachers? Librarians? School administrators? The school board? Students? Parents? Concerned citizens? Some combination of these? What criteria and procedures should be used in those decisions? Who, if anyone, should have the right to challenge such decisions? What procedures and criteria should be used in dealing with such challenges? Charges of censorship may sometimes be justified, but often serve only to mask the genuine difficulty of answering these questions.

History and current status of the issue
Controversy over school books and curricula is by no means a recent phenomenon: Challenges date back to the mid-1800s and have been a regular feature of public education since shortly after World War I (Yudof, 1984, pp. 537–538). Although there was virtually no litigation on this issue prior to the 1970s, there are now decisions from a

number of federal district courts and several courts of appeals. The courts have been sharply divided, with some emphasizing the First Amendment rights of students and others deferring to the extensive authority of school boards (for reviews and analyses, see Hentoff, 1980; Jenkinson, 1986; O'Neil, 1981; Shively, 1982; Sorenson, 1983; van Geel, 1983; Yudof, 1987). In its sole foray into this legal thicket, *Board of Education v. Pico* (1982), the Supreme Court strongly reflected the lower court divisions and failed to clearly settle the issue.[34]

In 1975, several members of the board of education of Island Trees, a school district on Long Island, New York, attended a conference sponsored by a conservative parents group, where they received a list of "objectionable" books. Upon returning to Island Trees, the board members arranged for a janitor to let them into a school library at night to check for these books. The board ultimately directed the removal of eleven books, including *Slaughter House Five* (Kurt Vonnegut), *The Naked Ape* (Desmond Morris), *Down These Mean Streets* (Piri Thomas), *Go Ask Alice* (anonymous), *Black Boy* (Richard Wright), *Soul on Ice* (Eldridge Cleaver), and *The Fixer* (Bernard Malamud). They later appointed a committee to recommend what to do about the books. After receiving the committee's report, they largely disregarded it and decided that most of the books should be permanently kept out of the school library.

Several students, including Stephen Pico, sued the school for abridging their First Amendment rights in removing the books. A Federal judge issued a summary judgment in favor of the school board, arguing that the board had authority to do as it pleased with respect to determining what books would be used in the school system and that there was thus no First Amendment issue. The Court of Appeals for the Second Circuit remanded the case for trial, arguing that students should have the opportunity to show that the school board's action was motivated by an unconstitutional intent to suppress ideas. The Supreme Court affirmed, 5-4, with the nine justices writing no fewer than seven distinct opinions.

Roughly, the court split 4-4-1. Four justices held that a school

---

34. Board of Education, Island Trees Union Free School District No. 26 v. Pico, 457 U.S. 853 (1982).

board's removal of books from a public school library could certainly violate the First Amendment and that the Second Circuit was thus correct in remanding the case for a full trial to determine the school board's motivation. Four justices disagreed, and the deciding vote upholding the Second Circuit was cast on procedural grounds.

The plurality opinion by Justice Brennan, signed by Justices Marshall and Stevens, argued that a school library is an intellectual marketplace in which students have a First Amendment right of access to information and ideas. A concurring opinion by Justice Blackmun argued against the view that students in public schools have a First Amendment right to receive information but concluded that the First Amendment does preclude school boards from suppressing certain views for the sole purpose of ideological indoctrination. Justice White, who cast the fifth vote for the majority, did not address the question of First Amendment constraint on school boards but simply argued that there should be a full trial to determine the school board's motivation. Implicit in this conclusion, however, is the notion that removal of books from a school library may, depending on the basis for removal, be unconstitutional.

The dissent by Chief Justice Burger, joined by Justices Powell, Rehnquist, and O'Connor, stressed the inculcative function of public schools and the authority of duly elected school boards to make decisions about school books. A separate dissent by Justice Rehnquist, joined by Justices Burger and Powell, acknowledged that certain hypothetical school board decisions—e.g., removal by a Democratic school board of all books written by or in favor of Republicans—would be unconstitutional, but argued that such an extreme situation was unlikely to occur and was certainly not relevant to the current case. Justices Powell and O'Connor each filed a brief additional dissent stressing judicial deference to school board authority.

In sum, the Supreme Court indicated that school library book removals may violate the First Amendment but the majority rejected Justice Brennan's broad conception of students' right to receive information. *Pico* was settled without further litigation when the school board voted to return the books to the library, but the underlying issues remain unresolved.

Application of the principles

"Censorship." Although it appears that *Pico* and similar cases have something to do with censorship, that term turns out to be surprisingly difficult to apply in the present context. To see why this is so, it is useful to start with more clearcut situations.

In the paradigm case of censorship, an individual wishes to express something and is forbidden to do so by the government. The first section of this chapter, "Students' Freedom of Expression," dealt with situations of this sort. In the case of children, and within the context of public schools, of course, there may be complicating factors. In order for education of all students to proceed without undue interference, school officials may set some constraints on the time, place, and manner of student expression. There may be reason for such constraints to be more severe in the case of students in a classroom than they would be for an adult on a public street. Nevertheless, although proper use of the term *censorship* with respect to student expression may become a bit complicated, it is not seriously problematical.

In the cases we are addressing in this section, however, government itself is the communicator (cf. Haiman, 1981, Chap. 17; Yudof, 1983, 1987). The issue is not what government allows students to express but what government expresses to them via its decisions about what textbooks to assign and what books to place on the shelves of the school library. How, then, is censorship involved?

One possible answer is to suggest that government is required to be content-neutral in dealing with ideas. Content-neutrality is in fact a useful concept in considering many censorship issues. If, for example, the school library requires students to speak in a whisper in order to permit other students to read in peace, this would normally be judged a reasonable restriction of expression. If, on the other hand, it requires students to speak in a whisper when discussing communism but allows them to shout joyfully about capitalism, it is no doubt acting as a censor. The difference is that in the second case it is violating content-neutrality: The library may require whispering but, if it does, it must do so without discriminating on the basis of the content of what students wish to say.

Should we then require that government be content-neutral in making book decisions and label it a censor when it violates this ideal? Such a principle would be ludicrous. Decisions about selection and removal of school books *must* be based on the content of the books. Educators make content-based discriminations in deciding what subjects to teach, what aspects of those subjects to cover, what points of view to emphasize, and what aspects or views not to incorporate into the curriculum. Education simply cannot be content-neutral (Gottlieb, 1987). To argue that government may never discriminate on the basis of the content of ideas is, at the very least, to argue against public education.

I am not suggesting that the First Amendment sets no constraints on school book decisions. My point is that in analyzing the nature of these constraints, the term *censorship* is of limited use. Although there are cases in this domain that justify the label, it is too often used merely as a rhetorical device for criticizing those who make selections one dislikes or challenge selections one likes. As Strike (1985, p. 239) puts it:

> Whatever censorship is, it is known to be a bad thing. This being so, in any debate about censorship it is strategically important to be sure that everyone knows who the censor is. It is your opponent. . . . To succeed in tagging one's opponent with the name *censor* is to succeed in bringing the collective weight of J. S. Mill, the First Amendment, the Supreme Court, and the liberal tradition crashing down on his head. In intellectual circles, few will survive such devastation.

Censors and censorship do exist, but in the present context it is not always so easy to determine whether censorship has occurred and, if so, who is the censor. In the words of Ira Glasser (1983, p. 19), Executive Director of the American Civil Liberties Union,

> everybody knows that government's role is just to let a hundred flowers bloom. The trouble in the schools is that there is room on the shelf for only ninety-five flowers and somebody has to decide which five don't get included.

Selection. Given that the school library physically cannot hold every possible book and that only one text or a small number of books can be assigned in any course, someone has to select which books to use. Each selection implicitly involves the rejection of those books that do not get selected. Are the rejected books being censored?

In general, I think the answer is *no*. Nonselection is not necessarily censorship. Students may have a right of access to ideas and information (Principle 3), but government is not required to facilitate that access. Selecting a book for inclusion in the curriculum or library facilitates student access to the book; failure to select a particular book does not facilitate access to that book. Unless the government actively forbids students to read the book, however, nonselection does not restrict access and thus does not violate Principle 3. To suggest that government must actively facilitate access to every book that is published would be absurdly impractical.

But what about the author whose book is not selected? Is government abridging his or her freedom of expression? I think not. Authors do have a right, of course, to publish and publicize their books. Government may not interfere with this, but neither is it required to assist. Specifically, government is not required to purchase any particular book or to use it in public schools; its failure to do so is not censorship and does not violate the First Amendment. The decision to use certain books and not others is, to be sure, a content-based distinction. But such distinctions are acceptable when government is not restricting expression but choosing what it itself wishes to communicate. The choice of what books to use in public schools fits in this category.

But the fact that nonselection is not inherently censorship does not mean that selection raises no First Amendment issues. Suppose, for example, the selector only chooses books that further the views of the Democratic Party or the Christian religion. Such choices would not violate Principle 3 in that there is no active restriction of access. Under some circumstances, however, facilitating access to certain ideas and not others may violate my Principle 5 (*Limited Inculcation*). Specifically, it will violate Principle 5a if there is no educational basis for the decision. It will violate Principle 5b if there is a deviation from religious neutrality. Finally, it will violate Principle 5c if the possibility of rational analysis is unnecessarily restricted.

Consider some examples. Clearly a textbook on American history need not—in fact, *cannot*—include every point of view ever proposed on the subject. An acceptable reason for including a particular view would be that it is taken seriously by most historians and is understandable to students. Acceptable reasons for excluding a particular view would include the following: (a) the view is not taken seriously by professional historians and thus its educational value is dubious; (b) the view is highly complex and cannot be explained to students who will be using the text; or (c) two distinct views on the topic are already included and a third would only confuse students. It would violate my construal of the First Amendment, however, to include or exclude a particular view because it is liked or disliked by the Republican Party, the Presbyterian Synod, the NAACP, Citizens for Excellence in Education, Concerned Women for America, the National Organization for Women, or members of the school board. Schoolbooks should, of course, be chosen by appropriate school officials, not by judges, but selections should, in my view, be subject to judicial reversal if they violate First Amendment restrictions on inculcation (Principle 5).

A single library book is much less likely than a single textbook to violate the First Amendment. A text is required reading and is students' main introduction to the area. A library book, on the other hand, is simply one of many books available; its biases may be balanced by other available books. Nevertheless, the selection pattern for the library as a whole may violate Principle 5 if it is designed to inculcate ideas that cannot be justified on educational grounds, if it deviates systematically from religious neutrality, or if it unnecessarily limits diversity in order to channel students' minds in a particular direction.

Removal. Removals differ from selections in that the book is already chosen and the government is taking an active step to remove it. Thus there is a more active restriction of access in these cases and Principle 3 may come into play. Government must, in my view, have a compelling reason for any decision to restrict access. Principle 5 may still be involved in book removals in that the removals may leave behind a biased selection of books. Moreover, the removal process itself may improperly indoctrinate students (e.g., if they get the idea that certain views have been deemed unacceptable).

With respect to textbooks, removal may be an integral part of a legitimate selection decision, as when a text is replaced by one deemed better (e.g., more accurate, more balanced, better written, or more up to date). Such replacements are best viewed as selections rather than as removals, unless there is reason to believe they were motivated by a desire to restrict access to certain ideas in the original text.

In the library, replacement is less likely in that a library typically includes a variety of books on a given topic and the selection of a new one does not mean one of the present ones must be removed. Some removals are obviously well justified: Nonfiction books do get outdated, for example, and yesterday's bestselling novel may simply no longer be read by today's students. Given that shelf space is finite, some books, at some point, will have to go. Nevertheless, removal of library books is probably the most suspect category of book decision. There should be clear procedures and criteria for all removals (Office for Intellectual Freedom, 1983). Reasons for removals should be scrutinized to be sure they are not subterfuges for violations of Principles 3 or 5.

Bases for strict scrutiny. The suggestion that certain book phenomena merit stricter scrutiny than others is worth pursuing. It is often difficult to determine whether the primary intent of a school official in selecting or removing a book is to maximize education or to indoctrinate students in his or her views. It is also difficult to decide whether a given text or library collection is reasonably balanced or shows some sort of systematic and unjustifiable bias in violation of Principle 5. In general, courts are rightly loath to second-guess the views of school officials about what constitutes good education or their determinations about how many views, and which views, students of a given age should be exposed to. School board members are, after all, democratically elected to represent the views of their communities about education, whereas judges are not. Administrators, teachers, and librarians have special expertise about children and education that judges do not necessarily have. Judicial deference to school officials is, in general, appropriate. The burden of proof should be on the plaintiff who claims that the school is violating the First Amendment.

There are at least two circumstances, however, where deference should be suspended and strict scrutiny applied. The first is revocation of delegated responsibility (Yudof, 1984). State legislatures typically delegate much of their responsibility for education to state education departments and local school boards. School boards hire and delegate responsibility to school administrators, who in turn hire and delegate responsibility to teachers and librarians. In some of these cases the delegation of responsibility is based on a law or written regulation; obviously, courts should require that such laws and regulations be followed. In other cases the specific nature and extent of the delegation may not be clear or may be a matter of custom. Although ad hoc revocations of delegated responsibility may be legal in such cases, they should be strictly scrutinized.

Suppose, for example, that a state legislature passes a law requiring that certain books be used in teaching history. Obviously, someone must make decisions of this sort; if the state legislature typically makes such decisions there is no special problem. Suppose, however, that— as seems likely—such decisions are typically made by the state education department, a state textbook commission, and/or local school boards and that the legislature itself virtually never makes textbook decisions of this sort. Obviously there is reason for suspicion here. Is the legislature trying to indoctrinate every student in the state in a certain view of history? If not, why this special law? In this situation there should be a burden of proof on the legislature to show an acceptable education-based motivation for its action.

Similarly, school boards and administrators generally delegate to librarians the responsibility of choosing appropriate books for the library. If a school board or principal suddenly demands that certain books be added to, or removed from, the library, there is reason for suspicion. Courts should engage in strict scrutiny of motivations in any situation (e.g., *Pico*) where delegated responsibility is unexpectedly reclaimed.

The second circumstance meriting strict scrutiny is closely related. All schools should have clear, written procedures and criteria for book selection and removal. Courts should require them to establish and follow such procedures.

> A student may not have a "right to know" and a publisher may have no right to government largesse, but they should have a right to compel a government entity to honor the procedures that

have been established for determining what is taught and which books will be used (Yudof, 1984, p. 556).

In cases where the procedures are too informal or the deviations too minor for a court to recognize inherent illegality, there may nevertheless be a basis for strict scrutiny of motivation. In any case where school (or other government) officials show an unusual intrusion into or deviation from normal selection or removal processes, the burden of proof should be on the official to show a permissible motivation for the action.

Empirical considerations

Evidence reviewed in Chapter 3 confirms common intuitions that young children are inclined to believe that adults have access to the absolute truths of the world and expect educators to provide them with those truths. They are less capable than adults of critically analyzing ideas and coordinating diverse points of view. There is thus some support for the view that textbooks for young children should often limit themselves to descriptive, factual accounts and avoid analyzing the weaknesses of those accounts and presenting alternative views.

It is important not to overstate this, however. Evidence from Chapter 3 also shows that children as young as six years have some ability to reflect on their own thinking, to consider the sources of ideas, to recognize legitimate differences of opinion, and to consider the evidence for and against a point of view. Moreover, most adolescents do not appear fundamentally different from many adults in this respect.

Even adults, of course, may be confused if they are confronted with too many viewpoints simultaneously or are asked to engage in detailed critical analysis of ideas they are first learning. Thus there are always legitimate educational grounds for limiting what is presented in introductory texts. Such limitations may reasonably be somewhat more stringent for secondary texts than for college texts, and substantially more stringent for elementary texts.

The ability to critically analyze ideas and coordinate diverse views does not magically appear, however. On the contrary, evidence reviewed in Chapter 3 (see "The Construction of Rationality") indicates that development of advanced intellectual abilities can be facilitated by providing diverse ideas and encouraging critical analysis. From an educational point of view, then, extreme restriction in what is presented may not only be unnecessary but may be contraindicated.

Obviously, school authorities must be given substantial leeway in choosing texts to make professional judgments on the basis of the subject matter in question and the intellectual abilities of children at the age in question. Even highly restricted coverage may be well justified, especially at young ages. Nevertheless, charges that coverage is restricted in order to indoctrinate students in particular views deserve serious consideration. Even elementary school students are not so intellectually limited as to justify narrowly partisan textbooks that systematically fail to raise significant issues or note important differences of opinion.

It is also worth noting that students can easily handle more diversity in a library than in a text. A text must be read and understood in its entirety, whereas students are free not to read library books that conflict with their views or otherwise confuse them. Thus, limited intellectual abilities provide little basis for restricting diversity in school libraries.

Conclusions

No justice in *Pico* disputed the idea that public schools may inculcate ideas and values. My own analysis similarly takes the legitimacy of inculcation as a given. Moreover, Justice Rehnquist's dissent (signed by Justices Powell and Burger) "cheerfully" acknowledged some constitutional limitations on inculcation. Thus there is general agreement that public schools have the authority to inculcate and that the Constitution sets some limits on inculcation.

Various analyses diverge with respect to the nature and extent of those constitutional limits. Justice Brennan's plurality opinion in *Pico* is, in my view, both too broad and too narrow. Its recognition of a general right of access to information is, it seems to me, too broad. Recognition of such a right could be used to require a school to purchase any book that any student wishes to have in the library and to give students unlimited power to choose their own textbooks. Recognizing this problem, the plurality was careful to note that the right of access only applied in school libraries, not in classrooms, and that it only applied to removals, not to selections. But this unduly limits the issue. The First Amendment is at stake in the classroom as well as the library and in selections as well as removals (Garvey, 1979; Gottlieb, 1987). What is needed is a coherent set of principles that can be applied to all of these cases.

My own analysis is closer to Justice Blackmun's concurring opinion. Public schools may facilitate access to books presenting anything that the government, on educational grounds, chooses to communicate (Principle 5a). The First Amendment is violated if and only if the intent or primary effect of the government's book decision is (a) to suppress certain books or ideas (Principle 3), (b) to deviate from religious neutrality (Principle 5b), or (c) to indoctrinate (Principle 5c).

For purposes of this analysis, "educational grounds" must be defined broadly, since it is, after all, part of the school board's responsibility to decide what counts as an education. Nevertheless, there are some real limits here: There is no educational basis for inculcating the views of a particular political party or a view of, say, history or biology that professionals in those fields agree is unjustified by current evidence.

"Indoctrination" should be defined fairly narrowly: It does not include all inculcation but only inculcation designed to permanently channel the mind in a certain direction by shielding the student from discrepant views and discouraging critical analysis. The distinction between legitimate inculcation and unacceptable indoctrination must be made on the basis of empirical evidence about how many views and how much evidence students of a given age are capable of comprehending. Limitations that may be educationally necessary in teaching nine-year-olds may be indoctrinative in teaching adolescents.

These principles, it should be emphasized, apply to decisions about curriculum and textbooks as well as library books and to both selections and removals. In addition, they recognize First Amendment issues not only when officials act from unconstitutional motives but when, regardless of motive, the resulting education is inappropriately restrictive or indoctrinative.

The following guidelines are consistent with this analysis:

1. Authority to select, replace, and remove schoolbooks should be delegated to relevant professionals.
2. There should be written procedures and criteria for all selection decisions, including ample opportunity for parental and community input.
3. There should be written procedures and criteria for responding to challenges to texts and library books, including opportunity for input from all interested parties.
4. Exclusions of books on the grounds that students are not mature enough for them and/or would be harmed by their content should be based on appropriate empirical evidence.

In implementing these guidelines, it is critical not only that the school system has fair procedures that provide an opportunity for adequate input from parents and the community but that the fairness and openness of the procedures are widely perceived by concerned individuals. This may mean that the school system should go out of its way to communicate to parents how its selection and removal processes operate and why it has made, upheld, or reversed particular controversial decisions.

It is also important to note that my principles and current judicial precedents provide school officials with a great deal of leeway. Only serious, systematic biases patently unrelated to legitimate educational purposes are likely to be successfully challenged in court. Such leeway should not be abused, however. Public schools should not merely attempt to avoid legal challenges but should be committed to the broad conception of intellectual freedom underlying the First Amendment. They should recognize a broad moral right of access to ideas and information (Principle 9) and should actively encourage diversity of perspective and critical analysis of all views (Principle 11). To the extent that selection and removal decisions are made on the basis of a genuine commitment to intellectual freedom and intellectual development, public schools have nothing to fear from the First Amendment.

Religion in Public Schools

The religion clauses of the First Amendment mandate that there be "no law respecting an establishment of religion" (establishment clause) "or prohibiting the free exercise thereof" (free exercise clause). Although the First Amendment initially limited only the federal government, the Supreme Court, since 1940, has consistently ruled that the Fourteenth Amendment extends the religion clauses of the First Amendment to cover actions by state and local governments.[35]

Many of the most intense controversies over religious liberty have involved the complex interrelations of church, state, and education. In fact, education is to a large extent the crucible in which current establishment clause doctrine has been forged. Controversies that have come before the courts may be divided into two major categories: (1) government aid to private (including religious) schools, and (2) religion in public schools.

Cases in the first category raise the general issue of whether public funds may be used to aid religion, and, if not, under what circumstances religion (as opposed to students or parents in general) is being unconstitutionally assisted. Although this is obviously an important and difficult issue, the religious liberty of students is only incidently involved and has not been a major consideration in resolving the various cases. Thus, this category of cases will not be further discussed.

The religious liberty of students is, however, directly involved in any case involving religious education or religious practices in school, and their First Amendment rights are implicated when the school in question is run by the government. May public schools inculcate religion? What practices constitute inculcation? May public schools require students to pray? May they encourage prayer? May they permit it at all? Must they? May they teach about religion? If they do, what sort of teaching is permissible? If they don't teach about religion, does this constitute anti-religious inculcation?

History and current status of the issue
Most schools in colonial America were established and run by particular religious denominations and were intended to inculcate religion.

35. Cantwell v. Connecticut, 310 U.S. 296 (1940).

As public schools began to be instituted during the late 1700s and as the modern public school system evolved during the 1800s, education remained largely religious in nature. Initially, this posed no constitutional problem in that public schools were state entities and the First Amendment applied only to the federal government. Despite this, many states added their own constitutional bans on establishment of religion and public schools became less pervasively religious and less narrowly sectarian. Nevertheless, religious influence, in a general Protestant sense, remained strong as late as the mid-1900s (McCarthy, 1983; Smith, 1987; Swomley, 1987; Tyack & James, 1985).

In the half-century since the Supreme Court declared the religion clauses of the First Amendment applicable to the states, there has been substantial litigation concerning religion in public schools, most of it involving the question of what practices constitute an unconstitutional establishment of religion. The legal history in this area can be summarized by presenting, in chronological order, seven major Supreme Court cases.[36]

In *McCollum v. Board of Education* (1948), the Court prohibited a common practice whereby public schools permitted release time for children to receive religious instruction on school premises. Although instruction was not mandatory, the Court ruled that the government was violating the establishment clause in using its facilities and its compulsory education laws to promote religious education. A few years later, however, the Court permitted a similar program of release time during school hours that differed only in that the religious education took place off school premises (*Zorach v. Clauson*, 1952). Six justices considered this an acceptable accommodation to, rather than unconstitutional promotion of, religious education.

In 1962, the Supreme Court ruled that school-sponsored prayers were an unconstitutional establishment of religion even if students had the option of not participating in them (*Engel v. Vitale*). The follow-

36. Karcher v. May, 108 S.Ct. 388 (1987); Wallace v. Jaffree, 472 U.S. 38 (1985); Stone v. Graham, 449 U.S. 39 (1980); School District of Abington v. Schempp, 374 U.S. 203 (1963); Engel v. Vitale, 370 U.S. 421 (1962); Zorach v. Clauson, 343 U.S. 306 (1952); McCollum v. Board of Education, 333 U.S. 203 (1948)

ing year it found devotional Bible-reading was equally objectionable (*Abington v. Schempp*). The Court was explicit in these cases, however, that it was not religion itself but government-sponsored inculcation that constituted the problem: Truly voluntary, individual prayers were not banned, nor was teaching *about* religion or having students read the Bible as literature. Applying the same reasoning in *Stone v. Graham* (1980), the Court ruled that, although consideration of the Ten Commandments was not inherently inappropriate in a public school, a law requiring its posting in every classroom had the intent and primary effect of promoting the Judeo-Christian religious tradition and was thus unconstitutional.

The school prayer decisions were highly controversial. As federal judge Warren Urbom put it in a 1987 speech to the Nebraska Conference of the American Association of University Professors, in the wake of the Supreme Court's 1962 and 1963 decisions, "whatever it is that hits the fan, hit the fan." Over the next two decades, there were strong but unsuccessful efforts in Congress to overturn the decisions via a constitutional amendment or by denying federal courts the authority to hear school prayer cases. There was also, as discussed earlier, a successful effort to pass a law permitting secondary students to meet on public school premises for religious purposes. At the state level, numerous legislatures passed laws requiring that public school teachers institute a daily moment of silence for silent prayer or meditation.

One such law, passed in Alabama, eventually reached the Supreme Court (*Wallace v. Jaffree*, 1985). The Court's reasoning relied heavily on a legislative history showing that the purpose of the law was to reinstitute as much school prayer as the Supreme Court would permit. Given the clearly religious motivation of the legislature in passing the law, the Court, by a 6-3 margin, ruled it unconstitutional. Two justices voting with the majority indicated, however, that an appropriately drafted moment-of-silence law with a legitimate secular purpose might pass constitutional muster. In 1987, the Court heard *Karcher v. May*, involving a moment-of-silence law in New Jersey, but for procedural reasons declined to rule on the merits. The constitutional status of mandatory moments of silence thus remains an open question.

Application of the principles

Neutrality vs. separation. The constitutional ideal with respect to religious liberty, I have argued earlier, is not separation of church and state but government neutrality with respect to religion (Beschle, 1987; Laycock, 1986; see also McConnell, 1986, 1987). Although the idea of a wall of separation between church and state helps us keep in mind the historical context and intent of the First Amendment, it is of limited use with respect to education controversies. Literal adherence to this concept would mean excluding all mention of religion and all religious practice from the public schools. This would greatly distort education in domains where religion has played a major role (e.g., American history and culture), would infringe on the voluntary religious activities of genuinely religious students who are required by compulsory education laws to spend much of their time in school, and might even inculcate an anti-religious ideology. If, however, we relax the wall of separation to alleviate these problems, we run into the problem of how much and in what ways we may relax it without rendering the establishment clause meaningless.

The solution, as I argued in Chapter 2, is to rely not on separation of church and state but on the concept of government neutrality with respect to religion. Principle 5 (*Limited Inculcation*) addresses the general problem that government inculcation poses for intellectual freedom by setting limits on such inculcation. With respect to most areas, the limits are not very strict, requiring only that inculcation have a legitimate educational purpose (Principle 5a) and that it fall short of indoctrination (Principle 5c). With respect to religion, however, the principle is far more exacting: It requires stringent neutrality on the part of the public school (Principle 5b). Government may neither promote nor hinder any particular religion or religion in general. This restriction applies to both the intent of its actions and their primary effect.

Application of this principle to actual cases requires that one make two critical distinctions. First, one must distinguish government sponsorship of religion from personal expression of religion. From a separationist point of view, this distinction is less critical: A public school is part of the state and thus religion, regardless of where it comes from, must be excluded. From a neutrality viewpoint, on the other hand, only government sponsorship is directly unconstitutional. If we are aiming for neutrality, personal expression of religion should not be discouraged any more than it is encouraged, except to the extent that there is a compelling reason to limit it.

Second, one must distinguish inculcation of religion (which violates neutrality) from teaching *about* religion (which, to the extent that it derives from normal educational considerations, does not). Again, from a separationist viewpoint, this distinction might not be made— the constitutional aim is simply to minimize any contact with religion in the public school.

Applications of neutrality. Any endorsement of religion by a public school or its representatives clearly fails the neutrality (as well as the separation) test. Public school teachers may not lead students in prayer, encourage them to pray, set aside time for prayer, institute devotional reading of Bible passages, or post religious symbols that appear to promote a particular religion or religion in general. Allowing students to opt out of religious activities does not solve the problem: Promotion may fall far short of compulsion and still constitute an unconstitutional deviation from government neutrality.

What about a student who says a quiet, personal prayer at her desk prior to a math exam? A strict and literal separationist approach might suggest that, since she is in a public school, she must not engage in any religious activity. The neutrality approach, on the contrary, would note that simply permitting a genuinely voluntary prayer does not promote religion; on the contrary, allowing her to do as she pleases constitutes the ideal of neutrality. The presumption is, in fact, in the student's favor: Any attempt to prevent or discourage her prayer is a deviation from neutrality. Such hindrance of religion must have a compelling purpose (Principle 2).

What if the student's prayer is loud enough to disturb other children? In this case, the compelling purpose of protecting other children's rights to an environment conducive to education may permit requiring that the prayer be quiet. What if several students regularly gather to pray together before or after class? There is danger here that other students may (mistakenly) perceive school endorsement or feel peer pressure to join in. The school may have a compelling reason to institute certain limits on group prayer in order to protect the right of other students—who are compelled by compulsory attendance laws to be present—to a religiously noninculcative environment (cf. the earlier discussion of equal access for religious groups in public schools). Limitations on voluntary religious expression are thus not necessarily in violation of the neutrality principle. What is critical is that there is strong reason for any action to limit religious expression; a simple intention to exclude religion from the school is not acceptable.

What about inclusion of religion in the curriculum? The school may not incorporate discussions of religion for the purpose of inculcating a positive attitude toward certain religions or toward religion in general. It may, however, teach *about* religion when there are legitimate educational reasons to do so. In teaching about American history, for example, it is certainly acceptable, perhaps even mandatory, to note the role of religion. Obviously, there is room for historians to differ on just how important religion has been in American history and what have been its positive and negative effects. As long as the treatment is professionally defensible and properly motivated, however, it does not raise any First Amendment problem.

May the school institute release time for inculcative religious instruction? Commitment to neutrality suggests not. Whether the instruction takes place on or off school premises, such a program uses the compulsory education apparatus for the purpose of advancing religion and should thus be unconstitutional.

Finally, what about moments of silence? On the face of it, a requirement that students be quiet for a minute has nothing to do with religion and may satisfy the requirement of neutrality. There is no constitutional problem if an individual teacher decides to get control of an unruly class by demanding a minute of silence. A general requirement that all teachers enforce a daily moment of silence, however, serves no such disciplinary purpose. In fact, it is disingenuous to suggest that state-mandated moments of silence serve any secular purpose at all. Their legislative histories invariably make it all too clear that their purpose is to encourage prayer (Conn, 1987; Melton, 1986). Since prayer has never been forbidden, such moments of silence are not merely accommodations to permit free exercise (Principle 2) but systematic efforts to promote religion, thus violating government neutrality (Principle 5b).

Empirical considerations

The Supreme Court has been stricter and more consistent in applying the establishment clause in public school contexts than in contexts primarily involving adults, apparently on the basis of assumptions about the impressionability of children. Psychological evidence reviewed in Chapter 3 generally supports this extra caution, especially with respect to young children. With respect to voluntary prayer, for example, even an adult might feel some compulsion to participate if nonparticipation requires a conspicuous deviation from what others are doing and from what authorities have indicated is the thing to do. Children's reliance on authorities (especially at early ages) and on peers (especially in early adolescence) suggests that the problem is even more serious when children are involved.

In the case of a moment of silence, of course, no one need know whether one is using it to pray, to engage in secular meditation, to plan one's day, or simply to daydream. Nevertheless, there is good reason to question the effects of moments of silence.

Melton (1986) discusses a challenge to a West Virginia moment-of-silence law that, unlike most such laws, had in fact been implemented.[37] He notes testimony from two children. Brent, a Catholic sixth grader, testified that he thought he should not sit during the moment of silence lest the teacher construe his behavior as disrespectful and give him demerits. Sally, an 11-year-old Jewish girl, had read a book during a moment of silence and was told by a classmate that she would go to hell with the other Jews. Although she was hurt, angry, and uncomfortable, she decided not to go to the teacher about this for fear of "bad publicity."

Melton himself testified in the case as an expert witness. Citing relevant psychological research (e.g., Elkind, 1970; Fowler, 1981; Goldman, 1964; Grisso, 1981; Melton, 1980), he noted a number of serious problems. First, elementary school children, especially in the first few years, are likely to have very concrete conceptions of prayer and may not understand, even if it is carefully explained, that they may, instead of praying, engage in "contemplation." Second, younger students might not understand their right not to participate at all or might

37. Walter v. West Virginia Board of Education, 610 F. Supp. 1169 (S.D. W. Va. 1985)

fear that they would be punished for exercising that right. Third, young children might feel pressure to conform to the expectations of adult authority (the teacher), and somewhat older children might feel pressure to go along with their peers. Finally, he argued, it was highly likely that nonconforming children would be subjected to substantial intolerance and that the resulting stigma could have long-term negative effects on their development.

Conclusion

The Supreme Court has often stressed separation of church and state in its establishment clause decisions. Nevertheless, it has recognized that strict separation is impossible and has frequently invoked considerations of neutrality in the public school religion cases. Most of the Supreme Court precedents are thus consistent with the conclusions that follow from Principles 2 and 5b. The Court has rightly banned religious manifestations that are obviously state-sponsored. Unfortunately, the sensitivity of religion in public schools has apparently led many schools and publishers, contrary to Supreme Court dicta, to eliminate all mention of religion. This has resulted in concern, especially among fundamentalist Christians, that public schools are not only failing to inculcate proper values but are in fact systematically inculcating an anti-religious ideology—secular humanism.

Secular Humanism

Court rulings in a variety of First Amendment establishment-of-religion cases have decreased the salience and impact of religion in public schools. Has the trend toward separation of church and school reached the point where religion is being unfairly singled out for exclusion from public education? Has this resulted in government inculcation of a systematically secularist or anti-religious ideology?

Many Americans, especially fundamentalist Christians, have argued that American public education in the late 20th century systematically inculcates "secular humanism"—an atheistic ideology that proposes that human welfare is the only basis for morality and that humanity can and must solve its problems via human reasoning. Is there really such a thing as secular humanism? If so, is it a religion? Is it being taught in the public schools? If so, does this establish a religion? Does it abridge the free exercise of religion?

History and current status of the issue

Fundamentalist Christians have argued that secular humanists, the intellectual progeny of John Dewey, have taken control of American public schools and are using public education to systematically spread their views. Most of the social problems of the 1970s and 1980s have, in fact, been attributed to this. In *The Battle for the Public Schools: Humanism's Threat to our Children*, for example, Tim LaHaye (1983) provides a diagram concerning "humanistic education" (p. 247). It consists of a circle with "humanism" at its core and shows, in concentric circles, the associated "philosophy" and "resultant lifestyles." The philosophy includes evolution, astrology, collectivism, socialism, Marxism, communism, Nazism, fascism, one worldism, liberalism, permissivism, meism, feminism, self-actualization, existentialism, and situation ethics. The resultant lifestyles include malnutrition, famine, ecology control, abortion, euthanasia, mind control, Keynesian economics, matriarchal society, witchcraft, prostitution, unemployment, inflation, extremism, terrorism, genocide, suicide, depression, incest, rape, drug abuse, homosexuality, pornography, communal living, easy divorce, and so forth.

Until recently, courts have not been sympathetic to claims that public schools inculcate secular humanism (Freed, 1986; Strossen, 1986). In one case, for example, it was alleged that *The Learning Tree*, a novel by Gordon Parks used in a high school literature class, should be prohibited because it promoted secular humanism. A federal court rejected this claim and its summary judgment was upheld unanimously by a three-judge panel of the Ninth Circuit Court of Appeals.[38] Without denying that certain sections of the novel might be offensive to some Christians, the Ninth Circuit concluded that, in the context of the class, the assignment of the novel did not constitute an establishment of either religion or anti-religion. It also concluded that, since

38. Grove v. Mead School District No. 354, 753 F.2d 1528 (9th Cir. 1985)

the student was permitted to read an alternate book and was not required to participate in class discussions of *The Learning Tree*, there was minimal burden on the free exercise of religion.

In two recent cases, however, charges of secular humanism were— at least initially—more favorably received by federal courts. In *Mozert v. Hawkins* (1986),[39] several Tennessee parents complained that a public school reading series fostered secular humanism and thus infringed on their own Christian religion. When the schools refused to permit any alternative, they sued in federal district court. In 1986, Judge Thomas Hull ruled that there was indeed an infringement on sincerely held religious beliefs and that the parents should be permitted to remove their children from the portion of the curriculum they found offensive. However, he rejected the parents' demand that the school provide an alternative curriculum acceptable to them, ruling that such accommodation would overly entangle government with religion. Instead, he ruled that the parents must take responsibility for their children learning to read and that the school could assess the children's progress. In addition, he specified that his ruling applied only to the claim involved in this particular case and should not be broadly construed.

This ruling was followed several months later by a more sweeping decision in Alabama. In *Smith v. Mobile* (1987),[40] a federal district court ruled that secular humanism is a religion and that several dozen textbooks commonly used in the Alabama public schools were fostering that religion by systematically omitting religious material and urging students to form their own values and reach their own conclusions. Judge W. Brevard Hand ordered that those books be removed from the curriculum of all Alabama public schools, except for use in courses, such as comparative religion, where the purpose is to teach *about* various religions including secular humanism.

The Tennessee and Alabama cases both received intense national publicity. Many fundamentalists regarded them as the first major victories in a long and difficult battle against the anti-religious forces that

39. Mozert v. Hawkins County Public Schools, 647 F. Supp. 1194 (E.D. Tenn. 1986)
40. Smith v. Board of School Commissioners of Mobile County, 655 F. Supp. 939 (S.D. Ala. 1987)

have controlled public schools for several decades. Many educators, on the other hand, regarded both decisions as serious threats to the future of public education and were much relieved when, in August 1987, both decisions were overturned on appeal.[41]

Application of the principles

Secular humanism. Many critics of the anti-humanist movement have argued that there is no such thing as secular humanism; they maintain that the term is simply a catch-all label for whatever fundamentalist Christians object to. Terms such as "secular," "humanism," and "secular humanism" are indeed used by a variety of people in a variety of contexts to mean a wide range of different things. Nevertheless, there do seem to be some core meanings to these terms. Yes, Virginia—and Alabama and Tennessee—there *is* such a thing as secular humanism.

It will be useful for our purposes to distinguish "humanism" (in a broad sense of the word) from "secular humanism" (which I will use in a narrower sense). Humanism may be defined as the point of view that human beings should be concerned about human welfare and should promote it through the use of human reasoning. Humanism in this broad sense is a philosophical view that can be traced back at least to the ancient Greeks and has been highly influential since the Renaissance (Abbagnano, 1967). Indeed, the United States Constitution is arguably a humanist document in that it views itself as the product of "We the People," is intended to serve humanist goals such as to "establish Justice, insure domestic Tranquility, provide for the common defence, promote the general Welfare, and secure the Blessings of Liberty," and attempts to serve these goals by constituting institutions, such as Congress and the courts, where human beings will consider evidence, debate possibilities, and make decisions. If public schools may inculcate basic American values (Principle 5a), they may surely inculcate humanism in this broad sense.

Why should one be a humanist? A religious argument might run as follows: Human beings were created in the image of God and com-

41. Mozert v. Hawkins County Board of Education, 827 F.2d 1058 (6th Cir. 1987), *cert. denied*, 56 U.S.L.W. 3569 (1988)); Smith v. Board of School Commissioners of Mobile County, 827 F.2d 684 (11th Cir. 1987) (not appealed)

manded to love one another. In pursuing humanitarian goals, we should use the reasoning with which God endowed us. Such views are commonly labeled *religious* humanism. An anti-religious argument might go this way: God either does not exist or does not care about us. We are on our own. In the absence of commandments from a higher authority we must forge our own morality out of our commitment to human beings. In pursuing our humanitarian goals we must use the best tool available to us: our reasoning. This is the essence of *secular* humanism (Kurtz, 1980, 1983).

To avoid some common confusions, it is critical, at this point, that we clearly distinguish two meanings of the term *secular*: (1) religiously neutral and (2) anti-religious. The Constitution is secular in the first sense. It neither affirms nor denies a religious basis for its humanism. Some might support its humanistic perspective for religious reasons and others for reasons that have nothing to do with religion. On this question of the ultimate basis for its humanism, the Constitution is conspicuously silent.

Secular humanism, on the other hand, is secular in the second sense. It is a systematically anti-religious ideology. Secular humanists believe that appeals to God, the supernatural, or the spiritual do not provide an adequate basis for the good life. They attempt to convince people that, for reasons that have nothing to do with God, morality should be based on a commitment to humanity and human goals should be pursued through the use of human reason (Freed, 1986; Kurtz, 1980, 1983).

Is secular humanism a religion? On first glance it appears that secular humanism is obviously not a religion: "Secular" means nonreligious or even, in the case of secular humanism, anti-religious. The Supreme Court has, nevertheless, suggested in dictum that secular humanism, like Buddhism, may be classified among "religions in this country which do not teach what would generally be considered a belief in God. . . ."[42]

One is tempted to reply that if belief in God and nonbelief in God are both religion, then everything is religion. Religion, then, ceases to

42. Torcaso v. Watkins, 367 U.S. 488, 495 n. 11 (1961)

be a meaningful concept and the religion clauses of the First Amendment either have no application at all or apply so broadly as to forbid
any conceivable government action.

But this is too quick. Ideologies that do not involve a belief in God
may nonetheless serve the same role in the life of the nontheist that a
conventional theistic religion (such as Christianity, Judaism, or Islam)
serves in the life of the theist. If the First Amendment is to prevent
government intrusion into people's religious lives, it must require government neutrality not only among religions (narrowly defined) but
between religion and anything that serves as an alternative to religion.
In other words, government should maintain a stance of neutrality
not only with respect to traditional theistic religions but with respect
to functionally equivalent sets of beliefs.[43] For purposes of the First
Amendment, then, it is appropriate to define a religion not simply as a
belief in God but as any self-reflective system of beliefs that addresses
ultimate concerns such as the meaning of life, the existence of God,
the purpose of humanity, or the proper way to live (cf. Freed, 1986;
Mason, 1988). Such a definition does not include every idea or system
of ideas. It does, however, include secular humanism.

If, as I have argued, the Constitution requires government neutrality with respect to religion (Principle 5b), it follows that public
schools may not endorse or favor secular humanism. In fact, at least
with respect to the public school controversies of present concern, it
seems to me to make no difference whether we define secular humanism as a religion or not.[44] Since secular humanism is clearly a point of
view with respect to traditional religious issues (such as the existence
of God), government may neither inculcate nor disparage this point
of view. Whether or not we label secular humanism a religion, public
schools may neither support nor oppose it.

Do public schools inculcate secular humanism? The crux of the issue,
then, is not whether secular humanism is a religion but whether it
is being inculcated in the public schools. Principle 5b suggests there

---

43. United States v. Seeger, 380 U.S. 163 (1965)
44. cf. Smith v. Board of School Commissioners of Mobile County, 827 F.2d 684 (11th
Cir. 1987)

is an unconstitutional deviation from religious neutrality if anything public schools do either is intended to promote secular humanism or has the primary effect of doing so.

The claim that public school officials are *purposely* inculcating secular humanism—that is, the systematically anti-religious ideology discussed above—is clearly unfounded. It is estimated that the several secular humanist organizations in the United States have a combined membership of no more than 10,000 (Kurtz, 1983). Prior to the publicity of the Tennessee and Alabama cases since 1986, it is unlikely that more than a handful of teachers had even heard of secular humanism; even today, there are probably very few who have ever knowingly talked to a secular humanist or have more than the vaguest idea of what secular humanists believe (Jenkinson, 1986). The vast majority of public school teachers are Christians, not secular humanists. The suggestion that there is an ongoing conspiracy to inculcate American children with the atheistic doctrine of secular humanism (e.g., LaHaye, 1983) is either a cynical attempt to manipulate concerned Christian parents or a paranoid delusion.

Anti-humanists have criticized textbooks, curricula, and class exercises that encourage students to think for themselves, arguing that this may promote secular humanism by lessening their reliance on God, the Bible, and appropriate authorities. It is true that having students engage in reasoning may inculcate the idea that reasoning about problems is a good way to solve them. But such inculcation is constitutionally acceptable: Its purpose and primary effect is to develop students' reasoning abilities, a clearly permissible educational goal (Principle 5a). Reliance on reasoning may be consistent with secular humanism and perhaps certain other religions; encouragement of reasoning may thus provide some benefit to those religions. This is, however, an unintended and incidental result. The First Amendment would only be violated if there were a purposeful or direct promotion of secular humanism—if students were expressly told, for example, that they must develop their reasoning because one cannot rely on God.

Anti-humanists have also criticized texts and curricula for systematic exclusion of religion. Of course, even complete exclusion of religion is not the same as teaching students the specific doctrines of secular humanism, much less inculcating that belief system. Never-theless, exclusion of religion may constitute an unconstitutional de-viation from government neutrality, depending on why, how, and to what extent religion has been excluded. This is thus a serious charge that raises important empirical questions about current textbooks.

Empirical considerations
The legal analysis raises several empirical questions that I will take up in this order: (1) Do contemporary textbooks encourage students to think for themselves and form their own ideas? (2) If so, is there reason to believe that this serves the asserted purpose of developing reasoning abilities? (3) Do contemporary textbooks justify their em-phasis on reasoning by presenting a secular humanist rationale for the need to reason? (4) Do contemporary textbooks systematically exclude religion? (5) If so, why do they do this and what is the primary effect of the exclusion?

Encouragement of reasoning in textbooks. Contemporary textbooks in many fields often inform students that people hold a variety of dif-ferent views on many controversial issues and urge them to consider the possibilities for themselves and make their own judgments. Psy-chologists and educators, especially those associated with the "critical thinking" movement (Baron & Sternberg, 1987; Siegel, 1988), often stress independent analysis by students as a way of promoting de-velopment of their reasoning abilities. Development of reasoning is clearly a constitutionally acceptable goal of education; evidence re-viewed in Chapter 3 under the heading "The Construction of Ratio-nality" indicates that encouraging reasoning is a reasonable means for achieving this goal. There is no evidence that current texts or reason-ing curricula posit the nonexistence of God as a reason for thinking for oneself or in any other way inculcate a secular humanist point of view. With respect to the first three empirical questions then, it appears that, although public schools do, to some extent, promote reasoning, they have legitimate educational reasons for doing this; any promotion of secular humanism or denigration of religious faith is unintended and incidental.

Exclusion of religion. Do current textbooks and curricula system-atically exclude religion? Content analyses sponsored by a variety of liberal, conservative, governmental, and professional sources—including the U.S. Department of Education, Americans United for Separation of Church and State, People for the American Way, the Association for Supervision and Curriculum Development, and the American Federation of Teachers—have generated what appears to be a consensus on this issue: They do (e.g., Davis, Ponder, Burlbaw, Garza-Lubeck, & Moss, 1986; Sherman, 1988; Vitz, 1986).

Clearly it would be unconstitutional to write and choose texts and curricula in such a way as to understate the role of religion in the United States if one's purpose were to get public school students to underestimate the role of religion in American history and culture so they would be more disposed toward a secular humanist view. A broader analysis of textbooks in a variety of disciplines, however, suggests that this is not what is going on. Instead, it appears that in choosing texts schools have a strong tendency to avoid controversy and that publishers, well aware of this and interested in selling their books in as many states as possible, avoid dealing not only with religion but with anything seriously controversial (Gottlieb, 1987; People for the American Way, 1987c; Sewall, 1988). As a matter of educational policy, avoiding controversy may not be wise; as a purpose, however, it is at least religiously neutral. There is no reason to suspect a systematic intent to bias students against religion or in favor of secular humanism.

Nevertheless, we need to consider the educational effects of excluding religion (Mason, 1988). How, for example, do students construe history books that fail to note the role of religion in the lives of the Pilgrims or in the work of Martin Luther King, Jr.? Although there is no clear evidence on this, it is reasonable to suppose that the resulting understanding of American history is systematically distorted with respect to the role of religion. Bad education in itself, of course, is not unconstitutional. But if we think of any accurate account of the role of religion in American history as religiously neutral, systematic underemphasis (or overemphasis) of that role may be considered a deviation from religious neutrality. Even if the deviation does not have an anti-religious purpose, it may nevertheless have a systematically anti-religious effect. There is no need to quibble about whether this effect is meaningfully characterized as the promotion of secular humanism. Whether it is or not, it constitutes a systematic deviation from religious neutrality (Principle 5b).

Conclusions

In sum, it seems clear that public schools may inculcate humanism in the broad sense—that is, they may promote a commitment to human welfare and may encourage students to think for themselves and form their own opinions. Whether they should do this is an important question of educational policy but is not, in itself, a constitutional issue.

I have argued, however, that public schools may not inculcate *secular* humanism—that is, a humanist ideology explicitly rooted in an atheistic worldview. For the most part, evidence indicates that public schools do not, in fact, inculcate secular humanism. Concerns about the systematic exclusion of religion from textbooks and curricula, however, do seem to me to raise a legitimate constitutional issue.

With respect to the Alabama decision, then, I have no problem with Judge Hand's conclusion that secular humanism is, for First Amendment purposes, a religion. This is less crucial than he and many of his critics realize, however, in that inculcation of secular humanism would be a clear violation of religious neutrality whether or not we define secular humanism as a religion in itself. Evidence does not support the view that the textbooks at stake in the suit were intended to inculcate the doctrine of secular humanism or that such inculcation was their primary effect. Judge Hand's paranoid analysis and his sweeping decision to ban use of the books was widely criticized as judicial censorship and it is no surprise that his ruling was quickly reversed upon appeal.

Nevertheless, there is a genuine and important constitutional issue involved in the case. The systematic exclusion of religion from public school textbooks may not be intended to inculcate secular humanism but it nevertheless constitutes a significant deviation from government neutrality toward religion. Needless to say, experts differ about the role of religion in American history and culture. Those who choose texts must be accorded substantial leeway in deciding what content is educationally most appropriate. Nevertheless, they violate the neutrality principle (5b) when they systematically exclude religion. Banning a set of texts may be a crude and inappropriate remedy, especially without analysis of what other texts are available, but it is not unreasonable for courts to require public schools to work toward correcting this problem.

The Tennessee district court decision was lumped with the Alabama district court decision as a victory for fundamentalists and sharply criticized by many liberals and supporters of public schools. The circumstances of the case, however, were radically different (Sherman, 1988). Although the fundamentalist parents did claim that the texts used by the school took a secular humanist perspective, they did not claim this violated the establishment clause and did not ask that the books be removed. They simply claimed that requiring their children to read those books violated the free exercise of their religion and that they should be permitted an alternative. In other words, they did not ask for the curriculum to be changed to suit their views but simply claimed the right to opt out of a curriculum they found religiously objectionable.

Most Americans have no problem with most books challenged by fundamentalists; indeed, fundamentalist objections are widely perceived as absurd. Constitutionally, however, this is irrelevant. The claims of the Tennessee fundamentalists were made in good faith on the basis of sincerely held religious beliefs. Given no apparent conflict between the parents and their children, we may take the parents to be acting on behalf of their children. Principle 2 suggests that— absent a compelling reason—the state may not infringe on religiously motivated choices of what to read and what not to read.

The books in this particular case were a series intended to teach students to read. Given the critical importance of basic reading in our society, we may accept the government's assertion that it has a compelling interest in children learning to read, both for the sake of society as a whole and for the sake of the individual children. It is clear, however, that use of any particular series of readers is not necessary to learn to read. Provided parents are willing to teach reading and are demonstrably successful in doing so, government should permit their children to be excused from its reading curriculum. Judge Hull correctly added, however, that, to avoid church/state entanglement, government could not fulfill the parents' request that it provide a religiously acceptable alternative curriculum.

The school also asserted that, even though parents are allowed to opt out of public education entirely, to allow them to opt out of particular books or parts of the curriculum would be a bureaucratic nightmare. But meeting the demands of the particular parents involved in this case would not have been unreasonably difficult. Far greater individualization of education is common in most school systems and does not impose an impossible burden (Glenn, 1987). If many parents wished to remove their children from a variety of different segments of the curriculum, the school could formulate a set of rules regarding how and under what circumstances such removal was permitted. Provided such rules constitute a good-faith effort to accommodate all parents as much as possible without an impossible burden on the school, courts should permit them. Principle 2 cannot, however, countenance unnecessarily inflexible requirements: Administrative inconvenience or minor expense are not sufficient to justify infringing on the free exercise of religion.

A final comment. The Supreme Court has been clear in its decisions that religious inculcation in public schools (which is impermissible) must be distinguished from teaching *about* religion (which is constitutionally acceptable). Schools have too often assumed that the best way to avoid religious inculcation is to avoid religion altogether. Religion is, however, an important aspect of American and world history and culture. Even if its exclusion does not constitute secular humanism, it is poor education and may, if sufficiently systematic, be an unconstitutional deviation from religious neutrality. A major challenge for public schools is to find non-inculcative ways to teach about religion. Needless to say, genuinely neutral treatment must include discussion of negative as well as positive influences. There will be disagreement about what constitutes neutrality and schools may find themselves embroiled in controversy with respect to their treatment of religion. That, however, would be nothing new.

Evolution and Creation

The publication of Charles Darwin's *The Origin of Species* in 1859 is widely regarded as one of the major events of intellectual history. His evolutionary perspective not only revolutionized the field of biology but had extraordinary impact in a variety of natural sciences, social sciences and humanities (e.g., Dixon & Lerner, 1984). Indeed, Darwin's conception of human beings as having evolved from other organisms via natural processes, like the earlier discovery that the earth is not the center of the cosmos, forced humanity to radically reconsider its entire conception of itself and its role in the universe.

Not everyone, however, wished to take part in that radical reconceptualization (Numbers, 1982, 1987). Although most religions accommodated the evolutionary perspective with little difficulty (e.g., by proposing that God set the process in motion), fundamentalist Christians found evolutionary biology inconsistent with their literal reading of Genesis. Their view, generally known as creationism, holds that the earth was created by God about 6000 to 10,000 years ago. With respect to living things, they hold that a finite number of distinct "kinds" were created at that time and that such kinds are immutable. If evolution occurs at all, it is only within kinds. In particular, human beings were created by God and are sharply distinct from all other organisms.

By contrast, although there is disagreement about specific mechanisms of evolution, virtually all modern scientists agree that the earth is about 4.6 billion years old and that, over most of that period, organisms have been evolving. Although human beings are obviously different from any other species, they are part of the natural world and, like all contemporary organisms, evolved from earlier organisms.

Creationists have bitterly opposed the concept of evolution, believing it is not only factually incorrect about the age of the earth and the mutability of species but morally reprehensible in its conception of humanity. Although opposition to evolutionary concepts is much older than the anti-humanist movement, in recent years evolution has been condemned as a fundamental tenet of secular humanism. Is teaching evolution anti-religious, anti-Christian, or pro-humanist? May it thus be banned? If evolution is taught, do fairness and academic freedom require that it be balanced with the creationist point of view? Is this constitutional? How about a scientific version of creationism that makes no reference to God or the Bible?

History and current status of the issue

In the early 20th century, a number of states, concerned that teaching evolution would undermine Christianity, banned the teaching of evolution in public schools (Tyack & James, 1985). One of the most publicized trials in history was the 1925 trial of John Scopes, a biology teacher who, contrary to Tennessee law, taught his students about evolution. Scopes was convicted of violating the law, and the constitutionality of the law was upheld upon appeal.[45] Moreover, the controversy surrounding evolution led teachers, administrators, and publishers in many states to avoid all mention of evolution for decades afterward.

Finally, in 1968, the Supreme Court considered and struck down an Arkansas law forbidding the teaching of evolution. Such a law, it held in *Epperson v. Arkansas*, had no purpose other than to support Christianity, a purpose that clearly violates the establishment clause.[46]

Accepting that the teaching of evolution could no longer be directly banned, creationists hit on the strategy of insisting, on the basis of fairness, that, if evolution is taught, it must be balanced by teaching creationism. The obvious problem with this was that creationism is a religious doctrine and thus may not be taught in public schools. The solution was to sanitize the creationist view of all religious references and claim that what remained was a scientific theory. The result was "scientific creationism," a theory that parallels Biblical creationism in all respects except that it omits all mention of God or supernatural causation. Scientific creationism posits that the geological phenomena and fossil record explained by evolutionism are explained at least as well as the result of Noah's flood.

Bills mandating balanced treatment of evolution and scientific creationism were introduced in numerous states and passed in Arkansas and Louisiana. The Arkansas law was immediately challenged in federal district court. In a 1982 decision, Judge William Overton concluded that the law violated the establishment clause in that, given

45. Scopes v. State, 154 Tenn. 105, 289 S.W. 363 (1927); State of Tennessee v. John Thomas Scopes, Nos. 5231 and 5232, Circ. Ct. Rhea County, Tennessee (1925)
46. Epperson v. Arkansas, 393 U.S. 97 (1968)

the absence of any scientific basis for teaching creationism, the sole purpose and primary effect of the law was to promote fundamentalist Christianity.[47] The state decided not to appeal.

The Louisiana law had a longer history but was ultimately no more successful. It was struck down by a federal district judge in a summary judgment. That judgment was upheld by the Fifth Circuit Court of Appeals and the U.S. Supreme Court. In a 7-2 decision, the Supreme Court ruled in *Edwards v. Aguillard* (1987) that the Louisiana legislature's claimed purpose of promoting academic freedom was a sham; there was no need to remand the case because, even without a full trial, it was all too clear that the sole purpose of the Louisiana legislature was patently religious.[48]

Application of the principles

The great age of the earth and the reality of evolution are virtually unquestioned among reputable scientists. In fact, evolution is not simply an important topic in the field of biology; it is the key concept that ties all of biology together, making it an explanatory science rather than a purely descriptive one (Eldredge, 1982; Futuyma, 1983; Kitcher, 1982). There is thus no question that, on educational grounds, discussion of evolution should be an important part of science education. Even if this casts some doubt on fundamentalist views, there is no violation of the First Amendment. The purpose and main effect of teaching about evolution is educationally reasonable and religiously neutral: To foster understanding of modern science. Any problem this creates for religious faith is unintended and incidental (cf. Principle 5b).

Given that the content of science courses is normally determined by scientists and educators, state laws and school board directives banning the teaching of evolution constitute a revocation of delegated responsibility and should be subject to strict scrutiny. It is clear they cannot survive such scrutiny: The only conceivable purpose for any such law would be to aid particular religious views, a violation of religious neutrality (Principle 5b).

47. McLean v. Arkansas Board of Education, 529 F. Supp. 1255 (E.D. Ark. 1982)
48. Edwards v. Aguilard, 107 S.Ct. 2573 (1987)

What about balancing evolution with discussion of scientific creationism? It is often good educational practice to present students with competing theories, consider the relevant evidence, and encourage them to make their own judgments. Courts should generally defer to the decisions of relevant professionals (e.g., scientists and educators) about what theories and data are worth presenting in a given area and how these should be presented. In the case of creationism, however, the absence of any scientific support for this view, and the detailed resemblance of this view to the creation stories in Genesis, make the purely religious nature of scientific creationism—and the unconstitutionality of teaching it as science—clear (Eldredge, 1982; Futuyma, 1983; Kitcher, 1982; La Follette, 1983). The case against scientific creationism is, of course, even stronger when the mandate of balanced treatment comes not from the relevant professionals to whom responsibility for curriculum decisions is normally delegated but rather from a school board or a state legislature.

The First Amendment, it must be recalled, does not mandate equal treatment of all ideas. Public schools may choose which ideas to teach and which to exclude on the basis of appropriate educational criteria (such as scientific merit) (Principle 5a). Where an idea has little or no credibility, and especially when it also deviates from religious neutrality (Principle 5b), giving it equal time is not only *not* required but may in fact be unconstitutional.

This is not to say, however, that evolution should be presented as an indisputable fact and creationism banned from the classroom. On the contrary, to the extent that time and students' cognitive abilities permit, education in evolution should include presentation of relevant evidence and open discussion of limitations of that evidence and other scientific uncertainties (Principle 5c) rather than relying on appeals to authority (Principle 5c) and censorship of creationist views (Principle 3). Students should be permitted to express views of their own, including creationist views, without penalty or ridicule (Principle 1a). Although students may be assessed and graded on their *understanding* of evolution, it should be clear to them that they are not required to *believe* in it (Principle 1b).

Empirical considerations

Research reviewed in Chapter 3 showed that over the course of child-hood and adolescence there is a dramatic increase in the ability to distinguish facts from hypotheses, to consider hypotheses in relation to relevant evidence, to test them against such evidence, and to co-ordinate multiple perspectives. In view of the intellectual limitations of elementary school children, there may be reason to simply tell them the age of the earth and the evolutionary history of various organisms (e.g., how eohippus evolved into the modern horse). By the time students take high school biology, however, they are much more capable of grasping relevant evidence, considering discrepent evidence, and weighing competing ideas.

Conclusions

The decisions striking down anti-evolution laws and balanced treatment for "creation science" are clearly well justified and are rightly considered major victories for both the First Amendment and science education. Nevertheless, evolutionists should not get too carried away. Although they need not—and should not—give "balanced" treatment to evolution and creationism, neither should they regard the Supreme Court's decisions as sanctioning indoctrination in evolution (Moshman, 1985a). To the extent allowed by students' cognitive abilities, teachers should respect students' moral right of access to information (Principle 9), including reasons for what they are expected to believe, and should avoid indoctrination (Principle 5c). Science should be presented responsibly, with due attention to the nature and limitations of scientific evidence (Moshman, 1985a).

Moreover, although teachers may expect creationist students to read about evolution, try to understand it, and demonstrate their knowledge of it on tests, they should respect the right of creationist students to express their own views (Principle 1a) and, ultimately, to make their own decision about whether to change or maintain their views (Principle 1b). There may even be value in teaching *about* creationism (e.g., in a course or unit on philosophy of science or the relation of science and society), and, if this is done responsibly, there is no constitutional objection (Moshman, 1985a).

Science educators should continue to monitor creationist activities. Although the anti-evolution movement suffered a serious blow in 1987, it has survived such blows in the past and appears to be surviving this one. The effort to pass statewide balanced-treatment laws is probably dead but creationists continue to press individual teachers, administrators, and school boards to implement portions of their agenda. Even if they only succeed in generating controversy, that is often enough to get evolution out of a curriculum. Science educators must monitor not only the blatantly unconstitutional teaching of creationism but the more subtle harm to science education that derives when key scientific concepts are omitted in order to avoid controversy and protect religious sensibilities.

Values and Morality in Public Education

We have thus far considered a variety of issues, including what students may believe and express, with whom they may associate and for what purposes, and what they may be exposed to in books, curricula, and classroom activities. Underlying all of these issues is the recognition that students are likely to be substantially influenced by what goes on in the schools and that public schools, for better or worse, are doing much more than teaching simple and uncontroversial facts. Intentionally or not, public schools are undoubtedly influencing students' values (Arons, 1983; Moffett, 1988; People for the American Way, 1987b; Raven, 1987).

This raises a number of difficult questions. Is the teaching of values desireable? Given the close association of values with religion, at least in our culture, does inculcation of values threaten religious liberty? Should public schools be value-neutral? *Can* they be? If values are to be taught, which values should we teach? Who should decide, and on the basis of what criteria? How should the values then be taught?

For our purposes, the central issue is the role of the First Amendment in answering these questions. Intuitively, there do seem to be critical issues of intellectual freedom involved. Does the First Amendment require or forbid certain answers to the above questions? Does the First Amendment permit values education? Does it require a particular approach to values education? Is there a range of constitutionally acceptable approaches? What, if anything, lies outside that range?

If there is a range of constitutionally acceptable choices, does the First Amendment provide any guidance with respect to what constitutes wise educational and social policy?

History and current status of the issue

Schooling has always included efforts to promote particular values and ideologies. Right from the start, American public schools have been subject to politically- and religiously-based pressures in this regard. There have been systematic efforts to legislate the inculcation of particular values and ideologies since the late 1800s. By the turn of the century, for example, every state and territory had laws requiring public schools to teach the evils of alcohol, many of these including specific—and scientifically unjustifiable—provisions regarding the content of textbooks (Tyack & James, 1985). The government used public education to promote Americanism during World War I, and, after the war, a variety of groups expanded on these efforts:

> Were Darwinism and skepticism undermining traditional patterns of faith? Then forbid the teaching of evolution and require the teaching of the Bible. Was the United States a nation of hyphenates? Then outlaw the teaching of foreign languages in elementary schools. Were Bolsheviks plotting to corrupt the minds of the young? Then weed out teachers who could not prove their patriotism. Was a cynical spirit abroad in the land? Then pass laws requiring textbook writers and teachers to be reverential toward the Founding Fathers. If society seemed centrifugal, schools must be clamped into narrow circles of orthodoxy. (Tyack & James, 1985, p. 514)

In recent decades, the direct inculcation of Christianity has been disallowed by the Supreme Court and promotion of patriotism has tended toward more subtle techniques. Although schools remain concerned about basic values, many educators have favored approaches, such as the well-known values clarification and Kohlbergian curricula, in which students consider a variety of moral dilemmas and are encouraged to formulate and reflect on their values and reasons. No effort is made by the teacher to have students adopt or reject any particular values. These approaches are thus seen as a way for schools to play a role in moral education and yet remain, themselves, value-neutral.

The question of values and morality in education nevertheless remains as vexing as ever. Critics of values clarification charge that it promotes ethical relativism by encouraging the view that, as long as your values are clear, they are as good as anyone else's values (Strike, 1982a). There is also controversy about the presence or absence of values in other aspects of the curriculum. Sex education courses, for example, are commonly charged either with discussing sexuality in a purely factual manner, and thus neglecting its moral dimension, or with inculcating the wrong values with respect to sexuality. Similar concerns have been expressed about drug education and about curricula dealing with death.

Some disputes over values hinge on what values should be taught or what values are most important. Nuclear war curricula, for example, are often charged with improperly valuing peace over freedom. Similarly, curricula concerning international relations ("global education") are charged with valuing tolerance over patriotism.

Other disputes concern who should have the authority to make decisions about values education. The National School Boards Association, for example, believes that each community must determine for itself what values to impart and that basic decisions should thus be made by school boards, representing their communities, rather than by state government, national government, or individual teachers or administrators (National School Boards Association, 1987).

Still other disputes concern the basis for and manner of inculcation (Benninga, 1988). William Bennett, for example, as Secretary of Education in the second Reagan administration, argued vigorously for direct inculcation similar to the purposeful Americanization mandated by many state legislatures earlier in the century. Distinguishing the "American common culture" from "the perverted culture of our adversaries," he proposed the educational system as a "vital instrument for the transmission of the common culture." Public schools, he argued, should be designed to inculcate an explicit American ideology that would serve "as a kind of immunological system, destroying the values and attitudes promulgated by our adversaries before they can infect our body politic (Bennett, 1986)."

Most educators accept the general view that schools cannot avoid dealing with values and should not try to do so (Association for Supervision and Curriculum Development, 1988; National School Boards Association, 1987; see also People for the American Way, 1987b). Many, however, remain leary of approaches that smack of indoctrination. The American Federation of Teachers, for example, sponsored a project that produced a 1987 statement entitled *Education for Democracy: Guidelines for Strengthening the Teaching of Democratic Values* (American Federation of Teachers, 1987). The statement called for schools to "purposely impart to their students the learning necessary for an informed, reasoned allegiance to the ideals of a free society." The statement was signed by a wide variety of liberals and conservatives (including Secretary Bennett and former presidents Jimmy Carter and Gerald Ford) and reflects the continuing efforts of public schools to achieve a consensus approach that reflects the concern of conservatives that American schools teach American values and the concern of liberals that American schools not become centers of indoctrination.

Application of the principles
The First Amendment requires government to respect the intellectual freedom of its citizens. Government-run schools are an obvious threat to such freedom: Clearly, we must be concerned about the prospect of each generation being channeled, via compulsory education laws, into schools where they are indoctrinated in values systematically chosen by government officials to reflect their political or religious agendas. On the other hand, as noted in Chapter 2, it is absurd to insist that education be value-neutral. If government is to run schools at all, it will necessarily be involved in inculcating values. This raises fundamental philosophical questions regarding the justifiability of public education (Cragg, 1988; Strike, 1982a). Even in schools committed to neutrality, rationality, and a free market of ideas, it is unavoidable that political power will play a major role in determining what is presented and even defining what constitutes neutrality and rationality (Proefriedt, 1985). Some regard the First Amendment problems in this area as so intractable that they can be handled only via substantially increasing government support for private school options (Arons, 1983).

Central to resolving the legal problem is how broadly we construe the First Amendment. An overly broad interpretation, in which government simply may not inculcate, favor, or oppose any ideas, is obviously untenable (Gottlieb, 1987). It would rule out not only the possibility of public schools but most other government activities as well. On the other hand, an overly restrictive interpretation would subvert the intellectual freedom that the Framers considered critical to democratic government and intended the First Amendment to protect. What we need is a middle-ground interpretation that draws a reasonable and workable line between permitted and forbidden activities with respect to values and morality in public schools. I believe Principle 5 provides such an interpretation.

Principle 5 expressly permits government inculcation of values but requires inculcation in public schools to meet three criteria: (a) it must have a legitimate educational purpose; (b) it must be religiously neutral in intent and primary effect; and (c) it must be nonindoctrinative.

The legitimate educational purpose test is the easiest to meet. The Constitution does not even require that children be educated, much less define what such education consists of. State legislatures, local school boards, and other school officials have substantial authority to determine the purposes of education in any given state, community, or school. This gives them the authority to decide that public education should be used to inculcate values and to decide what values should be inculcated. They may, for example, decide that children should learn constitutional values such as a commitment to liberty, equality, justice, due process, or the rule of law. They may decide children should learn to share community values such as honesty, courtesy, compassion, autonomy, tolerance, courage, responsibility, or respect for persons. If people disagree with the values chosen, they may elect new legislators or a new school board or urge the school board to hire different school officials.

Principle 5a does, however, imply certain limits. Government, it suggests, may not determine what values to inculcate on the basis of the platform of a particular political party or in order to increase support for a controversial law or political position. A core purpose of the free expression clauses of the First Amendment was to guarantee the intellectual freedom necessary for democratic self-government (Bogen, 1983; Garvey, 1979; Haiman, 1981). Government may not define education in such a way as to purposely or directly undercut this intent (Harpaz, 1986; Kamiat, 1983; van Geel, 1983, 1986). Thus, I would argue, a public school may seek to inculcate respect for personal autonomy but may not teach that this requires government to permit abortion. Similarly, a public school may seek to inculcate a general respect for life, but may not maintain that abortion should therefore be illegal.

Principle 5b construes the establishment clause as forbidding purposeful or direct inculcation of religion. This does not mean public schools may not inculcate any values associated with religious doctrines or beliefs. Virtually all values have religious connections of some sort. What Principle 5b requires is that there is a genuinely nonreligious purpose for the inculcation—for example, to promote constitutional values, commitment to society, or social cohesion—and reason to believe that the primary effect of the inculcation will be to serve that secular purpose. Any advantage or disadvantage to religion in general or any particular religion must be unintended and incidental. This would allow a great deal of values inculcation but would rule out direct reliance on religion in determining the values to be emphasized, systematically religious formulations of those values, or pervasive use of religious examples as a mode of inculcation.

Principle 5c goes beyond the question of what may be inculcated to the question of *how* such inculcation may be accomplished. It distinguishes and forbids certain strong versions of inculcation that are labeled indoctrination.

Respect for intellectual freedom does not entail the relativistic view that all values and all moral perspectives are equally acceptable. Quite the contrary, one may, consistent with a commitment to intellectual freedom, consider one's own values more adequate or defensible than those of another person and vigorously attempt to convince the other to adopt your point of view. Intellectual freedom does require, however, that such an attempt be a good faith effort to *convince* the other by communicating the reasons for your values, rather than to force acquiescence via ridicule, power assertion, distortion of facts, or withholding of relevant information (Siegel, 1986, 1988).

Efforts to convince are, of course, limited by the rationality of the other, a consideration that is particularly important with respect to children. As discussed in Chapter 2, fairly direct inculcation may be the only way to get a young child to believe certain things or act in certain ways (Snook, 1972). To the extent that the child is capable of considering the reasons certain things are considered immoral, however, reasons should be provided. To the extent that the child is capable of understanding alternative moral perspectives, such perspectives should be presented. To the extent that the child is capable of dealing with diverse considerations, rich sources of relevant information (including contrary facts and ideas) should be included. Naturally, educators must have substantial leeway to make professional judgments about how to present material on the basis of their analysis of the intellectual competence of their students. Imposition of limits that cannot be justified on the basis of relevant developmental and educational considerations, however, constitutes indoctrination and is inconsistent with Principle 5c.

Empirical considerations
Evidence reviewed in Chapter 3 indicates that moral development proceeds along a fairly predictable course, though the rate of change and the highest level achieved is highly variable. Even those who doubt the specific stages postulated by Kohlberg generally agree that moral understanding proceeds from a relatively naive view of absolute rights and wrongs to principled reasoning based on increasingly sophisticated insights into human interactions, the nature of social institutions, and the abstract requirements of justice. Relativistic rejection of any basis for moral evaluation appears to be a common (and perhaps unavoidable) phenomenon along the way but does not seem to be the end state of moral development. The process of change appears to be a gradual construction of new understandings that is facilitated by contradiction, active reflection, and open discussion with others.

Society is, of course, concerned at least as much with how people actually behave as with their mode of reasoning. Evidence indicates that behavior, though influenced by one's moral values and reasoning, cannot be precisely predicted from these. Morality appears to be not simply a bag of virtues or an abstract ideology but a complex, multifaceted aspect of the personality. It includes one's general modes of analyzing social interactions, one's specific values and reasoning, one's ability to translate moral decisions into behavior, and one's moral character, including commitment to determining what is moral and acting on this (Blasi, 1980, 1983, 1984; Rest, 1983, 1984).

Conclusions

A variety of approaches to values and moral education in the public schools are consistent with Principle 5. Direct inculcation of particular values is generally acceptable, provided there is a legitimate educational basis for inculcating those values, the purpose and main effect of the inculcation are religiously neutral, and the inculcation is non-indoctrinative in that it appeals to reasons and encourages critical analysis to the extent that children's emerging rationality permits.

Direct inculcation does have the potential problem that it is associated with the view that some things are just inherently right and others inherently wrong. Such a view is more associated with some religious traditions than with others. Educators should not explicitly endorse this sort of absolutist view of morality. Provided they do not, however, and provided any assistance the inculcative curriculum gives to absolutist religions is thus unintended and incidental, direct inculcation is, in my view, constitutionally acceptable.

It should be noted, of course, that constitutionally acceptable forms of value inculcation are not necessarily wise from the viewpoint of educational policy. Students may perceive and react against authoritarian attempts to alter their values. Even if they accept the inculcated values they may not understand them in the way intended or may be unable to implement them behaviorally in novel situations. Given the complexity of human morality, direct inculcation, even when constitutionally permissible, may be educationally naive and ineffective in achieving its own stated goals (A. C. Lewis, 1987).

An alternative family of approaches to values and moral education—including values clarification and Kohlbergian programs—emphasizes moral discussion and encouragement of student reasoning. Although such an approach is relatively noninculcative, it may lead students to the relativistic view that all values are equally acceptable or to the secular humanist view that, in the absence of God, we must rely exclusively on human reasoning. Explicit endorsement of either of these views would, in my view, be an unconstitutional violation of religious neutrality (Principle 5b). Simple exploration of value differences and encouragement of reasoning, however, are typically intended to foster awareness and tolerance of diversity and to develop the ability to reason, and have the primary effect of furthering these legitimate educational goals. To the extent that this is the case, any advantage such curricula give to religions that emphasize tolerance, diversity, and reasoning is unintended and incidental, and thus presents no constitutional problem.

Recognizing the sensitivity of moral issues and values, it would certainly be wise for school officials to avoid even the perception that something devious is going on in the public schools. There should be clear and open criteria for deciding what to inculcate, ample opportunity for student, parent, and community input prior to major decisions, and open communication with all concerned. Moreover, school and government officials should make it clear that, even though the schools accept the task of facilitating values and morality in the next generation, they should not and cannot have prime responsibility in this area. Values and morality are too deeply rooted in particular cultures, religions, and worldviews for public schools, working within the legal and ethical constraints of the First Amendment, to comprehensively address them (Strike, 1982a). Moral development is and must remain a fundamental concern within families, religious settings, and other social institutions (Howe, 1987). The State, especially when it sets up public schools, is unavoidably involved in the realm of values, but society is making a serious mistake if it leaves the burden in this area to the government.

Finally, for schools addressing these difficult issues, the First Amendment should not be considered merely an irritating legal constraint. Underlying the First Amendment are fundamental moral values of intellectual freedom (Principles 7–13). If American public schools are to inculcate any values at all—and that, we agree, is unavoidable—First Amendment values should be prime candidates for inclusion. Browbeating students about the importance of freedom of speech and religion, however, will probably not do the trick. The best way to facilitate a genuine and lasting commitment to these constitutional values may be insuring that, throughout their years in American public schools, students experience an environment that truly encourages intellectual freedom.

Government Regulation of Private Education

There has always been dissatisfaction with the public schools. Many dissatisfied parents have attempted to modify public education to suit their own educational philosophies, thus yielding many of the controversies we have covered in this chapter. Others, however, have taken a different tack: They have decided to educate their children outside the public school system, either in private schools or, on their own, at home.

The major impetus for private education in the 19th century was the Protestant bias of the public schools, leading American Catholics to set up their own system of private schools. Although the number of Catholic students has been declining (Peshkin, 1986), Catholic schools remain the major system of private education in the United States. Lutherans and other Christians have also set up major systems of private schools.

In the 1980s, however, the most rapidly growing segment of private education has been fundamentalist Christian schools. The typical fundamentalist school (Peshkin, 1986) provides a conservative Christian worldview that pervades all aspects of the curriculum. Not only are all courses taught from a religious perspective but there is a systematic effort to direct students' moral and political views and, indeed, their entire lives. Although students typically go home on evenings and weekends, the school urges a sharp physical and psychological separation from the secular world in their choice of friends, clothing, movies, records, television shows, and so forth. The ideology is highly authoritarian—teachers must submit to administrators, students to teachers, children to adults, wives to husbands, and everyone, of course, to the Will of God.

Underlying the entire program is an absolutist version of Christianity. In the words of the head of Bethany Baptist Academy in Illinois,

> This is not a place where there are alternative world views, competing and confronting cosmologies. . . . [W]e put ourselves in

a position of being the first and only among the religions of the world. There is one truth. Truth, as we see it, is singular (Peshkin, 1986, p. 9).

Given this perspective, the intense commitment of many fundamentalist ministers, teachers, parents, and students to their schools is not surprising. In the words of one Bethany Baptist teacher, "How could the Christian school not be superior when teachers are free to shout the Word of God and say, 'This is Truth'?" (Peshkin, 1986, p. 85).

Another important trend of the 1980s has been a dramatic increase in home schooling. The rationales for home schooling are diverse (Holt, 1981; Lines, 1987). Many parents who choose to educate their own children are fundamentalist Christians who object to the public schools for fostering secular humanism and excessive intellectual freedom and wish to provide at home the sort of education that fundamentalist Christian schools attempt to provide in a group setting. Others, however, have different reasons; some, ironically, choose to educate their own children because they believe the public schools are insufficiently humanistic and fail to challenge their children's intellects.

The best-known curriculum used in fundamentalist private and home schools is Accelerated Christian Education (ACE) (Fleming & Hunt, 1987). ACE aims to teach the "truth from God's point of view" (Facts about Accelerated Christian Education, 1979, p. 4). This includes not only the inculcation of absolute moral values derived from the Bible but a variety of specific, right-wing political ideas. The 10th-grade U.S. history curriculum, for example, teaches that

> The United Nations was created by Communists and has always been used by the Communists to further Communist goals. Even most of the United States delegates to the San Francisco Convention to found the UN were later discovered to be members of the Communist party.

The section further notes that "Satan is the real force behind man's efforts to achieve world government" (quoted by Fleming & Hunt, 1987, pp. 522–523). ACE itself readily acknowledges its intent to provide students with a "pro-American analysis of world events" and its view that "communism and socialism are . . . antithetical to theism, and the two cannot coexist peacefully" (Johnson, 1987, p. 520).

A number of questions are raised by the existence of private schools. May government require that children be educated? May it require them to attend public schools? If not, may it regulate the schools they do attend? Do compulsory education laws raise First Amendment issues? Does government regulation of private education raise First Amendment issues? How much regulation is constitutionally acceptable?

History and current status of the issue

Parents of widely varied political and religious views have long been concerned about the right to educate their own children as they see fit. There has been equal concern about the potential of private schools to undermine the purpose of public education. Passions run high on these issues. In Nebraska, for example, the Faith Baptist Church, which housed the unaccredited Faith Christian School, was actually padlocked and its minister, Everett Sileven, jailed several times. Not one to turn the other cheek, Reverend Sileven publicly prayed for God to kill the offending state officials (Moshman, 1985b).

The U.S. Supreme Court has held that states may not forbid private education. In *Pierce v. Society of Sisters* (1925),[49] it ruled that states must permit parents to send their children to private schools. Although the decision emphasized the economic interests of the private schools, it also noted the fundamental right of parents to make major choices concerning their children's education. The Court suggested, however, that the State may require education and may regulate private schools. In *Wisconsin v. Yoder* (1972),[50] the Supreme Court required an exception to compulsory education beyond grade 8 for children of the Amish. This decision was, however, based on particular characteristics of the Amish religion and society and thus has little general applicability. It is safe to say that the Supreme Court views compulsory education as constitutionally acceptable but compulsory attendance in public schools as unacceptable.

49. Pierce v. Society of Sisters, 268 U.S. 510 (1925).
50. Wisconsin v. Yoder, 406 U.S. 205 (1972)

Given that government may require children to be educated but must permit this to take place in private schools, to what extent and in what ways may it regulate those schools? May it, for example, require that certain subjects be taught, determine what must be included in various curriculum areas, determine testing standards students must meet, or set standards for teachers? The question of what regulations the state may impose has been extensively litigated in both state and federal courts. Most challenges to state regulation have been unsuccessful and the U.S. Supreme Court has declined several opportunities to consider the issue (van Geel, 1987).

The United Nations Universal Declaration of Human Rights endorses compulsory education but specifies that "parents have a prior right to choose the kind of education that shall be given to their children" (Article 26, Section 3). The United Nations International Covenant on Economic, Social, and Cultural Rights expands on this in highlighting

> the liberty of parents and, when applicable, legal guardians, to choose for their children schools, other than those established by the public authorities, which conform to such minimum educational standards as may be laid down or approved by the State and to ensure the religious and moral education of their children in conformity with their own convictions. (Article 13, Section 3)

Application of the principles

In analyzing government regulation of private schools it is critical to distinguish three sets of interests (Moshman, 1985b). First, there is the right of parents to educate their children in accord with their own religious or philosophical views. The concept that parents have a right to raise their children as they see fit is a well accepted part of our legal tradition (Rush, 1985; van Geel, 1987).[51] Parental choice is arguably a fundamental liberty protected by the Fourteenth Amendment. The family, moreover, may be construed as a zone of privacy between the State and the individual, protected by a generalizable right to privacy underlying the specific protections of the First, Third, Fourth, Fifth,

51. Meyer v. Nebraska, 262 U.S. 390 (1923); Pierce v. Society of Sisters, 268 U.S. 510 (1925)

and Fourteenth Amendments. The suggestion that parents have fundamental rights even though this is not directly specified in any particular clause of the Constitution is consistent with the Ninth Amendment, which provides that "the enumeration in the Constitution of certain rights shall not be construed to deny or disparage others retained by the people." When the parents have a religious motivation, the above arguments are reinforced by the free exercise clause of the First Amendment: For many religions, education of one's children in accord with certain principles is a fundamental religious obligation.

The community as a whole, however, also has a stake in children's education. The welfare—and even the continuation—of any society depends on the socialization of the next generation. Children who are inadequately educated may become a burden on society. Moreover, to the extent that a large number of children fail to receive an adequate education, there may be a failure to maintain the traditions and institutions of that society. Government, then, acting on behalf of society as a whole, has a compelling interest in the education of each new generation.

A generation, however, consists of individuals, and those individuals, even if they are too immature to realize it, have interests that are not necessarily identical with those of their parents or of society as a whole. A third consideration, then, is the rights and interests of the children involved. In the case of young children, this consideration is further complicated by the fact that they may not be sufficiently mature to recognize and act in behalf of their own interests. The question, then, is whether we should depend on their parents or on the government to protect those interests.

In general, we rely on parents, rather than government, to raise children. Parents are presumed to have their children's best interests at heart, to have more detailed knowledge of their own children than could any government official, and to be psychologically better suited for childrearing than any government agency. With respect to education, then, respect for both parental rights and child rights suggests that we should permit parents substantial leeway in choosing the best form of education for their own children.

Parental rights are not absolute, however. We allow parents substantial discretion in disciplining their own children, for example, but we nevertheless have laws against physical abuse. Similarly, with respect to education, parental choice should be limited by the government's compelling interest in seeing that no child is denied a minimally adequate education. This rationale, it seems to me, is the only adequate legal justification for compulsory education.

First Amendment considerations. How does this involve the First Amendment? Suppose a parent wishes to send his or her child to a private school where children are discouraged from forming or expressing their own ideas, are systematically indoctrinated in views favored by the school, and are completely deprived of access to any contrary opinions. We may ask three constitutional questions about this. First, are parents constitutionally permitted to foist such an education on their children? Second, is government constitutionally *required* to do anything about this? Third, is government constitutionally *permitted* to do anything about this?

The answer to the first question, it seems to me, is that parents are indeed constitutionally permitted to arrange for their own children to be educated in this way. The First Amendment limits only government, not parents (van Geel, 1986). The sort of indoctrinative education described here is fundamentally at odds with First Amendment values of intellectual freedom (Principles 7–13) and may thus be criticized on moral grounds. Such education does not, however, violate the First Amendment when it is imposed by parents, or by schools they have chosen, on their own children.

With respect to the second question, it does not appear that government is required to do anything about this. Government may not itself restrict the intellectual liberties guaranteed by the First Amendment but it is not required to actively prevent such restriction by private agents.

Government may, however, choose to actively promote intellectual freedom. With respect to the situation described, it may argue that it has a compelling interest in the intellectual freedom of all people, including children. Acting on behalf of society as a whole, it may even argue that its interest in promoting intellectual freedom is particularly compelling with respect to children in that a democratic society requires citizens who, in their formative years, have had access to a wide range of information and ideas and are thus capable of forming and expressing their own views (cf. Garvey, 1979). In other words, although government is not required to respect the broad moral formulation of intellectual freedom embodied in Principles 7–13, it may choose to do so and, in some circumstances, may even assert a compelling interest in doing so.

It does not follow, of course, that government may control private schools in any way it pleases. On the contrary, parents should have substantial leeway in educating their own children either on their own or via schools of their own choosing. Government may, however, regulate these schools. To the extent that a given regulation infringes on the fundamental right of parents to determine their own children's education, it is constitutional, it seems to me, if and only if government can demonstrate that the regulation in question serves a compelling educational purpose (such as furthering intellectual development) and is the least restrictive way of serving that purpose.

Empirical considerations

The above analysis rules out extreme solutions to the issue of government regulation of private education, such as the view that government may not regulate education at all or the view that it may impose any regulation rationally related to an educational purpose. In evaluating any given regulation for constitutionality under the proposed standard, a court would need to look at the particulars of the regulation and would almost always need to consider detailed empirical evidence.

Consider, for example, the continuing controversy over whether private school teachers and homeschooling parents must meet the same certification standards as public school teachers. In weighing a challenge to a state certification law, a court should consider the following: (a) What are the requirements for attaining certification? (b) Is there empirical support for the assertion that students will be better educated if their teachers have met these requirements? (c) Is it plausible, on the basis of available evidence, that alternative requirements, or a more flexible set of standards, would be adequate to achieve the intended quality of education? (d) Is it plausible, on the basis of available evidence, that regular use of achievement tests would be sufficient to ascertain student achievement and render it unnecessary to consider teacher qualifications at all?

These are difficult questions and have rarely been adequately considered (Moshman, 1985b). Available data are highly complex and not amenable to brief review (see Wittrock, 1986). The evidence is, however, consistent with the general conclusion that state regulations concerning private schools are rarely either (a) so obviously necessary to achieve compelling educational aims that courts must immediately accept them without detailed scrutiny of possible alternatives or (b) so patently irrelevant to good education that courts may immediately strike them down without careful inquiry into potential consequences.

Conclusions

However fair and constitutional the public schools try to be, not everyone will be satisfied with the education they provide. Government may require education and, for this to be meaningful, must have substantial power to determine what counts as an education. Parents, however, have a fundamental right to educate their own children according to their own religious or other views. For this to be meaningful, private schools must not only be permitted to exist but must be permitted to differ substantially from government schools.

In setting up regulations that all schools, including private and home schools, must meet, government may and should consider the fundamental values underlying the First Amendment. It may and should require that schools have an atmosphere that will foster an appreciation for intellectual freedom and that will facilitate intellectual development. To the extent that such regulations are challenged as restricting parental choice, government may note its compelling interest in the intellectual freedom of all individuals and in the intellectual development of the next generation of voters and citizens. The burden of proof should be on the government, however, to show, on the basis of empirical research on teaching and learning, that the regulations in question can be expected to achieve the asserted educational purposes and are the least restrictive way of doing so.

5 : Children, Government, and Society

Parents almost always play central roles in the socialization of their children. Indeed, to a large extent, children are valued by their parents as a means to extend themselves into the future and/or to perpetuate their own ideas and values. It is important for parents to keep in mind, however, that no one can accurately predict the precise nature of the world in which their children will be adults. Accordingly, it is critical that, in addition to teaching particular skills and values, parents facilitate the development of more general intellectual competencies that will help their children adapt. Even more fundamentally, although children are born years after their parents, this temporal distinction in no way diminishes their ultimate moral standing as persons. Treating one's children as extensions of oneself accords them the status of means rather than ends. Respect for children's personhood requires according them substantial and increasing intellectual freedom.

The same argument can be made at a societal level. It is the nature of human society that each generation socializes the next and it is natural that such socialization will treat each generation as a means of furthering the ends of the generation that socializes it. At the same time, however, moral considerations suggest limits on such use of later generations. From a teleological point of view, concern for the welfare of future generations requires a broader view of socialization that allows for adaptive change across the generations. Deontological considerations, moreover, require that each generation acknowledge the next as having the same right as each preceding generation to determine its own values and destiny.

Over the past two centuries, our society has increasingly relied on the government to play a central role in the socialization of children. Governmental socialization is an important aspect of socialization in general and raises all the same moral issues. In addition, however, to the extent that socialization involves influencing beliefs, governmental socialization has the potential to violate First Amendment protections of intellectual freedom against government intrusion and restriction. It is at this point that the moral issues take on constitutional dimensions.

Governmental Socialization

Public education
Public schools are the most important arena in which government comes in contact with children. Given that public schools are directly concerned with the intellect, it is inevitable that they will be the focus of complex First Amendment issues. Of course, public schools involve much more than government and children. Parents who send their children to public schools have good reason to be concerned about what happens there. They may intensely disagree with each other not only about how best to achieve educational goals but, more fundamentally, about what those goals should be. Moreover, not only do parents disagree with each other, but the community as a whole has a legitimate interest in its public schools that may conflict with the interests of some parents. Finally, recognition of children's First Amendment rights, as potentially distinct from their parents' First Amendment and childrearing rights, further complicates an already complicated situation.

One part of the solution must be to recognize that, although there are issues of policy involved here, to be settled by compromises among school officials and by election of school board members who share community views and values, there are also issues of moral and constitutional principle. With specific reference to children's side of the equation, I have proposed a set of principles that public school officials should apply, regardless of the political situation, and have considered in detail the application of those principles to a wide variety of public school issues. Reasonable people may, of course, disagree with some of my conclusions. There is no reason, however, to doubt the centrality of the First Amendment to these issues of intellectual freedom.

Public schools, moreover, are not simply the main arena in which children's First Amendment rights are important. They are, in fact, responsible for that importance. It is precisely due to the rise of public education that the issue of children's First Amendment rights has become so critical. As noted in Chapter 1, the framers of the Bill of Rights failed to consider its application to children not because they wanted government to have unbridled control over children but, quite the contrary, because they assumed government would have little to do with children. With the rise of public schools, it is now relevant —in fact, crucial—to consider whether the Constitution should be construed as providing children with the same protection as adults—or, instead, more protection, less protection, or different protections —against government intrusions into their beliefs and regulation of their expression.

It might be argued that children should indeed have First Amendment rights but that the public school is a special setting in which such rights have limited relevance. Judges, the argument goes, in order to permit school officials the leeway to perform their delicate educational functions, should not interfere unless the school's actions are patently irrational (cf. Rose, 1988). After all, provided children have clear rights to express themselves outside of the school, restrictions within the school do not *prohibit* the expression of any views. They merely restrict *where* and *when* children may communicate. Forbidding a child to express certain things *in school*, then, is comparable to refusing a permit to a group that wants to parade or demonstrate in a major street at a highly traveled time of day. There is no restriction of what one may say, only of where or when one may say it. First Amendment law is generally lenient about restrictions on the time, place, or manner of expression, requiring only that they be content-neutral and reasonable.[1]

But restrictions on speech within schools are often far from content-neutral. Moreover, public schools differ from streets or parks in that

1. Perry Education Association v. Perry Local Educators' Association, 460 U.S. 37 (1983)

students must spend a substantial portion of their waking hours there. In fact, not only is there mandatory attendance but one is required to learn what is being taught (Gottlieb, 1987). Given the intimate and extended involvement of public schools in children's beliefs and modes of thinking, it seems clear that this is a context crying out for strict scrutiny of any restrictions on children's intellectual freedom. It is not enough, I have argued, that such restrictions be reasonable means toward some legitimate end. The purpose must be compelling and it must be pursued in a manner that controls belief and restricts expression no more than absolutely necessary.

Any argument that the First Amendment simply does not apply to children within the school environment was definitively put to rest by *Tinker*.[2] *Hazelwood*, however, suggests that even though children do not forfeit their First Amendment rights upon physically entering the school, such rights have minimal application within the school's curriculum.[3] But it is precisely within the curriculum that we have the most reason for concern about government socialization of our children. It is here above all that we need the First Amendment to limit governmental inculcation of ideas and values by limiting unjustifiably indoctrinative presentations and by protecting the expression of students' own ideas.

Available evidence provides no support for the view that education requires highly focused exposure to a single point of view. On the contrary, as we saw in Chapter 3, exposure to diverse viewpoints, even to conflict and contradiction, often facilitate learning and development, especially at the secondary level. Public schools may choose not to present certain viewpoints for a variety of legitimate reasons, but this does not mean they have a legitimate interest in insuring that students will not encounter views the school has omitted. In restricting expression by some students in order to shield other students from ideas inconsistent with those of the curriculum, government is pursuing a purpose that is not even legitimate, much less compelling.

Children are not, of course, the only communicators within the school. The school has its own messages to communicate, and the First

2. Tinker v. Des Moines Independent Community School District, 393 U.S. 503 (1969)
3. Hazelwood School District v. Kuhlmeier, 108 S.Ct. 562 (1988)

Amendment issues raised by such communication are indeed intricate and difficult. Public schools constitute a complex setting in which well-educated professionals (administrators, teachers, and librarians) extend and implement the policies of elected officials (school board members, legislators). With respect to communication by the school, judges, who are neither elected to set school policy nor trained about children, teaching, and learning, should generally defer to school officials and hesitate to second-guess their decisions. Nevertheless, public schools are settings in which government is directly teaching individuals who, because they are still children, are particularly vulnerable to programs of religious or political indoctrination. Such indoctrination could severely compromise their present and future ability to form and express their own beliefs. The potential threat to the First Amendment is clear and substantial.

The public school is a constitutionally sensitive interface between government, in one of its most active roles, and the individual, at a time of life when she or he is most cognitively vulnerable. The resulting controversies are of fundamental significance not only for the cognitive development of individual children but for the intellectual vitality of society as a whole.

Intellectual freedom and intellectual diversity

Imagine a national education system in which a central board makes all decisions regarding books, curriculum, personnel, and so forth. Such a system would have serious pragmatic difficulties: How much can a single group of people be expected to do? More important for our purposes, such a system would be a serious threat to intellectual diversity.

Our own system is, of course, much different from this. Although there is a federal Department of Education, public education is primarily run by each of the 50 states. Moreover, each state includes a large number of semi-autonomous school systems, each with its own school board. Furthermore, each school board delegates much of its responsibility to hired administrators, who in turn hire teachers and librarians and delegate much responsibility to them. This system may have evolved largely for practical reasons but it also serves as an important guard against imposition of a single ideology on all American schoolchildren.

Underlying the First Amendment is a concern not only with the intellectual freedom of each individual but with the intellectual diversity of society (Harpaz, 1986). Even if the system of multiple centers of power and extensively delegated responsibility is not constitutionally required, it plays an important role in preventing an enforced conformity that would be deadly to genuine democracy. Responsibility need not always be delegated, but, once it is, ad hoc revocation of the delegated responsibility should provide grounds for strict judicial scrutiny. Although judges should not routinely second-guess the actions of state legislatures, elected school officials, or professional educators, they should be sensitive to suspicious situations, such as a decision by a high-level government institution to make specific decisions of a sort it would not normally make. Decisions by school boards or administrators about individual library books and decisions by state legislatures about the specific content of, say, the biology curriculum fall in this category.

One key aspect of the usual chain of delegation is that as one moves down the line from legislators to school board members to administrators to teachers and librarians one is usually moving in the direction of less political motivation and more academic/professional training. Respecting the academic freedom of teachers and librarians to make independent educational decisions thus not only protects the intellectual diversity of society (as a result of having many decision makers) but also protects the intellectual freedom of individual students by insulating their education, to some extent, from inappropriate political considerations.

It is important to keep in mind, however, that a single authoritarian teacher can be at least as effective as a national school board in narrowly indoctrinating a particular student. Diffusion of academic decision-making is clearly not enough to guard against unconstitutional motivation. Educators' academic freedom thus should not be absolute. Decision-makers at all levels should be bound to follow well-established procedures and to employ clear criteria in their original decisions and in responding to challenges of such decisions. Such procedures and criteria should be in place before a controversy arises and should not be modified during the course of a specific controversy. Deviations from established criteria or procedures, or failure to establish such criteria and procedures, should be a basis for strict judicial scrutiny, with a burden on the decision-maker to show constitutionally acceptable motivations and consequences.

There is an understandable yearning in the United States for the sort of social consensus that perhaps characterizes smaller and more homogeneous societies. There may indeed be value in working toward such consensus, but there is grave danger in efforts to achieve it through governmental indoctrination. Attention to criteria, procedures, and delegation of responsibility in public schools is critical to protecting children, their parents, and society against governmental power to coerce conformity.

Religious socialization

In the realm of intellectual freedom, no aspect is more sensitive than religious liberty. The intense and continuing controversy over religion in public schools directly illustrates this.

Government neutrality. The religion clauses of the First Amendment are often interpreted as requiring a strict separation of church and state, or at least as strict a separation as is practically possible. Given that the public school is an agency of the state, separation of church and state suggests that public schools must systematically exclude religion. But systematic exclusion of religion from a setting where most children are required to spend a large part of their waking hours during most of their childhood is itself a threat to the religious liberty both of the children themselves and of their parents.

I have argued we would do better to construe the First Amendment as requiring government neutrality toward religion. This is similar to separation of church and state as that concept is commonly interpreted and my analyses of various issues usually lead to the same conclusions reached by church/state separationists. The neutrality principle suggests, however, that when government goes out of its way to exclude or discourage religion (without a compelling reason to do so) it is violating the First Amendment, even if the intent was to separate church from state. Children may come to school with religious views, may desire to express those views, and may desire to associate with others who share those views. Religion, moreover, has been an important part of American culture since the beginning; it is a distortion of history to exclude discussion of this.

Many attempts to get more religion into public schools are, to be sure, intended to get the school to endorse, encourage, or facilitate religion. Such efforts should be scrupulously resisted. It is important to avoid even the *perception* of government support for religion. Nevertheless, it is possible to go so far in avoiding any possible perception of endorsement that the school is, in effect, acting against religion. In applying the religion clauses of the First Amendment to the public schools, the guiding ideal should be government neutrality, not the exclusion of religion.

Fundamentalist Christians as a religious minority. At the center of the controversy over religion in public schools has been fundamentalist Christianity. Fundamentalists interpret the Bible literally and believe that, through their religion, they have access to absolute, complete and final knowledge:

> When I say Christianity is true I mean it is true to total reality—the total of what is, beginning with the central reality, the objective existence of the personal-infinite God. Christianity is not just a series of truths but *Truth*—Truth about all of reality. (Schaeffer, 1982, pp. 19–20, capitalization and emphasis in original)

Armed with the Truth, fundamentalists have been highly active and vocal on public school issues, as well as abortion and other social issues. Moreover, given the political power they have been able to muster on many issues, due to the support of many conservatives and moderates for aspects of their agenda, they have been perceived by many as a powerful political force. Americans concerned about constitutional liberties have been right to oppose them on school prayer and many other issues.

Nevertheless, it is important to remember that fundamentalist Christianity is a religion and that genuine fundamentalists, though substantial in numbers, money, and political influence, are a minority. Like other minorities, they often find themselves unable to count on the democratic process to secure their rights and are forced to rely on the Constitution. Government schools, run by school boards elected by political majorities and by education professionals with mainstream views, may genuinely offend their religious sensibilities. When they suggest that, as parents, they have a right to more say in their children's education, their objections are commonly the object of national derision. If, in despair over the public schools, they decide to educate their children in private schools that share their religious orientation or to take the time to educate them at home, they sometimes find themselves frustrated by government insistence on controlling even these efforts in order to achieve its secular—in their view, secular humanist—aims.

Not all of the fundamentalist agenda involves unconstitutional efforts to impose their religion and morality on others. Some of their demands simply amount to asserting that their own religious views with respect to the education of their own children should be legally recognized. This includes the issues of voluntary prayer groups for Christian students, withdrawal of their own children from aspects of the public school curriculum they find religiously offensive, and freedom of private and home schools from government regulation. Government must, of course, protect other parents and children from the fundamentalist agenda and may choose to protect the children of fundamentalists from harmful intellectual restrictions their own parents would impose. It should be recognized, however, that many fundamentalist complaints are analogous to the complaints of other minority groups and, whatever one's view of the fundamentalist Christian religion, deserve equal consideration (Moshman, 1985c).

The First Amendment applies to all religions and points of view, and we must be especially sensitive in recognizing genuine constitutional claims from groups that are widely feared, ridiculed, or despised. Fundamentalist ideology is authoritarian, dogmatic, and self-righteous; much of the fundamentalist agenda would undermine basic constitutional liberties. Nevertheless, the First Amendment applies even to belief systems contemptuous of intellectual liberty. With respect to freedoms of belief and expression, the Constitution requires us to tolerate the intolerant.

Recommendations

Public school educators are government officials. This gives them an obligation to act in accord with the Constitution, including the First Amendment. Interpretation of the First Amendment is, of course, complex, and there is much disagreement even among legal experts about the meaning and application of various precedents. Fortunately, for the educator genuinely committed to intellectual freedom this is rarely a problem. The broad spirit of the First Amendment and of the historic Supreme Court decisions is reasonably clear. Adherence to this broad spirit will keep any teacher, librarian, administrator, or school board member well within the range of constitutionality. Educators should keep in mind that children are not "mere creature[s] of the State"[4] or "closed-circuit recipients of only that which the State chooses to communicate."[5] They must fight the temptation to "prescribe what shall be orthodox,"[6] recognizing that such prescription may "strangle the free mind at its source."[7] They must resist those forces, inside and outside the school, that would "cast a pall of orthodoxy over the classroom."[8]

Interpreted broadly, such guidelines go beyond the requirements of the Constitution. Educators should follow them even with respect to day-to-day interactions with students that would be difficult or impossible to challenge in court. Moreover, even private school educators should, for ethical reasons, respect the intellectual freedom of their students.

Educators should recognize that parents, and other members of the community, have a genuine and legitimate interest in what happens in the schools. Complaints should be taken seriously; concerned parents, even if their concerns are absurdly misguided, should not be dismissed out of hand as censors, fundamentalists, ideologues, or fanatics (Strike, 1985). Their concerns deserve serious consideration and meaningful response.

4. Pierce v. Society of Sisters, 268 U.S. 510, 535 (1925).
5. Tinker v. Des Moines Independent Community School District, 393 U.S. 503, 511 (1969).
6. West Virginia State Board of Education v. Barnette, 319 U.S. 624, 642 (1943).
7. *Id.* at 637.
8. Keyishian v. Board of Regents, 385 U.S. 589, 603 (1967).

This is not to say, however, that educators should routinely accede to the will of parents or concerned citizens who challenge books, curricula, or school activities. Even when the number of complaints is large, this may only reflect a well-organized minority. Moreover, even if the complaints represent a majority view, public education raises First Amendment issues that should not be settled by majority opinion. Every school should have clear procedures for handling challenges. The procedures should be set up to allow a fair hearing and a possibility of genuine change if the complaint is justified. If the complaint is deemed unjustified, the reason for what the school is doing and will continue to do should be explained as carefully as possible.

Finally, with respect to students, it is important to avoid the hypocrisy of professing respect for the Constitution in an authoritarian environment that shows contempt for intellectual freedom. If we want students to believe in intellectual freedom, it is crucial to show them how much we value it ourselves. To the extent that school officials censor "inappropriate" speech or restrict the school newspaper to "acceptable" topics and ideas, students will learn that, lofty rhetoric notwithstanding, freedom of expression in America only extends to ideas that don't offend the authorities.

Socialization and Society

Given the central importance of the socialization of the next generation for any society, public education is obviously an important concern not only for students and parents but for all Americans. Given the sensitivity and complexity of issues involving children, education, freedom of expression, and religious liberty, it is not surprising that public schools, involving all of these, are such a center of controversy. Much of the controversy in recent years is due to the efforts of fundamentalists and their allies. But it would be a mistake to view them as the source of the problem. The source of the problem is the genuine dilemma of how, in a country including an extraordinary diversity of religious and political views, the government can educate an entire generation without intruding on intellectual freedom.

We should acknowledge at the outset that there is no perfect answer. Our religious, political, and philosophical views are so diverse, so radically incommensurable, that it is difficult even to find enough common ground to begin a meaningful discussion. Considering all the potential pitfalls, we have probably been doing about as well as any two hundred and fifty million people could be expected to do.

I suggest, predictably enough, that we have done as well as we have because of the First Amendment. Two hundred years after its formulation, its basic fairness remains compelling. We will muddle through, despite our differences, provided government makes no law respecting an establishment of religion, or prohibiting the free exercise thereof; or abridging the freedom of speech, or of the press. And somehow, we will manage to educate the vast majority of our children in common schools, provided we insure that the schools act consistently in accord with those principles.

We will—and should—continue to argue about how the First Amendment applies to public schools. But perhaps we are making progress. We may not agree on the extent to which school officials may restrict student expression, but we have established that speech and press of students in public schools do enjoy some degree of First Amendment protection. We may not agree what books and curricula are appropriate, but we have established that even a properly elected school board may not choose to blatantly indoctrinate students in particular political views. We may not agree on what constitutes religious neutrality, but we have established that patent favoritism for particular religions, even religions favored by a majority, is constitutionally unacceptable.

Each of us, of course, would like the public schools to teach children what we ourselves consider, at the deepest level, to be good and true. Nevertheless, as a society, we must not allow public schools to be used for narrow indoctrination by whatever religious, political, or ideological group can get control of them. The key to avoiding this is a principled commitment to children's First Amendment rights.

But if concern for society as a whole directs us to attend to the treatment of children, meaningful attention to children brings us right back to the broader context. Children, especially at early ages, need adults, and cannot be understood, psychologically or legally, independent of their parents. Children and parents together form family units that are something more than the individuals composing them and give meaning and comfort to those individuals (Kegan, 1982; Maccoby & Martin, 1983). The moral significance of families cannot be reduced to the fundamental rights of the individuals that compose them and may even be lost in one-dimensional talk of such rights (Schoeman, 1980; cf. O'Neill, 1988).

Similarly, society is not a collection of individuals but a complex system that gives shape and meaning to the lives of its members. Moreover, society itself is not a static entity but a succession of generations. In more ways than we can consciously fathom, as individuals and as a society, we derive identity from our continuity with the past and construct meaning through our active efforts to shape a future that preserves and extends that continuity (Erikson, 1963; Lifton, 1987; Schell, 1982).

But continuity does not mean stagnation. Change is inevitable, and commitment to continuity need not be resistance to change. What continuity requires is the identification and preservation of those core characteristics and values that make the future *our* future and thus reflect positively on the significance of our own lives and activities. Intellectual freedom, in this context, means both the freedom to criticize aspects of the present and propose a different future and, equally important, the freedom to defend aspects of the present against the inevitable forces of change.

As individuals and as a society, then, each generation is faced with the daunting task of balancing stability and transformation, of adapting to the unexpected and, simultaneously, identifying and preserving those aspects of the past that are central to who we are and that make the future, however different from the present, a continuation. How are we to do this? There is no simple formula for providing the next generation with just the right balance of freedom, guidance, challenge, and support. From the broadest point of view, that task is the task of coordinating where we have come from and where we are going.

We fight bitterly over this not only because the intellectual dilemma is so extraordinarily complex but because its emotional roots go so deep and because the stakes are so great. Distinctions of children from adults, individuals from society, and society from government all break down. The issues are simultaneously personal and social, moral and historical, exhilarating and terrifying. Every choice we make limits some possibilities and opens others. We search for alternatives that will leave us flexible enough to face challenges we cannot anticipate and simultaneously provide sufficient continuity to link the generations and thus secure the meaning and significance of our lives.

Socialization raises issues of fundamental identity, of psychosocial existence. It forces us to consider who we are and whom we want to be. And at the heart of such consideration lie two questions, inextricably locked in an uneasy embrace: What will become of us if we fail to transmit the knowledge, values, and principles that have brought us this far? But what will become of us if, in our zeal to inculcate, we blindly cast a pall of orthodoxy over the future?

References

Abbagnano, N. (1967). Humanism. In P. Edwards (Ed.), *The encyclopedia of philosophy*. New York: Macmillan.

Adams, G. R. (1985). Identity and political socialization. In A. S. Waterman (Ed.), *Identity in adolescence: Processes and contents. New Directions for Child Development*, No. 30. San Francisco: Jossey-Bass.

Alpern, P. L. (1987). Constitutional law: The First Amendment and offensive student speech—Bethel School District No. 403 v. Fraser, 106 S.Ct. 3159 (1986). *Harvard Journal of Law and Public Policy, 10*, 259–265.

American Federation of Teachers. (1987). *Education for democracy—A statement of principles: Guidelines for strengthening the teaching of democratic values*. Washington, DC: American Federation of Teachers.

Amigues, R. (1988). Peer interaction in solving physics problems: Sociocognitive confrontation and metacognitive aspects. *Journal of Experimental Child Psychology, 45*, 141–158.

Arons, S. (1983). *Compelling belief: The culture of American schooling*. New York: McGraw-Hill.

Association for Supervision and Curriculum Development. (1988). *Moral education in the life of the school*.

Astington, J. W., Harris, P. L., & Olson, D. (Eds.). (1988). *Developing theories of mind*. New York: Cambridge University Press.

Baron, J. (1985). *Rationality and intelligence*. New York: Cambridge University Press.

Baron, J. B., & Sternberg, R. J. (Eds.). (1987). *Teaching thinking skills: Theory and practice*. New York: Freeman.

Basseches, M. (1984). *Dialectical thinking*. Norwood, NJ: Ablex.

Baumrind, D. (1986). Sex differences in moral reasoning: Response to Walker's (1984) conclusion that there are none. *Child Development, 57*, 511–521.

Bearison, D. J., Magzamen, S., & Filardo, E. K. (1986). Socio-cognitive conflict and cognitive growth in young children. *Merrill-Palmer Quarterly, 32*, 51–72.

Bennett, W. J. (1986, May 15). "In defense of the common culture." Speech to the American Jewish Committee, Washington, DC. Excerpted in *Education Week*, May 28, 1986, p. 10.

Benninga, J. S. (1988). An emerging synthesis in moral education. *Phi Delta Kappan, 69,* 415–418.

Berkowitz, M. W. (Ed.). (1985). *Peer conflict and psychological growth. New Directions for Child Development,* No. 29. San Francisco: Jossey-Bass.

Bersoff, D. N. (1987). Social science data and the Supreme Court: *Lockhart* as a case in point. *American Psychologist, 42,* 52–58.

Beschle, D. L. (1987). The conservative as liberal: The religion clauses, liberal neutrality, and the approach of Justice O'Connor. *Notre Dame Law Review, 62,* 151–191.

Black, B. (1988). Evolving legal standards for the admissibility of scientific evidence. *Science, 239,* 1508–1512.

Blasi, A. (1980). Bridging moral cognition and moral action: A critical review of the literature. *Psychological Bulletin, 88,* 1–45.

Blasi, A. (1983). Moral cognition and moral action: A theoretical perspective. *Developmental Review, 3,* 178–210.

Blasi, A. (1984). Moral identity: Its role in moral functioning. In W. M. Kurtines & J. L. Gewirtz (Eds.), *Morality, moral behavior, and moral development* (pp. 128–139). New York: Wiley.

Bogdan, D., & Yeomans, S. (1986). School censorship and learning values through literature. *Journal of Moral Education, 15,* 197–211.

Bogen, D. S. (1983). The origins of freedom of speech and press. *Maryland Law Review, 42,* 429–465.

Boston, G. R. (1988). Unanswered prayers: Equal access and the courts. *Church and state, 41,* 28–30.

Bowers, K. (1983). Banning books in public schools: *Board of Education v. Pico. Pepperdine Law Review, 10,* 545–578.

Boyes, M. C., & Walker, L. J. (1988). Implications of cultural diversity for the universality claims of Kohlberg's theory of moral reasoning. *Human Development, 31,* 44–59.

Brabeck, M. (1983). Moral judgment: Theory and research on differences between males and females. *Developmental Review, 3,* 274–291.

Braine, M. D. S., & Rumain, B. (1983). Logical reasoning. In J. H. Flavell & E. M. Markman (Eds.), P. H. Mussen (Series Ed.), *Handbook of child psychology: Vol. 3. Cognitive development* (pp. 263–340). New York: Wiley.

Brink, D. O. (1988). Legal theory, legal interpretation, and judicial review. *Philosophy & Public Affairs, 17,* 105–148.

Broughton, J. M. (1978). Development of concepts of self, mind, reality, and knowledge. In W. Damon (Ed.), *Social cognition* (pp. 75–100). *New Directions for Child Development,* No. 1. San Francisco: Jossey-Bass.

Broughton, J. M. (1983). Women's rationality and men's virtues: A critique of gender dualism in Gilligan's theory of moral development. *Social Research, 50,* 597–642.

Brown, D. (1970). *Bury my heart at wounded knee.* New York: Holt, Rinehart, and Winston.

Byrnes, J. P. (1988). Formal operations: A systematic reformulation. *Developmental Review, 8,* 66–87.

Campbell, R. L., & Bickhard, M. H. (1986). *Knowing levels and developmental stages.* Basel, Switzerland: Karger.

Case, R. (1985). *Intellectual development: Birth to adulthood*. Orlando, FL: Academic Press.

Clark, E. V. (1983). Meanings and concepts. In J. H. Flavell & E. M. Markman (Eds.), P. H. Mussen (Series Ed.), *Handbook of child psychology: Vol. 3. Cognitive development* (pp. 787–840). New York: Wiley.

Clinchy, B. M., & Mansfield, A. F. (1986). The child's discovery of the role of the knower in the known. Paper presented at the meeting of the Jean Piaget Society, Philadelphia.

Cohen, L. J. (1981). Can human irrationality be experimentally demonstrated? *The behavioral and brain sciences, 4,* 317–370.

Coleman, J. C. (1980). *The nature of adolescence*. New York: Methuen.

Coles, R. (1986). *The moral life of children*. Boston: Atlantic Monthly Press.

Commons, M. L., Richards, F. A., & Armon, C. (1984). *Beyond formal operations: Late adolescent and adult cognitive development*. New York: Praeger.

Conn, J. L. (1987). The sounds of silence: Supreme Court agrees to hear dispute over New Jersey's moment of silence. *Church and State, 40,* 52–53.

Cox, A. (1987). Storm over the Supreme Court. In N. Dorsen (Ed.), *The evolving Constitution: Essays on the Bill of Rights and the U.S. Supreme Court* (pp. 3–23). Middletown, CT: Wesleyan University Press.

Cragg, W. (1988). Public education, liberalism, and the pursuit of moral autonomy. *Interchange, 19,* 46–53.

Crosby, D. (1970). Almost cut my hair. In D. Crosby, S. Stills, G. Nash, & N. Young, *Déjà vu* (record). New York: Atlantic Recording.

Cummins, J. (1978). Language and children's ability to evaluate contradictions and tautologies: A critique of Osherson and Markman's findings. *Child Development, 49,* 895–897.

Darwin, C. (1859). *On the origin of species*. London: John Murray.

Davis, O. L., Jr., Ponder, G., Burlbaw, L. M., Garza-Lubeck, M., & Moss, A. (1986). *Looking at history: A review of major U.S. history textbooks*. Washington, DC: People for the American Way.

Dawidowicz, L. S. (1975). *The war against the Jews: 1933–1945*. New York: Holt, Rinehart and Winston.

Dixon, R. A., & Lerner, R. M. (1984). A history of systems in developmental psychology. In M. H. Bornstein & M. E. Lamb (Eds.), *Developmental psychology: An advanced textbook* (pp. 1–35). Hillsdale, NJ: Erlbaum.

Doise, W., & Mugny, G. (1984). *The social development of the intellect*. Oxford, Eng.: Pergamon.

Donaldson, M. (1978). *Children's minds*. New York: Norton.

Dworkin, R. (1978). *Taking rights seriously*. Cambridge, MA: Harvard University Press.

Dworkin, R. (1985). *A matter of principle*. Cambridge, MA: Harvard University Press.

Dworkin, R. (1986). *Law's empire*. Cambridge, MA: Harvard University Press.

Eldredge, N. (1982). *The monkey business: A scientist looks at creationism*. New York: Washington Square Press.

Elkind, D. (1970). The origins of religion in the child. *Review of Religious Research, 12,* 35–42.

Emerson, T. I. (1970). *The system of freedom of expression*. New York: Vintage.

Erikson, E. H. (1963). *Childhood and Society*. New York: Norton.

Erikson, E. H. (1968). *Identity: Youth and crisis*. New York: Norton.

Evans, J. St. B. T. (1982). *The psychology of deductive reasoning*. London: Routledge and Kegan Paul.

Evans, J. St. B. T. (Ed.). (1983). *Thinking and reasoning: Psychological approaches*. London: Routledge and Kegan Paul.

Faaborg, K. K. (1985). High school play censorship: Are students' First Amendment rights violated when officials cancel theatrical productions? *Journal of Law and Education, 14*, 575–594.

Fabricius, W. V., Sophian, C., & Wellman, H. M. (1987). Young children's sensitivity to logical necessity in their inferential search behavior. *Child Development, 58*, 409–423.

Facts about Accelerated Christian Education (1979). Lewisville, TX: Accelerated Christian Education, Inc.

Fallon, R. H. (1987). A constructivist coherence theory of constitutional interpretation. *Harvard Law Review, 100*, 1189–1286.

Feinberg, J. (1980). The child's right to an open future. In W. Aiken & H. LaFollette (Eds.), *Whose child? Children's rights, parental authority, and state power*. Totowa, NJ: Littlefield, Adams.

Fischer, K. W. (1980). A theory of cognitive development: The control and construction of hierarchies of skills. *Psychological Review, 87*, 477–531.

Flavell, J. H. (1985). *Cognitive Development* (2nd ed.). Englewood Cliffs, NJ: Prentice-Hall.

Flavell, J. H. (1986). The development of children's knowledge about the appearance-reality distinction. *American Psychologist, 41*, 418–425.

Flavell, J. H., Green, F. L., & Flavell, E. R. (1986). Development of knowledge about the appearance-reality distinction. *Monographs of the Society for Research in Child Development, 51*(1, Serial No. 212).

Flavell, J. H., Green, F. L., Wahl, K. E., & Flavell, E. R. (1987). The effects of question clarification and memory aids on young children's performance on appearance-reality tasks. *Cognitive Development, 2*, 127–144.

Fleming, D. B., & Hunt, T. C. (1987). The world as seen by students in Accelerated Christian Education schools. *Phi Delta Kappan, 68*, 518–523.

Fowler, J. (1981). *Stages of faith: The psychology of human development and the quest for meaning*. New York: Harper & Row.

Frankena, W. K. (1973). *Ethics* (2nd ed.). Englewood Cliffs, NJ: Prentice-Hall.

Franks, B. A. (1986). Children's intellectual rights: Implications for educational policy. In D. Moshman (Ed.), *Children's intellectual rights* (pp. 75–87). *New Directions for Child Development*, No. 33. San Francisco: Jossey-Bass.

Freed, E. C. (1986). Secular humanism, the establishment clause, and public education. *New York University Law Review, 61*, 1149–1185.

Freeman, B. A. (1984). The Supreme Court and First Amendment rights of students in the public school classroom: A proposed model of analysis. *Hastings Constitutional Law Quarterly, 12*, 1–70.

Friedman, L. M. (1986). Limited monarchy: The rise and fall of student rights. In D. L. Kirp & D. N. Jensen (Eds.), *School days, rule days: The legalization and regulation of education*. Philadelphia: Falmer Press.

Furth, H. G. (1981). *Piaget and knowledge: Theoretical foundations* (2nd ed.). Chicago: University of Chicago Press.

Futuyma, D. J. (1983). *Science on trial: The case for evolution*. New York: Pantheon Books.

Garvey, J. H. (1979). Children and the First Amendment. *Texas Law Review, 57*, 321–379.

Garvey, J. H. (1981). Freedom and choice in constitutional law. *Harvard Law Review, 94*, 1756–1794.

Gelman, R., & Baillargeon, R. (1983). A review of some Piagetian concepts. In J. H. Flavell & E. M. Markman (Eds.), P. H. Mussen (Series Ed.), *Handbook of child psychology: Vol. 3. Cognitive development* (pp. 167–230). New York: Wiley.

Gibbs, J. C., Arnold, K. D., & Burkhart, J. E. (1984). Sex differences in the expression of moral judgment. *Child Development, 55*, 1040–1043.

Gilligan, C. (1982). *In a different voice: Psychological theory and women's development*. Cambridge, MA: Harvard University Press.

Gilligan, C. (1987). Adolescent development reconsidered. In C. E. Irwin, Jr. (Ed.), *Adolescent social behavior and health* (pp. 63–92). *New Directions for Child Development*, No. 37. San Francisco: Jossey-Bass.

Ginsburg, H., & Opper, S. (1988). *Piaget's theory of intellectual development* (3rd ed.). Englewood Cliffs, NJ: Prentice-Hall.

Glasser, I. (1983). The role of the schools. In Office for Intellectual Freedom, American Library Association (Ed.), *Censorship litigation and the schools*. Chicago: American Library Association.

Glenn, C. L. (1987). Textbook controversies: A 'disaster for public schools'? *Phi Delta Kappan, 68*, 451–455.

Goldman, R. (1964). *Religious thinking from childhood to adolescence*. London: Routledge & Kegan Paul.

Gopnik, A., & Astington, J. W. (1988). Children's understanding of representational change and its relation to the understanding of false belief and the appearance-reality distinction. *Child Development, 59*, 26–37.

Gottlieb, S. E. (1987). In the name of patriotism: The constitutionality of "bending" history in public secondary schools. *New York University Law Review, 62*, 497–578.

Grisso, T. (1981). *Juvenile's waiver of rights: Legal and psychological competence*. New York: Plenum.

Haan, N. (1985). Processes of moral development: Cognitive or social disequilibrium? *Developmental Psychology, 21*, 996–1006.

Haiman, F. S. (1981). *Speech and law in a free society*. Chicago: University of Chicago Press.

Harpaz, L. (1986). Justice Jackson's flag salute legacy: The Supreme Court struggles to protect intellectual individualism. *Texas Law Review, 64*, 817–914.

Harris, P. L., Donnelly, K., Guz, G. R., & Pitt-Watson, R. (1986). Children's understanding of the distinction between real and apparent emotion. *Child Development, 57*, 895–909.

Hartup, W. W. (1983). Peer relations. In E. M. Hetherington (Ed.), P. H. Mussen (Series Ed.), *Handbook of Child Psychology: Vol. 4. Socialization, personality, and social development* (pp. 103–196). New York: Wiley.

Hawkins, J., Pea, R. D., Glick, J., & Scribner, S. (1984). "Merds that laugh don't like mushrooms": Evidence for deductive reasoning by preschoolers. *Developmental Psychology, 20*, 584–594.

Hechinger, F. M. (1986). Political shift on 'vulgar' speech. *New York Times*, July 15.

Hentoff, N. (1980). *The first freedom: The tumultuous history of free speech in America*. New York: Delacorte.

Hill, J. P., & Holmbeck, G. N. (1986). Attachment and autonomy during adolescence. In G. J. Whitehurst (Ed.), *Annals of child development*, Vol. 3 (pp. 145–189). Greenwich, CT: JAI Press.

Hogrefe, G.-J., Wimmer, H., & Perner, J. (1986). Ignorance versus false belief: A developmental lag in attribution of epistemic states. *Child Development, 57*, 567–582.

Holland, A., & Andre, T. (1987). Participation in extracurricular activities in secondary school: What is known, what needs to be known? *Review of Educational Research, 57*, 437–466.

Holt, J. (1981). *Teach your own: A hopeful path for education*. New York: Dell.

Houlgate, L. D. (1980). *The child and the state: A normative theory of juvenile rights*. Baltimore: Johns Hopkins University Press.

Howe, H. (1987). Can schools teach values? *Teachers College Record, 89*, 55–68.

Huffman, J. L., & Trauth, D. M. (1981). High school students' publication rights and prior restraint. *Journal of Law and Education, 10*, 485–505.

Ingelhart, L. E. (1986). *Press law and press freedom for high school publications*. Westport, CT: Greenwood.

Inhelder, B., & Piaget, J. (1958). *The growth of logical thinking from childhood to adolescence*. New York: Basic Books.

Jenkinson, E. B. (1986). *The schoolbook protest movement: 40 questions and answers*. Bloomington, IN: Phi Delta Kappa.

Johnson, D. W., & Johnson, R. (1985). Classroom conflict: Controversy versus debate in learning groups. *American Educational Research Journal, 22*, 237–256.

Johnson, R. E. (1987). ACE responds. *Phi Delta Kappan, 68*, 520–521.

Kamiat, W. A. (1983). State indoctrination and the protection of non-state voices in the schools: Justifying a prohibition of school library censorship. *Stanford Law Review, 35*, 497–535.

Kant, I. (1959). *Foundations of the metaphysics of morals*. New York: Macmillan. (Orig. pub. 1785.)

Kegan, R. (1982). *The evolving self: Problem and process in human development*. Cambridge, MA: Harvard University Press.

Keil, F. C. (1981). Constraints on knowledge and cognitive development. *Psychological Review, 88*, 197–227.

Kilpatrick, W. H. (1972). Indoctrination and respect for persons. In I. A. Snook (Ed.), *Concepts of indoctrination: Philosophical essays* (pp. 47–54). London: Routledge & Kegan Paul.

Kitchener, K. S., & King, P. M. (1981). Reflective judgment: Concepts of justification and their relationship to age and education. *Journal of Applied Developmental Psychology*, *2*, 89–116.

Kitchener, K. S., & Wood, P. K. (1987). Development of concepts of justification in German university students. *International Journal of Behavioral Development*, *10*, 171–185.

Kitcher, P. (1982). *Abusing science: The case against creationism*. Cambridge, MA: MIT Press.

Kleiman, D. (1981). Parents' groups purging schools of "humanist" books and classes. *The New York Times*, May 17.

Kohlberg, L. (1984). *Essays on moral development: Vol. II. The psychology of moral development*. New York: Harper and Row.

Komatsu, L. K., & Galotti, K. M. (1986). Children's reasoning about social, physical, and logical regularities: A look at two worlds. *Child Development*, *57*, 413–420.

Kristof, N. D. (1983). *Freedom of the high school press*. Lanham, MD: University Press of America.

Kuhn, D., Amsel, E., & O'Loughlin, M. (1988). *The development of scientific thinking skills*. New York: Academic Press.

Kurtines, W. M., & Gewirtz, J. L. (Eds.) (1984). *Morality, moral behavior, and moral development*. New York: Wiley.

Kurtines, W. M., & Gewirtz, J. L. (Eds.). (1987). *Moral development through social interaction*. New York: Wiley.

Kurtz, P. (Ed.). (1980). *A secular humanist declaration*. Buffalo, NY: Prometheus.

Kurtz, P. (1983). *In defense of secular humanism*. Buffalo, NY: Prometheus.

La Follette, M. C. (Ed.). (1983). *Creationism, science, and the law: The Arkansas case*. Cambridge, MA: MIT Press.

LaHaye, T. (1983). *The battle for the public schools: Humanism's threat to our children*. Old Tappan, NJ: Revell.

Laycock, D. (1986). Equal access and moments of silence: The equal status of religious speech by private speakers. *Northwestern University Law Review*, *81*, 1–67.

Lerner, R. M. (1986). *Concepts and theories of human development*. New York: Random House.

Lewis, A. C. (1987). A word about character. *Phi Delta Kappan*, *68*, 724–725.

Lewis, C. C. (1987). Minors' competence to consent to abortion. *American Psychologist*, *42*, 84–88.

Lifton, R. J. (1987). *The future of immortality, and other essays for a nuclear age*. New York: Basic Books.

Limiting what students may read. (1981). Sponsored and printed by the Association of American Publishers, the American Library Association, and the Association for Supervision and Curriculum Development.

Lines, P. M. (1987). An overview of home instruction. *Phi Delta Kappan*, *68*, 510–517.

Locke, J. (1960). *Two treatises of government*. New York: Cambridge University Press. (Orig. pub. 1690.)

Lyons, D. (1987). Substance, process, and outcome in constitutional theory. *Cornell Law Review, 72,* 745–764.

Maccoby, E. E., & Martin, J. A. (1983). Socialization in the context of the family: Parent-child interaction. In E. M. Hetherington (Ed.), P. H. Mussen (Series Ed.), *Handbook of child psychology: Vol. 4. Socialization, personality, and social development* (pp. 1–101). New York: Wiley.

Mason, C. A. (1988). "Secular humanism" and the definition of religion: Extending a modified "ultimate concern" test to *Mozert v. Hawkins County Public Schools* and *Smith v. Board of School Commissioners. Washington Law Review, 63,* 445–468.

McCarthy, M. M. (1983). *A delicate balance: Church, state, and the schools.* Bloomington, IN: Phi Delta Kappa.

McConnell, M. W. (1986). Neutrality under the religion clauses. *Northwestern University Law Review, 81,* 146–167.

McConnell, M. W. (1987). You can't tell the players in church-state disputes without a scorecard. *Harvard Journal of Law and Public Policy, 10,* 27–35.

Melton, G. B. (1980). Children's concepts of their rights. *Journal of Clinical Child Psychology, 9,* 186–190.

Melton, G. B. (1983). Toward "personhood" for adolescents: Autonomy and privacy as values in public policy. *American Psychologist, 38,* 99–103.

Melton, G. B. (1983–84). Developmental psychology and the law: The state of the art. *Journal of Family Law, 22,* 445–482.

Melton, G. B. (1986). Populism, school prayer, and the courts: Confessions of an expert witness. In D. Moshman (Ed.), *Children's intellectual rights* (pp. 63–73). *New Directions for Child Development* No. 33. San Francisco: Jossey-Bass.

Melton, G. B. (Ed.). (1987a). *Reforming the law: Impact of child development research.* New York: Guilford.

Melton, G. B. (1987b). The clashing of symbols: Prelude to child and family policy. *American Psychologist, 42,* 345–354.

Melton, G. B., Koocher, G. P., & Saks, M. J. (Eds.). (1983). *Children's competence to consent.* New York: Plenum.

Melton, G. B., & Russo, N. F. (1987). Adolescent abortion: Psychological perspectives on public policy. *American Psychologist, 42,* 69–72.

Melton, S. L. (1987). Tinkering with high school press: *Kuhlmeier v. Hazelwood School District. Creighton Law Review, 20,* 1199–1224.

Mill, J. S. (1974). *On liberty.* New York: Penguin. (Orig. pub. 1859.)

Mill, J. S. (1957). *Utilitarianism.* Indianapolis: Bobbs-Merrill. (Orig. pub. 1861.)

Minuchin, P. P., & Shapiro, E. K. (1983). The school as a context for social development. In E. M. Hetherington (Ed.), P. H. Mussen (Series Ed.), *Handbook of child psychology: Vol. 4. Socialization, personality, and social development* (pp. 197–274). New York: Wiley.

Moffett, J. (1988). *Storm in the mountains: A case study of censorship, conflict, and consciousness.* Carbondale: Southern Illinois University Press.

Monahan, J., & Walker, L. (1988). Social science research in law: A new paradigm. *American Psychologist, 43,* 465–472.

Moore, M. S. (1984). *Law and psychiatry: Rethinking the relationship*. Cambridge, Eng.: Cambridge University Press.

Moshman, D. (1979a). Development of formal hypothesis-testing ability. *Developmental Psychology, 15*, 104–112.

Moshman, D. (1979b). To *really* get ahead, get a metatheory. In D. Kuhn (Ed.), *Intellectual development beyond childhood* (pp. 59–68). *New Directions for Child Development*, No. 5. San Francisco: Jossey-Bass.

Moshman, D. (1981). Jean Piaget meets Jerry Falwell: Genetic epistemology and the anti-humanist movement in education. *The Genetic Epistemologist, 10*(3), 10–13.

Moshman, D. (1982). Exogenous, endogenous, and dialectical constructivism. *Developmental Review, 2*, 371–384.

Moshman, D. (1985a). A role for creationism in science education. *Journal of College Science Teaching, 15*, 106–109.

Moshman, D. (1985b). *Faith Christian v. Nebraska*: Parent, child, and community rights in the educational arena. *Teachers College Record, 86*, 553–571.

Moshman, D. (1985c). The right to hold frivolous beliefs: A reply to Bandman. *Teachers College Record, 86*, 576–578.

Moshman, D. (Ed.). (1986). *Children's intellectual rights. New Directions for Child Development*, No. 33. San Francisco: Jossey-Bass.

Moshman, D. (1988, April). Equal access for religion in public schools? An empirical solution to a legal dilemma. Paper presented at the meeting of the Western Psychological Association, San Francisco.

Moshman, D. (1989). The development of metalogical understanding. In W. F. Overton (Ed.), *Reasoning, necessity, and logic: Developmental perspectives*. Hillsdale, NJ: Erlbaum.

Moshman, D., & Franks, B. A. (1986). Development of the concept of inferential validity. *Child Development, 57*, 153–165.

Moshman, D., Glover, J. A., & Bruning, R. H. (1987). *Developmental psychology: A topical approach*. Boston: Little, Brown.

Moshman, D., & Hoover, L. M. (1989). Rationality as a goal of psychotherapy. *Journal of Cognitive Psychotherapy, 3*, 31–51.

Moshman, D., & Lukin, L. E. (In press). The creative construction of rationality: A paradox? In J. A. Glover, R. R. Ronning, & C. R. Reynolds (Eds.), *A handbook of creativity: Assessment, theory, and research*. New York: Plenum.

Moshman, D., & Timmons, M. (1982). The construction of logical necessity. *Human Development, 25*, 309–323.

National School Boards Association. (1987). *Building character in the public schools: Strategies for success*. Alexandria, VA: NSBA.

Nemeth, C. J. (1986). Differential contributions of majority and minority influence. *Psychological Review, 93*, 23–32.

Note. (1983). The constitutional dimensions of student-initiated religious activity in public high schools. *Yale Law Journal, 92*, 499–519.

Numbers, R. L. (1982). Creationism in 20th-century America. *Science, 218*, 538–544.

Numbers, R. L. (1987). The creationists. *Zygon: Journal of Religion and Science, 22*, 133–164.

Nunner-Winkler, G. (1984). Two moralities? A critical discussion of an ethic of care and responsibility versus an ethic of rights and justice. In W. M. Kurtines & J. L. Gewirtz (Eds.), *Morality, moral behavior, and moral development* (pp. 348–361). New York: Wiley.

Oakes, J. L. (1987). The proper role of the federal courts in enforcing the Bill of Rights. In N. Dorsen (Ed.), *The evolving Constitution: Essays on the Bill of Rights and the U.S. Supreme Court* (pp. 169–195). Middletown, CT: Wesleyan University Press.

O'Brien, D. P. (1987). The development of conditional reasoning: An iffy proposition. In H. W. Reese (Ed.), *Advances in child development and behavior*, Vol. 20. Orlando, FL: Academic Press.

O'Brien, D. P., Costa, G., & Overton, W. F. (1986). Evaluations of causal and conditional hypotheses. *Quarterly Journal of Experimental Psychology, 38A*, 493–512.

O'Brien, D. P., & Overton, W. F. (1980). Conditional reasoning following contradictory evidence: A developmental analysis. *Journal of Experimental Child Psychology, 30*, 44–60.

O'Brien, D. P., & Overton, W. F. (1982). Conditional reasoning and the competence-performance issue: A developmental analysis of a training task. *Journal of Experimental Child Psychology, 34*, 274–290.

Office for Intellectual Freedom, American Library Association. (1983). *Intellectual freedom manual* (2nd Ed.). Chicago: American Library Association.

O'Neil, R. M. (1981). *Classrooms in the crossfire: The rights and interests of students, parents, teachers, administrators, librarians, and the community*. Bloomington: Indiana University Press.

O'Neill, O. (1988). Children's rights and children's lives. *Ethics, 98*, 445–463.

Osherson, D. N., & Markman, E. (1975). Language and the ability to evaluate contradictions and tautologies. *Cognition, 3*, 213–226.

Overton, W. F., Ward, S. L., Noveck, I. A., Black, J., & O'Brien, D. P. (1987). Form and content in the development of deductive reasoning. *Developmental Psychology, 23*, 22–30.

People for the American Way. (1987a). *Attacks on the freedom to learn: 1986–1987 report*. Washington, DC: People for the American Way.

People for the American Way. (1987b). *Values, pluralism, and public education: A national conference*. Washington, DC: People for the American Way.

People for the American Way. (1987c). *We the people: A review of U.S. government and civics textbooks*. Washington, DC: People for the American Way.

Peshkin, A. (1986). *God's choice: The total world of a fundamentalist Christian school*. Chicago: University of Chicago Press.

Pfeffer, L. (1984). *Religion, state and the Burger Court*. Buffalo, NY: Prometheus.

Piaget, J. (1965). *The moral judgment of the child*. New York: Free Press. (Orig. pub. 1932.)

Piaget, J. (1985). *The equilibration of cognitive structures: The central problem of intellectual development*. Chicago: University of Chicago Press.

Piaget, J., & Inhelder, B. (1969). *The psychology of the child*. New York: Basic Books.

Piattelli-Palmarini, M. (Ed.). (1980). *Language and learning: The debate between Jean Piaget and Noam Chomsky*. Cambridge, MA: Harvard University Press.

Pieraut-Le Bonniec, G. (1980). *The development of modal reasoning: Genesis of necessity and possibility notions*. New York: Academic Press.

Politzer, G. (1986). Laws of language use and formal logic. *Journal of Psycholinguistic Research, 15*, 47–92.

Powell, H. J. (1985). The original understanding of original intent. *Harvard Law Review, 98*, 885–948.

Pratt, M. W., Golding, G., & Hunter, W. J. (1984). Does morality have a gender? Sex, sex role, and moral judgment relationships across the adult lifespan. *Merrill-Palmer Quarterly, 30*, 321–340.

Proefriedt, W. (1985). Power, pluralism and the teaching of values: The educational marketplace. *Teachers College Record, 86*, 539–552.

Radke-Yarrow, M., Zahn-Waxler, C., & Chapman, M. (1983). Children's prosocial dispositions and behavior. In E. M. Hetherington (Ed.), P. H. Mussen (Series Ed.), *Handbook of child psychology: Vol. 4. Socialization, personality, and social development* (pp. 469–545). New York: Wiley.

Raven, J. (1987). Values, diversity, and cognitive development. *Teachers College Record, 89*, 21–38.

Rawls, J. (1971). *A theory of justice*. Cambridge, MA: Harvard University Press.

Reinstein, R. J. (1988). The evolution of individual rights from the Constitution's original intent. *Temple Law Review, 61*, 197–204.

Rescher, N. (1987). Rationality and moral obligation. *Synthese, 72*, 29–43.

Resnick, L. B. (1980). The role of invention in the development of mathematical competence. In R. H. Kluwe & H. Spada (Eds.), *Developmental models of thinking*. New York: Academic Press.

Rest, J. R. (1983). Morality. In J. H. Flavell & E. M. Markman (Eds.), P. H. Mussen (Series Ed.), *Handbook of child psychology: Vol. 3. Cognitive development* (pp. 556–629). New York: Wiley.

Rogan, J. M., & MacDonald, M. A. (1983). The effect of schooling on conservation skills: An intervention in the Ciskei. *Journal of Cross-Cultural Psychology, 14*, 309–322.

Rose, L. C. (1988). 'Reasonableness'—The High Court's new standard for cases involving student rights. *Phi Delta Kappan, 69*, 589–592.

Rotunda, R. D. (1987). Bicentennial lessons from the constitutional convention of 1787. *Suffolk University Law Review, 21*, 589–621.

Rotunda, R. D. (1988). Original intent, the view of the framers, and the role of the ratifiers. *Vanderbilt Law Review, 41*, 507–516.

Rush, S. E. (1985). The Warren and Burger courts on state, parent, and child conflict resolution: A comparative analysis and proposed methodology. *Hastings Law Journal, 36*, 461–513.

Russell, J., & Haworth, H. M. (1987). Perceiving the logical status of sentences. *Cognition, 27*, 73–96.

Rybash, J. M., Hoyer, W. J., & Roodin, P. A. (1986). *Adult cognition and aging: Developmental changes in processing, knowing and thinking.* New York: Pergamon.

Schaeffer, F. A. (1982). *A Christian manifesto,* Rev. Ed. Westchester, IL: Crossway.

Schell, J. (1982). *The fate of the earth.* New York: Avon.

Schoeman, F. (1980). Rights of children, rights of parents, and the moral basis of the family. *Ethics, 91,* 6–19.

Schwetschenau, C. M. (1987). Constitutional protection for student speech in public high schools: *Bethel School District No. 403 v. Fraser,* 106 S.Ct. 3159 (1986). *Cincinnati Law Review, 55,* 1349–1369.

Seuss, Dr. (T. S. Geisel). (1954). *Horton hears a who!* New York: Random House.

Sewall, G. T. (1988). American history textbooks: Where do we go from here? *Phi Delta Kappan, 69,* 552–558.

Sherman, E. F. (1988). The role of religion in school curriculum and textbooks. *Academe, 74,* 17–22.

Shively, S. B. (1982). Book banning in public schools: Don't tinker with *Tinker. Arizona State Law Journal, 1982,* 939–964.

Shultz, T. R., Wright, K., & Schleifer, M. (1986). Assignment of moral responsibility and punishment. *Child Development, 57,* 177–184.

Siegel, H. (1986). Critical thinking as an intellectual right. In D. Moshman (Ed.), *Children's Intellectual Rights* (pp. 39–49). *New Directions for Child Development,* No. 33. San Francisco: Jossey-Bass.

Siegel, H. (1987). *Relativism refuted: A critique of contemporary epistemological relativism.* Dordrecht, Reidel.

Siegel, H. (1988). *Educating reason: Rationality, critical thinking, and education.* London: Routledge.

Simson, G. J. (1987). The establishment clause in the Supreme Court: Rethinking the Court's approach. *Cornell Law Review, 72,* 905–935.

Skov, R. B., & Sherman, S. J. (1986). Information-gathering processes: Diagnosticity, hypothesis-confirmatory strategies, and perceived hypothesis confirmation. *Journal of Experimental Social Psychology, 22,* 93–121.

Smetana, J. G. (1984). Morality and gender: A commentary on Pratt, Golding, and Hunter. *Merrill-Palmer Quarterly, 30,* 341–348.

Smetana, J. G. (1985). Preschool children's conceptions of transgressions: Effects of varying moral and conventional domain-related attributes. *Developmental Psychology, 21,* 18–29.

Smith, M. E. (1987). Relations between church and state in the United States, with special attention to the schooling of children. *American Journal of Comparative Law, 35,* 1–45.

Snarey, J. R. (1985). Cross-cultural universality of social-moral development: A critical review of Kohlbergian research. *Psychological Bulletin, 97,* 202–232.

Snarey, J. R., Reimer, J., & Kohlberg, L. (1985). Development of social-moral reasoning among Kibbutz adolescents: A longitudinal cross-cultural study. *Developmental Psychology, 21,* 3–17.

Snook, I. A. (1972). *Indoctrination and education*. London: Routledge & Kegan Paul.

Sodian, B. (1988). Children's attributions of knowledge to the listener in a referential communication task. *Child Development, 59*, 378–385.

Sodian, B., & Wimmer, H. (1987). Children's understanding of inference as a source of knowledge. *Child Development, 58*, 424–433.

Somerville, S. C., Hadkinson, B. A., & Greenberg, C. (1979). Two levels of inferential behavior in young children. *Child Development, 50*, 119–131.

Sorenson, G. P. (1983). Removal of books from school libraries 1972–1982: *Board of Education v. Pico* and its antecedents. *Journal of Law and Education, 12*, 417–441.

Steinberg, L., & Silverberg, S. B. (1986). The vicissitudes of autonomy in early adolescence. *Child Development, 57*, 841–851.

Sternberg, R. J. (Ed.). (1984). *Mechanisms of cognitive development*. New York: Freeman.

Stevens, J. P. (1987). The life span of a judge-made rule. In N. Dorsen (Ed.), *The evolving Constitution: Essays on the Bill of Rights and the U.S. Supreme Court* (pp. 196–207). Middletown, CT: Wesleyan University Press.

Strike, K. A. (1982a). *Educational policy and the just society*. Urbana: University of Illinois Press.

Strike, K. A. (1982b). *Liberty and learning*. New York: St. Martin's Press.

Strike, K. A. (1985). A field guide of censors: Toward a concept of censorship in public schools. *Teachers College Record, 87*, 239–258.

Strike, K. A., & Soltis, J. F. (1985). *The ethics of teaching*. New York: Teachers College Press.

Strossen, N. (1985). A framework for evaluating equal access claims by student religious groups: Is there a window for free speech in the wall separating church and state? *Cornell Law Review, 71*, 143–183.

Strossen, N. (1986). "Secular humanism" and "scientific creationism": Proposed standards for reviewing curricular decisions affecting students' religious freedom. *Ohio State Law Journal, 47*, 333–407.

Strossen, N. (1987). A constitutional analysis of the equal access act's standards governing public school student religious meetings. *Harvard Journal on Legislation, 24*, 117–190.

Swomley, J. M. (1987). *Religious liberty and the secular state*. Buffalo, NY: Prometheus.

Taylor, M. (1988). Conceptual perspective taking: Children's ability to distinguish what they know from what they see. *Child Development, 59*, 703–718.

Thayer, E. S., & Collyer, C. E. (1978). The development of transitive inference. *Psychological Bulletin, 85*, 1327–1343.

Thoma, S. J. (1986). Estimating gender differences in the comprehension and preference of moral issues. *Developmental Review, 6*, 165–180.

Thompson, J. D. (1985). Student religious groups and the right of access to public school activity periods. *Georgetown Law Journal, 74*, 205–231.

Tremper, C. R., & Kelly, M. P. (1987). The mental health rationale for policies fostering minors' autonomy. *International Journal of Law and Psychiatry, 10*, 111–127.

Tribe, L. (1988). *American constitutional law* (2nd ed.). Mineola, NY: Foundation Press.

Tucker, D. F. B. (1985). *Law, liberalism and free speech.* Totowa, NJ: Rowman & Allanheld.

Turiel, E. (1983). *The development of social knowledge: Morality and convention.* New York: Cambridge University Press.

Tyack, D. B., & James, T. (1985). Moral majorities and the school curriculum: Historical perspectives on the legalization of virtue. *Teachers College Record, 86,* 513–537.

Urberg, K. A., & Rosen, R. A. (1987). Age differences in adolescent decision-making: Pregnancy resolution. *Journal of Adolescent Research, 2,* 447–454.

van Geel, T. (1983). The search for constitutional limits on governmental authority to inculcate youth. *Texas Law Review, 62,* 197–297.

van Geel, T. (1986). The Constitution and the child's right to freedom from political indoctrination. In D. Moshman (Ed.), *Children's intellectual rights* (pp. 7–23). *New Directions for Child Development,* No. 33. San Francisco: Jossey-Bass.

van Geel, T. (1987). *The courts and American education law.* Buffalo, NY: Prometheus.

Vasudev, J., & Hummel, R. C. (1987). Moral stage sequence and principled reasoning in an Indian sample. *Human Development, 30,* 105–118.

Vitz, P. (1986). *Censorship: Evidence of bias in our children's textbooks.* Ann Arbor, MI: Servant Books.

Walker, L. J. (1983). Sources of cognitive conflict for stage transition in moral development. *Developmental Psychology, 19,* 103–110.

Walker, L. J. (1984). Sex differences in the development of moral reasoning: A critical review. *Child Development, 55,* 677–691.

Walker, L. J. (1986a). Experimental and cognitive sources of moral development in adulthood. *Human Development, 29,* 113–124.

Walker, L. J. (1986b). Sex differences in the development of moral reasoning: A rejoinder to Baumrind. *Child Development, 57,* 522–526.

Weithorn, L. A., & Campbell, S. B. (1982). The competency of children and adolescents to make informed treatment decisions. *Child Development, 53,* 1589–1598.

Welfel, E. R., & Davison, M. L. (1986). The development of reflective judgment during the college years: A 4-year longitudinal study. *Journal of College Student Personnel, 27,* 209–216.

Wellman, H. M., & Estes, D. (1986). Early understanding of mental entities: A reexamination of childhood realism. *Child Development, 57,* 910–923.

Wilson, J. (1972). Indoctrination and rationality. In I. A. Snook (Ed.), *Concepts of indoctrination: Philosophical essays* (pp. 17–24). London: Routledge & Kegan Paul.

Wimmer, H., Gruber, S., & Perner, J. (1985). Young children's conception of lying: Moral intuition and the denotation and connotation of "to lie." *Developmental Psychology, 21,* 993–995.

Wimmer, H., Hogrefe, G.-J., & Perner, J. (1988). Children's understanding of informational access as source of knowledge. *Child Development, 59,* 386–396.

Wittrock, M. C. (Ed.). (1986). *Handbook of research on teaching: A project of the American Educational Research Association,* 3rd ed. New York: Macmillan.

Wringe, C. (1986). Three children's rights claims and some reservations. In D. Moshman (Ed.), *Children's intellectual rights* (pp. 51–62). *New Directions for Child Development,* No. 33. San Francisco: Jossey-Bass.

Yudof, M. G. (1983). *When government speaks: Politics, law, and government expression in America*. Berkeley: University of California Press.

Yudof, M. G. (1984). Library book selection and the public schools: The quest for the Archimedean point. *Indiana Law Journal, 59*, 527–564.

Yudof, M. G. (1987). Three faces of academic freedom. *Loyola Law Review, 32*, 831–858.

Zacharias, F. C. (1987). Flowcharting the First Amendment. *Cornell Law Review, 72*, 936–1024.

Table of Cases

Subject Index

Author Index